THE INNER LIMITS
OF OUTER SPACE

THE INNER LIMITS
OF OUTER SPACE

JOHN C. BAIRD

PUBLISHED FOR DARTMOUTH COLLEGE BY
UNIVERSITY PRESS OF NEW ENGLAND
Hanover and London, 1987

UNIVERSITY PRESS OF NEW ENGLAND

Printed in the United States of America

LIBRARY OF CONGRESS CATALOGING-IN-PUBLICATION DATA
Baird, John C.
The inner limits of outer space.

Includes index.
1. Life on other planets. 2. Life on other planets—
Psychological aspects. 3. Extraterrestrial anthropology.
I. Dartmouth College. II. Title.
QB54.B34 1987   577   86–40551
ISBN 0–87451–406–1
ISBN 0–87451–422–3 (pbk.)

5   4   3   2   1

Illustration by John Holmes

FOR CHILDREN

CONTENTS

PREFACE

The search for alien life and intelligence enjoys a dedicated following among a wide cross-section of the population. Whether this search ever will prove successful is an open question whose resolution turns on the uniqueness of human beings in the broader context of life throughout the universe. In the absence of evidence about life elsewhere, opinions about the special standing of humans must remain squarely within the domain of philosophy. Quite naturally, therefore, people have tried to discover empirical clues both here and in outer space that point more surely to the existence of extraterrestrial intelligence.

The layperson's means for gathering information about alien life is confined to direct observation and the statements of others. The bulk of such evidence arises from eyewitness reports of unidentified flying objects (UFOs) or from conjectures about an extraterrestrial influence on the construction of engineering marvels that date from the distant past (theory of ancient astronauts). Movies, television, radio, and the popular press are additional, primary sources of information about the search for extraterrestrial intelligence.

Despite most people's sympathetic response to nonscientific theories that pique our interest in alien life, the science community at large has roundly criticized the reliability of the supposed "facts" accepted by persons with little or no technical training. Many physical scientists feel the so-called evidence for extraterrestrial visitors is extremely scant and weak, that personality traits of nonscientists are probably responsible for their gullible acceptance of quack ideas, and that in any case, the layperson's beliefs about aliens are remarkably similar to stereotypical beliefs about their fellow humans.

In place of these "subjective" opinions, some engineers and astronomers are now attempting to contact extraterrestrials by deliberate physical means: deploying satellite probes to other star systems, using telescopes to search for messages that might be embedded in the radio activity emanating from distant and ancient civilizations, and—eventually—founding human settlements in space. The prospects for these ventures depend on the degree to which the scientific laws assumed by engineers and astronomers are seen as valid by other intelligent species existing elsewhere in the universe.

In this book I evaluate both the scientific and the nonscientific attitudes toward the search for extraterrestrial intelligence, and in the process I ask scientists the same pointed questions they have put to nonscientists: Is the basis of the search firmly established? Can physical science provide reasonable answers to questions concerning matters beyond its usual realm of application—for example, fixing the time course of technological societies, correctly guessing the motivation and intelligence of aliens, and understanding the means by which communication occurs among advanced organisms? When considered from the standpoint of social science, and of psychology in particular, the motives and actions of the scientist wrestling with these issues closely parallel those of the nonscientist. I expect that my frequent comparison of these two groups will provoke objections from both sides, especially from those whose livelihood and public status depend on keeping things the way they are.

The book is, however, more than a critical essay on the human quest to contact aliens. I offer many untested speculations about the probable success of this search in the light of social science knowledge, and I show wherever possible the positive contributions psychology can bring to such an endeavor. Perhaps the most important among these is the suggestion that the search for aliens may help us better appreciate human nature as it exists today on Earth. Once we see ourselves as members of a universal community of conscious beings, we may be more able to recognize and satisfy humanity's special needs and goals here and now.

The impetus for writing this book came from my participation in a 1979 NASA study group designed to explore the feasibility of detecting radio signals from extraterrestrial civilizations. Most of the twenty-five members of the team were engineers, physicists, and astronomers. Tyler Blake and I were the only psychologists, invited to furnish expertise about human perception that might be applied to a human-computer system for detecting patterns in radio waves.

What surprised many of us working on the project was that here we had a fascinating concept, alien intelligence, about which we knew absolutely nothing; and yet very detailed search plans were rapidly taking shape. As far as I can tell, the same conceptions of the search persist to this day. Such restrictedness does not augur well for future efforts to detect the presence of intelligent aliens. I wrote this book to encourage more parties, both within and outside the scientific community, to become involved in the ongoing debate surrounding this exciting enterprise. Indeed, I will be satisfied if my ideas stimulate others to look more deeply into this intriguing problem and consider the potential costs and benefits of a search which could have far-reaching consequences for all life on this planet, whether or not we ever find anything.

A major portion of the first draft was completed while I was on leave from Dartmouth College and a visiting scholar at Brown and Harvard universities. I am deeply appreciative of all these institutions for providing me with the time and resources to learn and reflect. During this period I lived in a lovely seaside cottage in Little Compton, Rhode Island. I want to thank all my friends there (including M. and P.v.P.P.) for enriching my visit.

I had many stimulating conversations with friends and colleagues about the content of this book, as I struggled to sort out the issues and state my conclusions clearly. In particular, I would like to thank Barbara Angelone, Carole Beal, Tyler Blake, Janis Bolster, Joan Hummel, William T. Jackson, R. Duncan Luce, Susan Miller, Robert Teghtsoonian, and Mark Wagner for their personal support and constructive suggestions. I am grateful as well to Frank Drake and Lynn Margulis, and to all the people who posed counter-points to some of my cherished ideas. I hope the present version of the manuscript alleviates their concerns, without extinguishing the spark of controversy that necessarily accompanies a critical essay of this sort.

In the later stages of preparing the manuscript for publication I re-

ceived expert and welcomed counsel from all the people associated
with the University Press of New England. My special appreciation
goes to Steve Marrone for encouragement and support when it was
needed most.

Hanover, New Hampshire   J.C.B.
November 1986

THE INNER LIMITS
OF OUTER SPACE

CHAPTER 1

THE HUMANIZATION OF SPACE

The single most important event in the history of the human race may occur at the instant we establish indisputable contact with extraterrestrial intelligence. From our current position the detailed impact of such a singular occasion can only be dimly appreciated, though it is almost certain that life on this planet will undergo significant and lasting changes as a result. But rather than attempt to foretell the future, it is perhaps more sensible to look to the present and, in particular, to examine the search techniques being considered in the quest to contact alien life on other planets in the Solar System and beyond—indeed, throughout the vast expanse of the Milky Way Galaxy. I hope to convince the reader that the search for extraterrestrial intelligence is in truth a search for human capabilities as well and, as such, is bounded by the psychological and social skills peculiar, if not unique, to human beings. If we are still the measure of all things, as some Greek philosophers claimed, then probing the depths and mysteries of the universe is synonymous with marking the limits and exploring the mysteries of the human mind. The laws of natural science leading one to entertain the possibility of communication with extraterrestrial life are a direct, inevitable consequence of the inherent complexity of intelligent life on Earth. Although physics and engineering may provide the tools to gain access to an alien consciousness, the degree to which we understand and profit from such an interaction depends critically on psychological and social factors that can only be approached by the "softer" paths of social science.

Apart from the eventual success or failure of the search for extraterrestrial intelligence, the process serves as an outlet for the emerging self of humanity, a means by which we can reach out and gain a more objective understanding of ourselves. By beginning to consider the capabilities and motivations of other civilizations, very different from our own, the species also engages, whether it likes it or not, in a thorough self-examination. Part of the reason we are often unable to break through societal pressures and realize our potential as human beings is that our worldly values are our only reference point for assessing what life has to offer when it comes to communicating our special view of the universe to others. In brief, we may well use the search process as a trigger to unlock the inhibitions that currently block the way to a full understanding of ourselves and the physical universe surrounding us.

If messages from outer space direct attention to matters of scientific interest, they may lead to a kind of self-actualization, insofar as the major questions of science are answered and laid at our doorstep in a comprehensible form. But the motivation for seeking contact with extraterrestrial intelligence may result from a desire to satisfy psychological needs as much as scientific ones. People have always been curious about communicating with forms of life totally unlike themselves, but until scientific study made it virtually certain that the sky above was populated with Sun-like bodies capable of supporting life on Earth-like satellites, this curiosity had to be restricted to forms which after all were originally designed and evolved according to the same biological blueprint. The physical and chemical conditions on Earth encourage some forms of life and absolutely forbid others. But technological advance in the past fifty years has rekindled interest in learning something about alien forms whose starting point and subsequent evolution may have found safe harbor within a totally different physical-chemical milieu existing elsewhere.

This heightened interest in other worlds is apparent in widely diverse quarters. Some people feel that we are being contacted by aliens on a regular basis, as evidenced by the proliferation of sightings of unidentified flying objects (UFOs), which may transport beings from outer space who are equally curious about the variety of life encountered in their galactic neighborhood. Others say that Earth has received space visitors throughout its history and that artifacts of past generations, such as the Egyptian Pyramids, testify to the exceptional intellect and engineering talents of these ancient astronauts.

Still others wishing to extend the limits of present-day engineering suggest that we send our own spacecraft on missions to explore outer space, or at least begin to extend the influence of humanity by constructing habitable space colonies located at successively greater distances from Earth. As we blanket an ever-increasing volume of space with humanity's cultural and technological values, it will be we who assume the role of an unidentified intruder into the worlds of alien species—if they exist—and consequently, it will be the human astronaut who is labeled the strange visitor from a distant, mysterious place.

Despite an ongoing debate among a diverse cross-section of the population concerning the likelihood of finding intelligent life in outer space, only a small segment is marshaling the considerable political and financial support required to underwrite a serious full-scale search. This segment is represented by a tiny, but influential, subset of the scientists and engineers who control the modern radio telescope. Their immediate plan, partly instituted already, is to scan the heavens in hopes of detecting messages amid the omnipresent background noise composed of charged particles and the remnants of the "big bang" of creation. Because the success of this venture could have far-reaching, yet inestimable, consequences for all life on this planet, it is crucial that the guiding assumptions of their program be thoroughly evaluated from as many perspectives as possible: scientific and political, economic and philosophical, social and psychological.

I believe it would be foolish to let research programs involving the radio telescope close the door on other approaches which offer even the faintest hope of success; that is, we should keep an open mind when considering reports of UFOs and past alien contacts. It seems clear, however, that we should carefully investigate those scientific avenues that already show promise, and the most fruitful avenue involves the modest, but growing, effort under way in radio astronomy, where practical questions are being raised about the feasibility of discovering concentrated beacons or scattered pockets of information embedded in the radio environment of outer space—information sent out, intentionally or not, by an extraterrestrial species possessing what we understand as intelligence.

The radio telescope represents an efficient and relatively inexpensive way to contact such a species. The argument favoring its use has even been buttressed by a mathematical formula to gauge the probability that a search for cosmic messages would pay dividends at this moment in history. The formula is variously known as the "Drake equation," the "Drake-Sagan equation," or the "Green Bank equation." Frank Drake and Carl Sagan are the astrophysicists most responsible for its development; Green Bank is the national laboratory in West Virginia where the first scientific conference was held to air these issues and bring them to public attention. The formula isolates the key steps necessary for communication with alien intelligence, the first step being the birth of stars able to support life on orbiting planets and the last being an estimate of the lifetime of a technological society with the will and wherewithal to build and use a radio telescope to exchange messages on an interstellar scale.

If reasonable probabilities of occurrence could be attached to each step in this chain of independent factors, we might gain insight into the chance of making contact by simply multiplying a string of numbers: one probability for each step between the requisite number of candidate stars (not especially difficult to estimate) and the lifetime of a technological civilization (easy to guess, impossible to calculate). The Drake equation expresses this product of probabilities. According to some estimates using the equation, there is a good chance that a technological community like ours is flourishing within easy reach of the larger radio telescopes, which can send and receive signals across immense distances, requiring thousands of light-years to traverse. In his book *Cosmos,* Carl Sagan says that there may be as many as 1 million advanced civilizations within the Milky Way Galaxy alone. If this conclusion is accurate, the universe is literally teeming with life, since there may be as many galaxies in the known universe as there are stars in the Milky Way—several hundred billion.

Not all astronomers, however, agree with this favorable assessment, and critical voices have been raised in opposition. Some who have weighed the same evidence feel that Sagan's early estimates are unwarranted and misleading. The newer figures paint a bleaker picture of the situation; according to the pressimists, there may be only a handful of civilizations in the Galaxy with the technical expertise to conquer the enormity of outer space and establish contact with kindred spirits elsewhere. In this event, there is no pressing reason for humans to initiate a search, except to derive ego satisfaction from knowing that it can be done. But the prospect of moving ahead in the face of heavy odds need not, and probably will not, spoil the dreams of dedicated space enthusiasts, even though it may affect the willingness of society to fund such projects on a large scale.

From the perspective of social science, a comparison of optimists and pessimists is of interest because their "scholarly" pronouncements nicely illustrate how scientists' personal beliefs and emotions influence the style and substance of a supposedly logical debate. As we peer through the window of time and space provided by the radio antenna, the assumptions behind the search process reflect back upon us, bringing home the truth that those assumptions are a function as much of the principles of human psychology as they are of engineering and physics.

This social science perspective is not the centerpiece of most scientific and popular accounts of the search for extraterrestrial intelligence. Perhaps the reason for ignoring social factors is the common belief that science is by definition "objective" and that personal opinion is by definition "subjective." For example, the rationale for launching communication satellites and building space colonies presumably rests on unassailable logical and empirical grounds, whereas subjective reports of alien UFOs and beliefs in ancient astronauts supposedly arise from the gullibility of people unfamiliar with the rudiments of scientific thinking. As far as I can gather, most mainline scientists would feel that the search for extraterrestrial intelligence with a radio telescope, though uncomfortably close to the brink of quack science, could not possibly be motivated by the factors that are behind first-hand reports of UFOs or behind the curiosity about the guiding hand of ancient astronauts in planning the Great Pyramid of Egypt.

Such skepticism is healthy and to be expected, but I think the differences between the views of the scientist and those of the layperson have been overblown. Although the details of what they say may seem incompatible, and the practicality of their ideas disparate, the styles of reasoning used by all types of people are surprisingly alike when considering space research and the possibility of extraterrestrial intelligence. One of my chief purposes in writing this book is to spell out and publicize these similarities. The many differences in attitudes between assorted scientists and laypersons have been amply described elsewhere by physicists and engineers.

Behind the scientific quest to intercept messages from outer space is a long heritage of scientific theory and experimentation. The methods of physical science are so imbued in public consciousness that they seldom undergo the revision characteristic of a dynamic set of ideas under continual scrutiny by outside critics. It is simply taken for granted that the "laws of nature" hold fast throughout the whole fabric of the universe; that use of the electromagnetic medium, including radio waves, is the most efficient way to communicate over great distances; that the coded message we receive someday will bear a close resemblance to mathematical or physical principles; and that, consequently, computers and telescopes working together provide the best means for detecting signals from extraterrestrial sources. On the other hand, it would not surprise me if every one of these assumptions fell wide of the mark or turned out to be just plain wrong. While being perfectly applicable to human communication, they may fail badly when applied to nonhuman communication. We must remember that the eventual goal is to understand an alien mentality, whose motivation for sending messages, for choosing a method of transport and message content, may well involve ways of thinking that are totally foreign to human beings.

In short, the usual strategies of physical science may be inappropriate for this problem. The remarkable success of modern technology results from its ability to move physical matter around at will; that is, large-scale engineering feats are the tangible outcomes of the logical thinking endemic to the scientific method. The physicist and philosopher of science John R. Platt has called this logical style of reasoning the method of "strong inference." He considers it to be the keystone of scientific breakthroughs in physics, chemistry, and biology. The crux of the inductive strategy is straightforward. Once a phenomenon is identified, a number of alternative hypotheses are formulated to explain it. By conducting a series of experiments, researchers eliminate

THE HUMANIZATION OF SPACE   **7**

all but one hypothesis; by strong inference, the surviving alternative is henceforth held to be correct. So from an initial multiplicity of plausible explanations we move quickly and confidently toward a single choice. Karl Popper and other philosophers have recently described such methods at great length.

This is the style of thought fueling the current plans to lift people and machines into semipermanent homes in outer space, as well as standing behind the techniques suggested to contact extraterrestrial intelligence from stations on Earth. Not all scientists unswervingly embrace the doctrine of strong inference, but it dominates the philosophical underpinnings of the space effort. Although seldom made explicit, the plan for the immediate future apparently is to conduct physical, chemical, and biological experiments, as funds permit, to test out notions about the nature of outer space and its potential inhabitants, and then to exploit those approaches that strike the richest lode. If there are unequivocal answers to questions about alien intelligence, this method is designed to find them.

Social science, on the other hand, generally operates with a complex network of explanations about any given phenomenon. Social science's experience with Platt's principle of strong inference is often disappointing. When dealing with problems of human learning, perception, cognition, and social behavior, one almost never ends up with a clear winner from among the pool of candidate explanations. To some degree this may be because the experiments in social science cannot be run with the rigor possible in the physics laboratory. I doubt, however, if this is the whole story. Either the alternative viewpoints stubbornly hold their ground in the face of new data, or else, as old ideas fade, new ones spring forth to take their place. Thus the number of alternative theories at any point in a research program stays pretty much constant. A likely outcome of a long investigation is that the remarkable flexibility of the human being is reaffirmed, a flexibility which demands that the theorist consider diverse opinions about how people approach everything from mathematics to child rearing, from ice fishing to bank accounts. There appear to be no absolute answers to many questions posed by social science. At least, such answers cannot be obtained with the methods presently available.

The theoretical psychologist develops conceptual models to elucidate various sides of human behavior, but in the cold reality of empirical facts none of these models can effectively sink its competitors. Different concepts are appropriate for different social situations, and so far, the method of strong inference has not led to a single broad theory of the human being that can account for behavior in even the most ordinary circumstances. It is in part because of this failure that social scientists are encouraged to think divergently and to retain an openness about opposing views, be they concerned with social, psychological, or physical matters.

Since I believe that the human mind creates the deeper melody to which the lyrics of natural science must be arranged, a variety of routes, including those of social science, must be pursued in treating the altogether novel issues arising in attempts to contact alien civilizations. At present, this is not the favored strategy of the scientists, administrators, and politicians most responsible for the world's major space programs. As far as I can tell, social scientists are rarely consulted in the planning stages of these programs, and consequently, the divergent thinking characteristic of their discipline is given less weight in making decisions than are the convergent methods familiar to the physical and biological sciences.

The result in practical terms is that only a small number of approaches are being explored, or even contemplated; and attempts by outsiders, social scientists and others, to extend the breadth of study are either ignored or met with frank disdain. In the opinion of some philosophers—for example, Paul Feyerabend—the past achievements of science in explaining selected aspects of the material world have gone to its head. Many people now have the unfortunate notion that physical science furnishes the conceptual tools to overcome every sort of obstacle encountered by the human race. I would like very much to see this trend moderated and redirected into a more balanced view about the conditions under which physical science is and is not applicable. Those aspects of existence about which we know almost nothing, including the higher functions of the human brain and the universal limits of intelligence, may in the long run prove totally opaque to methods found effective in dealing with the inanimate and with the biochemistry of life, or in dealing with small-scale biology and physiology at the cellular level.

Because of the comparative youth of human civilization when set against the billions of years available for the evolution of complex life throughout the universe, it is likely that contact with extraterrestrial intelligence will involve a being or entity far more advanced than ourselves. This conclusion is supported by the fact that humanity has been unable to journey very far from its home planet and has had the technical means to communicate over interstellar distances for only the past half century. We have barely crossed the threshold of technological competence required to complete goals which may have been reached long ago by civilizations elsewhere in the universe.

Most observers agree on this point. It is impossible to say how this advanced mentality would be manifested—whether it would be apparent in the power of raw intelligence, emotional expression, technological accomplishments, aesthetic awareness, or what. At this stage, of course, no one can tell, but it does appear likely that humans will occupy a subordinate position in any interchange of viewpoints. We will be like children at the knees of the family elders, listening to a story that may be only vaguely understood. Indeed, storytelling itself embodies all the requirements for comprehending a message when the give-and-take of normal conversation is minimized. The passive listener, child or adult, must have the proper sensory receptors to encode the separate parts of the story, the cognitive ability to assemble the parts into a whole, the knowledge to grasp its meaning, and the memory to retain the message over time. In addition, the listener feels more confident about interpreting the message if unfamiliar terms are thoroughly explained, the essence of the story is repeated every now and then, and ample opportunity is given to perform the integration needed to fit the implications of what is being said into a larger social context.

All these requirements hold when we consider listening to messages from extraterrestrial storytellers. Whether the listener is a person or a machine built to supplement human skills, the receiver's ability to observe patterns, decipher meanings, learn new concepts, and store critical ideas will set upper bounds on how much of the story is finally understood. And behind the generation of this list of requirements stand principles of social science and psychology. Although these principles are admittedly more obscure than those in the physical sciences, their implementation in the search for extraterrestrial intelligence will produce a more satisfying result, however the physical search is conducted.

High-powered technology does not alter this basic truth. Computers, telescopes, and electronic space probes are effective only insofar as they provide facts that can be understood by their human makers. As physical appendages to our capabilities, machines can reveal something new about only those dimensions of a physical world with which we are already somewhat conversant. Aside from purely speculative comments, computer specialists offer no evidence to convince us otherwise. The crucial philosophical point boils down to epistemology. If a machine in some way were able to collect information that was beyond the comprehension of human sensory and mental abilities, the relevance of such information would remain a puzzle forever. The numbers coming out of the machine would be seen as nothing more than random garbage.

While this is a truism, it is worth repeating every now and then, since those engaged in space research might unwittingly construct a false image of human omnipotence, shared among themselves and uncritically disseminated among the ranks of the uninformed. This image could prove detrimental to both science and the human species in the long term, because it will most assuredly be shattered by failures in key realms of social and political science. It is my contention that careful attention to psychological factors, in particular, will reduce the danger by fostering a sense of modesty about what humans can actually hope to accomplish, while simultaneously improving the chances of success in reaching out to other civilizations, whatever the means for doing so. Therefore, I spend a lot of time in this book noting the merits of search efforts within a larger societal and psychological context, which so far as I can tell has not previously been considered.

Things change quickly in the space program. A few years ago the United States' Viking lander visited Mars, conducted clever biological experiments, and returned valuable scientific data to Earth. In this way a new field of study was legitimized: exobiology, the study of biological systems in outer space—stars, planets, and the like. A sister discipline of exopsychology might emerge someday to concern itself with the behavior, attitudes, personalities, and thoughts of alien beings. But first we must be convinced that such beings exist and can be coaxed into some kind of profitable interaction. Until that happens, we will have to rest content with sketchy psychological profiles of the humans on Earth who desire contact and of those who actively develop the technical means for approaching this goal. Throughout this book I touch upon the traits and attitudes that seem to characterize these individuals, but of course only with respect to one particular facet of their activities and interests.

These preliminary analyses may quickly blossom and bear fruit if an interpretable message is ever discovered. Not only will exopsychology burst on the scene, but those areas of social science concerned with people's normal and abnormal reactions to world events of major significance will also suddenly be faced with a host of fresh material. The psychological pluralism that defines the human state guarantees a wide range of reactions.

In the early days following their reception, everyone may see alien messages as Rorschach inkblots from outer space; people will read the tea leaves according to their personal hopes, needs, and expectations. Most such reactions will be driven by normal curiosity, pure and simple. Some individuals, however, surely will treat the novel information, whatever its content, as a serious threat to the integrity of "the self" and perhaps to the survival of the human race, although psychological difficulties will probably subside once uncertainty is removed about the exact meaning of the communication, for better or worse!

Political consequences are interesting to think about as well. Security is likely to be tight. Governments may become more protective than usual about their proprietary rights to data gathered by their astronomers. There could be a dramatic increase in covert intelligence operations, and these activities could escalate in proportion to the perceived value of the messages being received. If we are fortunate, a message will proffer advice for dealing with the various political and military conflagrations that cosmic messages could ignite among competing nations. In such desired circumstances, nations may willingly choose to unite and cooperate in a common venture to understand extraterrestrial messages. But further speculations about the result of contact had best wait until we have covered the various search methods, scientific and otherwise, and the psychological factors involved in implementing each of them.

REFERENCES AND FURTHER READINGS

Feyerabend, P. *Against Method*. London: NLB, 1975.

Maslow, A. H. *Toward a Psychology of Being*. Princeton, N.J.: Van Nostrand, 1968.

Michener, J. A. *Space*. New York: Ballantine, 1982.

O'Neill, G. K. *The High Frontier: Human Colonies in Space*. New York: Morow, 1977; Bantam, 1978.

Platt, J. R. *The Step to Man*. New York: Wiley, 1966.

Popper, K. R. *The Logic of Scientific Discovery*. London: Hutchinson, 1959.

Regis, E., Jr. (Ed.) *Extraterrestrials: Science and Alien Intelligence*. Cambridge: Cambridge University Press, 1985.

Rood, R. T., & Trefil, J. S. *Are We Alone? The Possibility of Extraterrestrial Civilizations*. New York: Scribner, 1981.

Sagan, C. *Contact*. New York: Pocket, 1985.

Sagan, C. *Cosmos*. New York: Random House, 1980.

Sevastyanov, V.; Ursul, A.; & Shkolenko, Y. *The Universe and Civilisation*. Translated from the Russian by S. Syrovetkin. Moscow: Progress, 1981.

Von Däniken, E. *Chariots of the Gods?* New York: Putnam, 1969.

CHAPTER 2

ANCIENT ASTRONAUTS?

A recurring theme in the historical debate about the possibility of alien life is that the search for its existence need never leave Earth. Some say aliens have been arriving off and on over the millennia, and continue to do so today, thereby saving us the trouble of initiating a search program of our own. This optimistic attitude is common among people intrigued by the mysteries of outer space but unable or unwilling to consider these matters in scientific terms. Though open to the possibility of contacting alien intelligence, they draw heavily on inner feelings when trying to decide whether contact has already occurred. Rather than formulate a scientific argument or seek additional facts to resolve an issue, these people are likely simply to ask themselves: "Does this idea feel right to me? Do I really believe that extraterrestrials have visited Earth?" For many, the emotional response to both questions is a firm yes.

The validity of this conclusion is doubted by most scientists who have examined the evidence justifying belief in alien visits. They are not satisfied with the testimony used to further the extraterrestrial hypothesis, either as an explanation of the numerous sightings of UFOs or as support for the notion that "ancient astronauts" once roamed the face of the globe and civilized the primitive humans they met there.

With the exception of a few hard-core skeptics, scientists would be instant converts to an extraterrestrial explanation of the origin of UFOs if there were remnants of alien visits lying around for anyone's examination. Nothing would be more convincing than to have in hand a functioning alien spacecraft or, better yet, a genuine example of alien life. Such unmistakable clues have not surfaced, and until they do, scientists will continued to express strong reservations about the validity of UFO reports.

But scientific argument doesn't flow as smoothly when we entertain the possibility of visits by extraterrestrials in the far distant past, say four or five thousand years ago. The farther back in time we go the scarcer the facts become, and our historical perspective suffers accordingly. Perhaps it was to resolve this uncertainty that the theory of ancient astronauts was first developed and vigorously defended by the late Swiss writer Erich von Däniken.

The broad issue addressed by von Däniken is unique and fascinating. In the garden-variety UFO report we have the statements of human witnesses but no physical artifacts; in considering ancient UFOs we have no living witnesses, but there are artifacts that might be accepted as circumstantial evidence. These artifacts are large and obvious, represented by the lasting monuments attributed to the architectural and construction skills of ancient civilizations: the Pyramids of Egypt, the temples of Central America, the statues of Easter Island, and other engineering marvels of comparable vintage.

Before delving further into this topic, and into von Däniken's controversial theory, we should note that the average person of a nonscientific bent probably doesn't grasp the principles behind much of modern engineering. It is therefore not surprising that nonscientists in particular have difficulty seeing how an ancient society, working with primitive tools and relying on elementary science, completed engineering tasks which to our eyes seem quite impossible. Von Däniken himself was more a practicing novelist than a knowledgeable scientist, and he was no doubt genuinely amazed by the engineering feats he observed.

Each of us perceives modern technology as a standard against which to judge the achievements of the past. In this regard, a scientist may stand in awe of an ancient monument but still imagine ways it could have come about. Nonscientists have a harder time of it, because they must draw upon a different pool of options. Lacking comprehension of the engineering possibilities in their own era puts them at a still greater disadvantage when trying to determine the means by which ancient civilizations set and reached their goals.

Confusion often reigns when we speculate about the remote past of the human species and try to generate sufficient reasons for its cultural practices and artifacts. The inexorable forces of nature erode and distort all but the most massive edifices, built from the sturdiest materials, and located in climates favorable to their longevity. Consequently, the objects caught in the net of history do not necessarily reveal key facts about the people who created them. The size of an artifact need not correlate with its original importance, although the expenditures of human effort in constructing the Pyramids of Egypt or the Great Wall of China strongly suggest that these massive artifacts were considered very important by their creators. Such solid monuments are the only clues we have to aid the detective work required to spell out our ancestral lineage, and we can use only those clues available.

It is interesting to note that such material facts will not be around to aid future generations who might wish to understand the present technological state of humanity. A dim fate awaits today's engineering miracles. Many would agree that the most newsworthy products of a technological age are electronic computers. As these machines have diminished in size over recent decades, they have been made from proportionately smaller and more fragile components. So during a period when computer power has reached previously undreamed-of heights, the physical vulnerability of the machines responsible for this power has increased at a corresponding pace. In a throwaway society the fruits of advanced technology are easily produced and more easily discarded in favor of newer models. I doubt very much whether the desktop computer on which this book is being written will still function in the year 6000, although its tough exterior casing may be intact. An empty plastic shell will not provide many helpful hints to future archaeologists about the purpose or power of the original circuitry within, and will be even less useful in determining the substantive ideas being expressed with the help of the computer's word-processing program.

Scanning back in time, the vestigial traces of civilizations are composed of tougher stuff: immense stone artifacts found in climates where erosion from the weather is minimal. This is nowhere more apparent than in the case of the Egyptian Pyramids, von Däniken's prime example of the guiding hand of ancient astronauts. Although a sizable number of Pyramids attest to the vigor of Egyptian civilization at the time, modern writers show special interest in the so-called Great Pyramid, built approximately four thousand years ago by King Khufu (Cheops) on the west bank of the Nile near the present city of Cairo. Its vital statistics are impressive. The base covers some thirteen acres, and in a youthful state of grandeur the peak soared 480 feet above the ground. The individual blocks average two and a half tons, and there are approximately two and a quarter million of them. Yet one of the most remarkable characteristics of this structure is that despite its grand scale, it is also thought to be far and away the best example of the careful planning and workmanship represented by the pyramidal form. In his lively treatment of the history of engineering, L. Sprague DeCamp notes that the sides forming the base of the Great Pyramid are almost a perfect square (within seven inches) and are very nearly oriented in the true north-south and east-west directions (within six minutes of arc). Quite definitely, some individual or group spent a fair amount of time thinking about this project, well before a single block of stone was laid.

The combination of sheer mass and high precision embodied in the Great Pyramid begs us to ask questions about its mode of construction, as well as about the design and building skills of its creators. Is it possible that four thousand years ago a society had the physical resources, architectural competence, and technical skill needed to complete a project of such sophistication successfully? A large task force must have been assembled; the workers must have been well organized, housed, and fed and completely dedicated to the project for an extended time. In addition, trade skills would be necessary to mine and shape the stones, not to mention hauling them to the construction site and hoisting them up the sides of the pyramid. To many, the very thought of an engineering task of this scope, at such an early stage in the evolution of civilization, borders on the incredible. A modern construction firm would shudder at the prospect of fulfilling the job specifications for the Great Pyramid, and the project certainly would pose a formidable challenge for even the largest and best equipped construction firm of the year 2000 B.C.

When considering the present, a person has confidence that somebody in the local community possesses the background to understand and properly operate a device like a television set, a washing machine, or an elevator, but this confidence dissipates when we contemplate artifacts created long ago in an unfamiliar geographical and political context. Our familiar items of home and office are being manufactured and serviced on a regular basis by trained members of the community. But when the nonspecialist confronts the Great Pyramid, he or she is dealing with an exceptional object whose original purpose for being is quite obscure. And even among Egyptologists the validity of the common "tomb" theory of the Pyramids has come under occasional attack. The average person would not find it helpful to try to settle such controversies by seeking out "pyramid" in the business section of the local telephone book, nor would this person be likely to have friends and relations who know much about pyramids. Viewed in this light, the majority of people might not conjure up sufficient reasons to explain how the Great Pyramid was ever built. Why on earth was it put there? Who was responsible for its construction, and exactly how was it done? All such queries are quite logical and legitimate.

The typical citizen's uncertainty serves to illustrate what we might call the "Principle of Insufficient Options": *Scientists and nonscientists alike who do not have the benefit of all historical evidence are constrained in their ability to generate explanations for exceptional events which took place in the very distant past.* A corollary might be: *Alternative explanations of a bizarre and unusual kind are seen as more valid when applied to ancient events than when applied to current events of a similar level of complexity.*

One frequent option entertained by people when they find themselves in a state of scientific ignorance is that provided by religious teachings. In 1877 Joseph A. Seiss published a religious treatise on the Great Pyramid that is still cited by Egyptologists, though seldom in a flattering light. After noting the physical measurements and folklore surrounding the purpose and construction of the Pyramid, Seiss presented his thesis that God himself approved and oversaw its construction. Seiss was not at all pleased with the accepted views of his time; specifically, he denied that the Pyramid served any role as a burial chamber for Egyptian royalty. He proposed an alternative theory that the real architects were not Egyptians at all but a people who were the founders of the Christian faith. Detailed instructions on how to build the Great Pyramid were passed down by God as a special communication to a chosen people. The exact layout of the Pyramid, inside and out, was chosen for religious reasons only, and not as a means to pay homage to a "pagan despot." Seiss offered no special insights into the possible engineering methods used to erect the Great Pyramid, apparently leaving such details to scientific historians.

The religious theory of why the pyramids were built draws attention to the difficulty of making decisions under conditions of factual uncertainty. When human ingenuity in forming practical, ground-roots hypotheses fails, religious doctrine is sought to bring closure and meaning to an otherwise uncomfortable situation. Many people become anxious when the answers to philosophical questions are not clear-cut and definitive. In such states of agitation they often turn to religion for concrete answers, although they are less willing to accept such doctrine when applied to events of comparable complexity found in their immediate environment. For example, the existence of skyscrapers in New York City probably has never been attributed to the power of divine intervention.

The Great Pyramid of King Khufu is the most renowned edifice of Egypt, and to judge its true importance for those who built it requires scholarship and powerful imagination. Other monolithic structures of the Middle East pose engineering puzzles of equal complexity. For example, the old and beautiful Lebanese city of Baalbek, just north of Damascus, boasts a stone acropolis of mammoth proportions, a platform 440 feet wide by 880 feet long, supported by stone blocks mined and removed from a quarry a half mile away. Some of the blocks stand thirteen feet high, are ten feet thick, and stretch to a length of sixty-four feet. Each of these monsters is estimated to weigh in at roughly one thousand tons! Numerous observers have commented on the construction problems posed in erecting this platform, as well as in building the nearby temples, which in their original state were of comparable proportions. The same questions arise as with the pyramids: How were these massive blocks carved from the earth? Where did the energy come from to transport the blocks from the quarry to the construction site? How were stones cascaded to make columns for the temples and supports for the platform?

Similar hard questions occur to the observer of the Easter Island statues located quite literally in the middle of nowhere, about twenty-five hundred miles west of Chile and a comparable distance east of

Tahiti. According to Thor Heyerdahl, the statues were probably carved out of the slope of a dead volcano between A.D. 1100 and 1680. They consist of twelve-ton heads sitting atop what appear to be undersized torsos. Originally, the heads were adorned with red sandstone caps, but these have since been knocked from their pedestals thirty feet above ground. Although many inscriptions were uncovered on polished slabs found on the island, they do not help clarify why the statues were chiseled out of the volcano and hauled to their final location above the island's shore: The language on the wooden slabs has yet to be deciphered.

A more artistic riddle is created by a set of desert markings near the town of Nazca in southern Peru. Within a rectangular sector approximately sixty miles long by ten miles wide one finds what looks to be a giant child's sketch pad. Probably at least fifteen hundred years ago, large patterns of animals, plants, and simple geometric shapes were etched on the desert floor by removing rocks and thus uncovering the lighter subsurface. The fantastic dimensions of these patterns are such as to be appreciated in their entirety only from a great height. It is not obvious what the motivation would be for a society to expend effort on an art project whose full beauty could only be appreciated from an unattainable height, although a few nearby mountains do provide some distant vistas. Recent scholarship suggests that the drawings had nothing to do with their visibility from the ground, but rather were the result of a government "make-work" project with ceremonial tones. According to the anthropologist William H. Isbell, the particular patterns on the ground are also depicted on the pottery of the region attributed to that historical period.

With this brief historical background in place we can explore more fully the relevance of these ancient structures for recent pronouncements about visitors from outer space. The puzzlement induced by the stone monuments of the Middle East, the Easter Island heads, and the desert museum of Peru is what led Erich von Däniken to put forth some unorthodox ideas about the cultural heritage of human civilization. The heart of his thesis is religious. He claims unabashedly that a significant kernel of truth is found in Judeo-Christian doctrine suggesting, among other things, a comparatively recent origin for *Homo sapiens,* who, he argues, reached the current height of intelligence quickly and without benefit of Darwinian evolution. In addition, he feels that there is good reason to trust biblical stories about the natural disasters at the dawn of history and about the human manifestation of a god who came from on high, a god who walked the earth and freely distributed moral and technical advice to human beings. In this sense, von Däniken sounds like a twentieth-century version of Joseph Seiss.

There is, however, one mighty difference between pure religious doctrine and the viewpoint expounded by von Däniken: Namely, von Däniken argues that a careful reading of Genesis leaves the impression that there was a plurality of gods in ancient times and that these gods or their sons were in fact alien beings from another planet. As his thesis unfolds, these ancient astronauts visited Earth on several occasions and were so constituted biologically as to be able to communicate effectively with our ancestors.

According to von Däniken, it is this superior, alien species which deserves credit for the otherwise inexplicable monuments of the past. These god-astronauts either built the pyramids and other structures of ancient times or instructed people in the art and science of doing so. Supposedly, the remains of these civilizations are a lasting tribute as much to the commandments of space visitors as to the ingenuity and ceremonial traditions of our human predecessors. For example, he explicitly claims that the reason for devising the geometric patterns of the Nazca Plain was to establish landing strips to accommodate alien spacecraft.

Von Däniken further states that these visitors were especially interested in transmitting their genes in order to breed alien/human hybrids, and they did so by mating with selected humans met on one of their early visits, some ten thousand years ago. The rapid expansion of human intelligence and technology since then can be traced to the introduction of superior traits into the human gene pool at this comparatively recent epoch in history. As the Bible says, we were indeed created in God's image. But contrary to the literal interpretation of this statement, von Däniken thought the God of the Bible was a primitive people's image of an alien being, sent on a mission to Earth by a superior civilization in order to accelerate the growth of a fledgling civilization.

By referring to these extraordinary ideas as "speculative explanations," von Däniken invites scientists and laypersons alike to come up with alternative interpretations of the historical foundations of modern civilization. Basically, what he suggests is that the unadulterated, pre-alien version of humanity was incapable of the mental and physical dexterity required to design and build the structures of the past we now attribute to the people of those times. More interestingly, then, a search for extraterrestrial intelligence becomes in von Däniken's mind nothing less than an expedition into the depths of human consciousness. There is little point in looking for salvation beyond ourselves, except to trace our ancestry. If we are the superior extraterrestrials being sought, the human race is a chosen people, the end result of a colonization policy formulated long ago by a species intent on propagating its kind throughout the universe.

This rather fanciful view of the origins of humanity must strike a sympathetic chord in a large number of readers, since von Däniken's books have sold by the millions all over the world. It is likely that this popularity can be traced to the doorstep of psychology. In particular, widespread belief in these unorthodox notions seems to reflect a common reaction to situations in which we are asked to make decisions without the benefit of critical information. The principle of insufficient options suggests that perfectly reasonable, intelligent individuals are often willing to entertain really bizarre ideas about events which took place long ago, and about which they know very little.

Egyptologists and scholars of early civilizations offer more prosaic stories about the origins of ancient monuments. According to L. Sprague DeCamp the ancient engineers were people, not gods, and they regularly used techniques that evolved after extended periods of trial-and-error learning. For example, early stone burial tombs foreshadowed the pyramidal form, and partially collapsed pyramids attest to a learning phase over which the final shape was approached gradually. The pyramid is also a stable form. Because of the lack of arch and vault, towering structures can be stabilized by tapering the walls to a point in this manner. The Egyptians did this in their early buildings, and such a purely architectual concern might explain why the same form is encountered in widely separated regions of the world. Human builders with a common architectural problem tend to come up with similar, human, solutions. As for their purpose, in the opinion of DeCamp, the Great Pyramid and similar edifices of Egypt "were tombs pure and simple" (*The Ancient Engineers*, p. 29).

In his book *The Space-Gods Revealed* Ronald Story arrives at the same conclusion regarding the Pyramids and also surveys the archaeological views about how and why human beings erected the stone heads of Easter Island and laid out the curious patterns of the Nazca Plain. All his interpretations, based on accepted anthropological findings, lead him to believe that these structures were the products of human ingenuity and were painstakingly crafted without the spiritual or technical assistance of ancient astronauts.

In addition, Story and others have repeatedly asked the most poignant question of von Däniken's thesis: Why would aliens be partial to such monuments in the first place? We presume with some confidence that this superior species was technically advanced, or otherwise it wouldn't be cavorting about the Galaxy. Therefore, we can assume as well that these visitors would have little need for landing fields in the desert, stone statues of apparent religious significance on isolated islands, or gigantic pyramids whose purpose it was to serve as luxury hotels for enhancing the afterlife of Egyptian nobility. There are, then, some reasonable scientific theories about how these structures came into existence. Both Story and DeCamp offer sound arguments that invoke neither religious nor extraterrestrial influences to explain the actual construction of the monuments—though religious concerns may have played a key role in motivating people to undertake such time-consuming projects. Even if our human ancestors planned and built these structures, however, it still could be argued that they did so under the watchful eyes of alien advisers.

A rather amusing, but plausible, rendition of how the Pyramids were built is given by T. B. Pawlicki in a little book on speculative engineering. He describes in some detail how a relatively small band of workers could apparently defy gravity by lifting two-and-a-half-ton blocks of stone up the side of a pyramid. Briefly, the argument goes like this: If a pulley or device of similar function is fixed at the top, a rope can be strung down on both sides. Sleds can then be attached to each end of the rope. The block of stone is placed on one of the sleds while it lies flat on the ground. An appropriate counterweight is then assembled by placing small, manageable pieces of stone on the other sled, which has been dragged empty to the top of the pyramid. Now, as the counterweight is eased down one side and lowered to the ground, there is a corresponding ascent of the solid block of stone on the opposing sled. The physical principle behind this approach is in fact identical to that behind the operation of most elevators.

People nowadays may overlook obvious solutions to the problems suggested by the impressive structures of the past because they are not really aware of similar problems and solutions in their own time and immediate environment. A singular quality of human societies is the talent for inventing and building labor-saving devices. A curious spin-off of this activity is the equally strong desire to conceal the inner workings of these devices from the purview of the senses, that is, eyes, ears, and touch. The intended use of a device may be readily apparent, but the physical mechanism responsible for making it work is often hidden in such a way as to impede any serious effort to understand the physical principles involved in its operation. There is nothing extraordinary in this practice. The protection of the parts within and the people without are important concerns, as are the aesthetics of the product and the desire to protect trade secrets.

An illustrative example is a device I just mentioned, the ordinary elevator. When I was a child my parents took me on a guided tour of the wonders of New York City. One of the "must" stops on these tours was the Empire State Building, at that time the tallest in the city, from whose upper decks one enjoyed a commanding view of Manhattan. Somewhat to my parents' surprise, the magnificent view did not hold the same attraction for me as did the elevator used to transport people from the ground floor to the observation deck. I remember having doubts about entering a tiny room which presumably would fly up to the roof of this very large building. Even after a successful round trip, I had no idea how the elevator accomplished this stupendous feat, and upon asking, I was told something about giant cables, pulleys, and counterweights. The functioning of these various parts on such a grand scale remained unclear and slightly unbelievable. I would much have preferred to have the opportunity to see for myself, but thankfully no one was about to let a young boy explore the wonders of an elevator shaft.

It was not until years later in Paris that I gained firsthand knowledge of how most elevators work. I was staying in a small, family-run hotel whose elevator shaft was entirely visible above a side wall of the public bathroom. From a seated vantage point I could easily inspect the cables and counterweights moving in synchrony with the cage, and by looking up I could see a pulley system hooked into an electric motor. I imagined a similar arrangement applied as well to greater heights, for example, the Empire State Building. The extension of the basic principle would simply require an increase in the size and strength of all components to handle the vertical distance to be traversed.

Several years ago I happened to learn a little more about elevators and, in particular, about how they function in buildings with five or fewer stories. The occasion was the construction of a wing on a local office building. As a consequence of this project, the elevator in the old building had to be completely replaced. The architect told me that the new elevator car would be hydraulically lifted from below. A plunger would be raised by pumping oil into the bottom of an enclosing cylinder, sunk underground to a depth equivalent to the vertical distance required to raise the car.

His comments triggered a brief library search, from which I discovered that the first commercial electric elevator was in operation as early as 1850 and the hydraulic type was introduced in 1878. Many years of my life passed before I secured any intuition about the engineering behind a piece of equipment used every day by millions of people, whose essential features have remained the same for over a hundred years.

I relate this anecdote to ask whether I am alone in my ignorance of the principles behind the engineering achievements of a technological age. Naturally, I think not. To most people, scientists and laypersons alike, a familiar technology is taken for granted; they would be at a loss if asked to identify the energy source driving the electrical appliances in the home, the origin of the community drinking water or gas supply, or the destination of its waste products. Many of us would be further at sea if asked to explain how a radio or television set works, or even to describe what is seen when the back panel of a refrigerator or washing machine is removed.

Although somewhat shaky in our knowledge of applied science, we do not classify these engineering feats as unsolved puzzles. If the television set fails, we are confident that someone in the community can fix it. If a source of energy is sought, a friend or neighbor will know where and how to obtain it. The presence of a cadre of professional and amateur specialists provides the community at large with all the necessary expertise to understand and control even the most esoteric equipment, from high-rise elevators to high-speed computers. We ourselves could spell out the laws governing the machine age, if we were inclined to try hard enough, to undergo the necessary training, to hold an apprenticeship with a master electrician or plumber, to read and experiment on our own, and so forth. But time does not permit the indulgence of all our wishes, and adequate sources are available to elucidate what otherwise would be a hopeless mass of technical detail. For these reasons, most people are not in a state of constant disbelief over the engineering miracles of their familiar environment.

I would venture the guess that the majority of the Earth's literate population has only the foggiest notion of how an electric elevator works, and even fewer people have ever heard of the hydraulic type. It therefore comes as no big revelation to find that the engineering principles behind our modern conveniences, though obvious when pointed out, are not instantly seen as the basis for the engineering accomplishments of previous ages. Instead, we offer a sympathetic ear to all manner of alternative theories about how these events came to pass. Into this void of knowledge boldly steps the doctrine of outside assistance, of either a religious or an extraterrestrial flavor.

Acceptance of a theory of outside intervention implies that the limits of human capabilities have been extended in the past by forces of higher intelligence. On closer examination of the facts, however, this theory simply appears not to hold. Rather, humans often underestimate their own talents, more so in regard to the past than to the present. Given the available materials and equipment, the ambitious building programs of prior generations taxed human ingenuity in engineering, but it is nonetheless possible to understand how our predecessors managed to complete such programs.

In sum, a nontechnical person is unlikely to have a good grasp of the principles underlying the engineering feats of today, but at least this person has the belief that others, more technically competent, do understand these principles. When the nonscientist looks to the distant past, however, there appear to be no obvious facts to explain the meaning of the unusual artifacts found there. Thor Heyerdahl, who has commented extensively on this subject, feels that social scientists, in particular, should accept the blame for not making the agreed-upon facts more accessible to the nonscientist. Left in a state of uncertainty, nonscientists may turn to religious and quasi-religious sources in order to resolve annoying ambiguities. In doing so, these people are led to believe theories that they would see as utterly ridiculous if someone tried to apply them to current events engendering similar degrees of perplexity.

Some may argue that the popular belief in UFOs is a counter-example, but I really don't see it that way. Aside from the subjective reports of witnesses, the voluminous pages written in support of the extraterrestrial origin of UFOs fail to include discussion of solid physical evidence. It would be difficult to do otherwise, since so far as I can tell such evidence doesn't exist. We turn next to this topic.

REFERENCES AND FURTHER READINGS

DeCamp, L. S. *The Ancient Engineers*. New York: Ballantine, 1980.
Ebon, M. (Ed.) *The World's Great Unsolved Mysteries*. New York: Signet, 1981.
Heyerdahl, T. *Aku Aku*. Chicago: Rand McNally, 1958.
Isbell, W. H. The Prehistoric Ground Drawings of Peru. *Scientific American*, 1978, *239*, No. 4, 140–153.
Klass, P. J. *UFOs Explained*. New York: Random House, Vintage, 1976.
Krupp, E. C. (Ed.) *In Search of Ancient Astronomies*. New York: McGraw-Hill, 1978.
Pawlicki, T. B. *How to Build a Flying Saucer and Other Proposals in Speculative Engineering*. Englewood Cliffs, N.J.: Prentice-Hall, 1981.
Seiss, J. A. *The Great Pyramid: A Miracle in Stone*. Philadelphia, 1877. Reprint. San Francisco: Harper & Row, 1973.
Story, R. *The Space-Gods Revealed*. New York: Barnes & Noble, 1980.
Von Däniken, E. *Chariots of the Gods?* New York: Putnam, 1969.
Von Däniken, E. *Signs of the Gods*. New York: Berkley, 1980.

CHAPTER 3

SPACE PROBES
AND UNIDENTIFIED FLYING OBJECTS

The sentiment shared by most scientists is that Earth has not been visited by alien spacecraft in the distant past, and most probably is not being visited today. Contemporary reports of UFOs do not automatically bestow credibility on the extraterrestrial hypothesis concerning the genesis and nature of the objects being seen.

On the other hand, there is a subtle, but important, point to be made in favor of the extraterrestrial hypothesis. From an engineering standpoint we are now capable of dispatching spacecraft on missions beyond the borders of the Solar System and on to other stars in the Galaxy. In theory, then, it is natural to believe that aliens can do the same, and consequently, it is not surprising to find widespread support for the extraterrestrial hypothesis among people who are interested in outer space but who lack the scientific knowledge to evaluate the physical barriers such ventures pose for a sending civilization, wherever it happens to be located in the Galaxy. It is true that science sets limits on the expeditionary dreams of humans, but everyone admits that science cannot provide rational figures on the technical proficiency of alien societies.

Because of the impossibility of defining alien life, all of us have unbridled freedom to imagine whatever we choose. Belief in extraterrestrial messengers flows easily from unshackled imagination. Before examining this special belief in more detail, let me relate what some engineers think is possible in the way of sending spacecraft and satellite probes to other star systems. (Note that scientists and nonscientists alike usually talk as though human capabilities at this point in space and time are those available to all species at all points in space and time.) Once our own capabilities in this regard are reviewed, it will be easier to see why people are led to believe that UFOs have an extraterrestrial origin and purpose.

In recent years the space programs of both the United States and the Soviet Union have launched unmanned satellites to monitor the atmospheric and surface conditions of other planets in the Solar System. The cost of such endeavors would not jump sharply if these satellites were outfitted with electronic equipment to listen for radio activity generated by extraterrestrial civilizations. The long-range goal of such a listening program would be to eavesdrop on life residing in the vicinity of more distant, neighboring stars. Some foresighted engineers hope eventually to fix probes in enough strategic positions throughout the Galaxy to install a communication network that includes alien life—what there is of it—on a still wider scale.

The mathematical physicist Frank J. Tipler has detailed how an advanced civilization could populate the entire Milky Way Galaxy within the brief period (on a cosmic scale) of 300 million years. Self-reproducing computer-robots would be sent out as an expeditionary force to leapfrog from one star system to the next, until all systems with the potential for intelligent life were explored. The material to reproduce these space-faring machines would be found in the star systems encountered in the course of exploration. One of the questions posed by this scenario is why other civilizations, perhaps billions of years our senior, have not already embarked on this journey, in which case they should have arrived here by now. As the physicist Enrico Fermi once asked at a Los Alamos dinner party, "Where are they?" (Regis, *Extraterrestrials*, p. 129). The resolution of the Fermi paradox seems to depend critically on how fast such emigration can and does occur, and this is currently a matter of great debate (see, e.g., the articles by Carl Sagan and William I. Newman and by E. M. Jones).

The particulars of how such intersteller envoys might actually function have been discussed at some length by Ronald Bracewell and Robert A. Freitas, Jr. They reason that if we are not contacted in the near future by extraterrestrials, we should begin posting our own calling cards into outer space. Because we are probably a newcomer to the galactic club of long-distanced correspondents, however, the immediate future will find us on the receiving end of space probes deployed by more advanced civilizations. So chances are they will contact us before we contact them.

When considering the minimum equipment necessary for this task from the standpoint of the sender, engineers fall back on what would work if we chose to send probes. More specifically, if we were situated on a planet circling a distant star how would we proceed to make contact with life on Earth? As an engineer, Bracewell envisages a simple radio receiver on an incoming satellite whose purpose is to monitor and actually contribute to local radio broadcasts. Upon arrival in the Solar System the probe would fire a rocket to propel itself into stable orbit in close proximity to Earth. Once there, the probe's radio receiver would be turned on to listen for signs of intelligence in the transmissions it discovered within a band of preselected frequencies. Supposing an interesting signal were detected, the assumption would be that where there was a transmitter operating at a particular frequency there would be a receiver somewhere to decode the message. This is how communication is accomplished on Earth: Radio stations transmit information to people who have the appropriate receivers to pick up the radio frequencies over which information is being sent. After coming to this conclusion, the alien probe might be emboldened to announce its presence by broadcasting over the same frequency channels we use. In short, the probe would eavesdrop on our radio and TV programming and then interfere in some obvious way with the broadcasts in an effort to draw our attention and, it is to be hoped, not our fire.

What information might the probe transmit to advertise its existence? Bracewell notes that a reasonable strategy would be for the probe to repeat back to Earth exactly what it received. This would have an immediate and dramatic impact. For instance, suppose that at the time the probe began to play its little game you were listening to a nightly news program. Instead of the usual rendition of the day's events, you would actually hear the announcer say each word twice in rapid succession. The first signal would have been sent in the standard manner by a radio station; the second signal would arrive shortly thereafter and would have been generated by the orbiting probe. On that singular occasion you would be forced to hear all the news, good and bad, in duplicate. Recognition of this oddity would quite naturally arouse curiosity in some listeners and alarm in others, but with a little luck some clever person, probably a teenage ham radio buff, would discover the cause of the echo and try to make contact with the alien probe in a more deliberate way—for instance, by directing the probe's transmissions back again. Once both parties were aware of the other's presence, it might be possible to exchange technical facts; for example, discussions could proceed on the sensitivity of the radio equipment, the preferred bandwidth, or the best rate of transmission. After such engineering business had been settled and a common language established—no easy feat—we would be ready to converse in earnest about more substantive issues.

By this reckoning the first correspondence from the alien probe could be sent as television signals, with geometric shapes and patterns disclosing the location of the probe's home base in the Galaxy, its engineering sophistication, the key features of its language, and so forth. Since the guest probe would be close by, we could engage in two-way dialogue immediately. We might be urged to express preferences for radio frequencies and time and length of communication, and, of course, we could submit a list of discussion topics. If the probe contained a large computer memory, it might even be feasible to swap dictionaries of key words and mathematical symbols, together with instructions on how to interpret such symbols when used in combination—the grammar of the language, the rules of the mathematics.

So the advantage of an alien satellite in our neighborhood would be give-and-take over comparatively brief intervals, which would not be the case if the parties involved lived thousands of light-years apart. If we made a statement the probe misunderstood, it could request clarification by relaying the statement back in some altered form to indicate its tentative interpretation. Once mutual understanding was reached, according to Bracewell, the electronic messenger might let us in on some abstruse secrets (from our standpoint) about mathematics, physics, chemistry, and cosmology—when the universe began, how it did so, when it will end, and whatever else is deemed important by the alien society that sent the probe. After its on-board computer ascertained our biological makeup, it might also enlighten us on the fate of organisms like ourselves, perhaps revealing in the process effective ways to preserve healthy communities of intelligent life. Presumably, a super-smart probe might even drop hints about how to prevent a society from destroying itself once it has the technical ability to create high-powered devices—such as electronic probes that can be sent to eavesdrop on radio telecasts emitted by faraway planets.

An alien probe would have to have a finite capacity to perform all of these functions, but there is no telling what level of discourse might be possible. The assumption is that after contact was secured, the probe would begin transmitting the information it had gained from Earth back to its parent base in another star system. At least this is what we have our probes do on their missions within the Solar System. Since the distances among the stars are so incredibly large, and since nothing discovered so far travels faster than the speed of light, there would be a substantial lag between the time of initial contact and the time when the sending civilization received word of its success. If the probe made it transparent to us how and where to forward mail, and if we were desirous of direct conversation with its home, then we might choose to initiate a long-distance sending program to lay the foundation for more permanent communication.

The time lags of any ensuing dialogue would depend upon the distances to be traversed. In the average case, based on the size of the Milky Way Galaxy, the turnaround times for messages would be on the order of thousands of years, and so one would have to be prepared to accept the fact that any message would arrive at its destination well after the death of the sender. The return message would take just as long again to reach Earth, and so the optimist would need to assume that someone else would be alive and willing and able to receive and decipher the reply. This is indeed a monumental assumption!

Whether we would be "officially" in the galactic club the minute we started interacting with an alien machine, or whether we would have to await more direct word from its home of origin, is a question best left for the philosophers on either planet. The answer is probably of little consequence, especially if the probe arrived on the scene outfitted with fancy technology, and the required intelligence was there to transfer that knowledge to us in a meaningful form.

That which holds true for aliens seeking contact holds true for us. We have no workable examples yet, but the promise is great. After twelve years of reliable operation, the Pioneer spacecraft that recently drifted out of the Solar System has since stopped transmitting astronomical data back to Earth. In future expeditions of this kind we should be able to stay in touch with probes sent expressly to investigate star systems located hundreds and thousands of light-years away. The details of these missions cannot be predicted with any confidence, but there is no reason to believe that the broad strokes of future programs will not resemble those envisioned by Bracewell.

The space engineer and the average sky watcher have this much in common: They both believe in the feasibility of using messenger probes to foster communication between civilizations separated by huge spans of time and space. Ordinary citizens who follow the progress of the major space programs are positive that machines and human beings actually visited the Moon; that space vehicles landed on Venus and Mars; that satellite probes relayed scientific data about the planets Jupiter, Saturn, and Mercury; and moreover, that it is possible to obtain similar data by dispatching probes to other stars in the Galaxy. The nonscientist does not dispute these achievements and quite logically concludes further that whatever humans can do, aliens can do as well. Consequently, when this person sees an unfamiliar airborne object, the possibility of an extraterrestrial cause springs to mind as a very real option. In light of the facts made available through news media concerning our own efforts to explore outer space, the extraterrestrial hypothesis emerges as a fairly sensible candidate. For these reasons we should not be astonished by the high number of UFO reports, nor by the implied involvement of aliens when witnesses try to interpret sightings. The more we trumpet the successes of our own space research, the more we can expect to hear about alien UFOs.

The particular objects seen and the circumstances surrounding UFO reports vary greatly, but a common thread runs through them all—something was seen in the sky which did not fit a preconception of what people expected to see there. A concrete example will help focus attention on the sorts of issues that beg resolution from either a physical or a social science perspective. The following vignette, an illustration of a possible UFO incident, contains all the essentials of reports that commonly appear in the popular press.

One October evening a middle-aged couple drove home from a dinner party on New England's South Shore. Suddenly they noticed a large, luminous object hovering just above the ocean in the distance. It always seemed to be about a half mile away, even though they were driving in the opposite direction at a speed of fifty miles an hour. Several minutes later the car dipped into a valley, so that the object was blocked from view for the rest of the journey. Upon arriving home the couple realized that they had witnessed a strange event, an inexplicable celestial object of the type they had often read about in the news but had never really thought existed.

The next day a brief article appeared in the *South Shore News* relating the couple's experience and referring to the supporting testimony of some fellow townspeople who also saw the UFO. One of these witnesses, the owner of the local grocery store, is a well-respected and trusted leader in the community. His corroborative support gave a stamp of approval to the sighting and helped sway other residents to accept the couple's statements at face value.

The foregoing incident could easily be one of ten thousand appearing in the news over the past thirty years or so. The number of people who have actually seen what they thought was a UFO, said nothing about it, or told only friends and relatives must be many times larger than this figure. Public acceptance of UFOs is really quite striking. A recent Gallup poll (1978) found that more than half of the people of the United States believe in their existence, and many feel that UFOs pose a threat to the human race. To what should we attribute this intense belief and concern? As in the case of ancient astronauts, I think belief in UFOs is intimately connected with our own technical capabilities and with our failures to make proper inferences when we are handicapped by the lack of relevant evidence. There is a strong positive relationship between our technological competence and that attributed to aliens: Whatever we can do they can do. Moreover, the scarcer the evidence about technological achievement, the more exotic the inference. When coupled with the layperson's modest understanding of space research, such inferences are likely to include vivid references to extraterrestrials.

My conclusion is supported by commonplace examples. The three major physical "substances" open to human experience on this planet are land, water, and air. It is not coincidental that we know the most about the ground on which we spend the majority of our days; we understand far less about the depths of the sea; and the mysteries of the sky above are greater than those of either land or sea. Descriptions of unusual occurrences, be they ostensibly biological or physical in character, closely mirror our understanding of the medium in which these events supposedly occur.

There are very few tales nowadays of weird creatures roaming the continents. Exceptions portray animals, such as Bigfoot and the Abominable Snowman, as inhabitants of remote, inhospitable regions of the globe. Reports of strange underwater creatures are more prevalent, because, I would suggest, we know even less about what life-forms are capable of surviving in that medium. Most notably, many ocean and lakeside communities have evolved a rich folklore surrounding some harmless serpent who resides beneath the surface of the nearest lake or ocean. The Loch Ness monster of Scotland is a famous case, but there are many lesser-known celebrities.

Even communities near relatively small lakes boast of the innocent exploits of such creatures. For example, the visitor to the rural town of Burlington, Vermont, is sure to learn about a shy, serpentlike animal called "Champ" who supposedly lives in Lake Champlain. Anecdotal support for Champ's presence is plentiful, and every now and then some local entrepreneur distributes blurred photographs purporting to show Champ's sleek figure outlined against a late sunset.

The uncertainty of events taking place under foot and beneath the water seems minor when compared to the level of ignorance surrounding rare events in the sky. The truly astounding number of UFO sightings amply confirms this. The recent success in transporting men to the Moon and in landing spacecraft on Venus and Mars only serves to bolster the feeling that visits to Earth by alien beings are a definite possibility. In my view the wide public awareness of such technical accomplishment, more than any other factor, is at the root of the extraterrestrial hypothesis concerning the origin of UFOs. After all, if you were a citizen of Mars having a drink on the front porch when the United States' Viking lander descended and scooped up a clawful of Martian soil, then most certainly you would have been an instant believer in UFOs sent to Mars by an inquisitive society, intent on learning more about alien environments and their potential for sustaining intelligent life. To many people the hypothesis of visitation from other planets is eminently reasonable, because we ourselves accomplish similar feats. People project human qualities into space, and in particular attribute human motivation to aliens.

Quite apart from the issue of belief in UFOs, differing opinions have been expressed about their causes. Assuming that a large percentage of these events are valid—that is, people saw something in the sky—the specific interpretation appears to depend critically on a person's scientific and political inclinations.

As we have just seen, the most popular hypothesis among nonscientists claims that UFOs are actually spacecraft sent by alien civilizations with an apparent curiosity about life on Earth. Interestingly enough, the circumstances of the sightings, that is, the size, distance, shape, and speed of the objects, correspond very nicely to the familiar properties of human airplanes, space satellites, and meteorites. This resemblance to state-of-the-art technology has always been a hallmark of UFO reports. For example, Philip J. Klass describes a widespread flap occurring in the 1890s, when people claimed they saw imposing objects in the sky that resembled "gas-filled fabric airships" equipped to convey passengers in gondolas, attached to the underside of the vehicle. These reports faithfully reflected the technology of the times: It was the new age of airships defined by these very characteristics. More recently, wingless craft have dominated the UFO scene, in keeping with our current predilection for building spherical satellites, weather balloons, and tubular rockets. Every country's space efforts receive a great deal of news coverage, and the latest developments are followed assiduously by millions of people.

On those rare occasions when an extraterrestrial being is said to disembark from its craft and engage the witness in brief conversation, the alien is described by physical and psychological properties that resemble those of human beings to a remarkable extent. The creature usually stands upright on two legs, has a single head with a pair of eyes in front, and always demonstrates full command of the language native to the region. Often the special knowledge attributed to the alien corresponds to the level and type of knowledge we might well attribute to the witness. A deeply religious person might hear the alien tell how

God made the Sun and planets and how he moves unerringly to punish evil; the person concerned with social change learns how that goal might be efficiently realized; and so on. A similar kind of chauvinism is apparent in the recent spate of popular movies on the subject. The aliens depicted are like people in many respects, from physical appearance to social attitudes and emotional constitution—they are cast to show laughter, sadness, and sympathy and are often portrayed in hot pursuit of power, wealth, or inner peace.

As far as I can tell, nothing very startling has ever been learned from purported firsthand contacts with aliens. It is not surprising that most of those who champion the extraterrestrial hypothesis have little training in either the natural or the social sciences. This isn't a character flaw, but it really does restrict their ability to formulate imaginative hypotheses. Their knowledge of UFOlogy rests exclusively on the reading of magazine and newspaper accounts, usually of a sensational genre, and upon casual discussions with others of like persuasion. In other words, the extraterrestrial argument takes all its ammunition from space travel as understood by the nonscientist. Since these sketchy details are the only ones the observer is aware of, he or she has no choice but to use them in depicting hypothetical creatures in outer space.

Scientists who reject the extraterrestrial hypothesis do so partly because they realize that interstellar flight is exceedingly costly in both time and money. It has been estimated by a NASA study group, Project Cyclops, that using present-day chemical propulsion a space satellite would take about forty thousand years to reach a planet orbiting the nearest star (Alpha Centauri) and at a tremendous expenditure of energy. Eventual harnessing of nuclear power might keep the round trip to under a century, but the energy costs would still be staggering. On the other hand, these costs are figured in Earth terms; costs may be trivial in reference to the resources available to a highly advanced society.

The nearest star is slightly over four light-years away. By comparison, the spiral galaxy we call home is shaped like a wafer-thin Danish pastry of enormous proportions: approximately one hundred thousand light-years across and one thousand light-years thick. Under the assumption that intelligent life is at best scattered throughout the

Galaxy, we might have to examine millions of stars, many light-years apart, before finding one inhabited by creatures with the technical skill to engage us in productive conversation. It is unlikely that we would be the lucky target of even one alien probe, let alone the thousands which must be accounted for by the extraterrestrial hypothesis.

Accepting for the moment that physical constraints render this hypothesis untenable, we can look into simpler, though equally suspect, alternatives. According to the French astrophysicist and UFOlogist Jacques Vallee, the true cause of UFO sightings could be sitting right in our own backyard. He finds the available evidence consistent with the view that UFOs are part of a diabolical scheme of worldwide proportions, whose purpose is to foster social change through the manipulation of witnesses and contactees. In a recent book he alludes to the political agenda behind the UFO phenomenon: "They are physical devices used to affect human consciousness. They may not be from outer space; they may, in fact, be terrestrial-based manipulating devices. Their purposes may be to achieve social changes on the planet. Their methods are those of deception" (*Messengers of Deception*, p. 21).

According to Vallee, the wild claims about contacts between humans and extraterrestrials, though a vanishingly small fraction of all cases, succeed in warding off inquisitive scientists who prefer to deal with more tractable problems. Once the skeptical eye of this group is diverted, supposedly back to the laboratory, it is relatively easy to dupe the general public into believing that UFOs are the leading edge of an alien movement to change the world. The list of themes collected by Vallee in his interviews of self-proclaimed contactees upholds this conclusion. In fact, his theory is held firmly by the contactees themselves. They seem resigned to a dependent future. Because, in their opinion, personal motivation and diligence on Earth have not yielded a secure existence for the human race, we must switch allegiance to an extraterrestrial philosophy. Often the chief tenets of this philosophy, as related by the contactee, have totalitarian overtones, including a belief in economic policies antithetical to a free-enterprise system and democratic principles. Blind obedience to dictatorial authority is often included in the list of new demands. This kind of political structure is cited by contactees as the foundation of a more equitable world government—presumably one they would gladly embrace.

If the basis of UFO sightings is the work of a disenchanted splinter group intent on changing the direction of world politics, then it must be exceedingly powerful and very busy. How else can we explain its success in tricking thousands of people from all walks of life over the course of many decades? I would think the perpetrators of this giant hoax would be highly visible by now, easily trapped and unmasked. And yet Vallee offers no clues whatsoever about the identity of this clandestine group. The only organizations large enough, and with the requisite technical competence, to orchestrate such a sham would be the nations of the world heavily involved in legitimate space programs. Is the deception hypothesis just the result of a cynical view of established political systems? It would appear so. No other organization fits the part quite so well. But the world's political systems are presumably the target of this radical faction's outrage, and we would hardly expect them to turn the arrow of social change onto themselves in an act of self-immolation.

But if one of these political bodies is not responsible for the UFO hoax, then who is? Vallee's analysis leaves us groping for a satisfactory answer to this pivotal question. In my view, the answer probably rests with his contactees' personal belief systems. It is they who are reading the tea leaves of the heavens to fit preconceptions of how they think modern political institutions should be run.

The scientific hypotheses heard most often to explain UFO reports also are conditioned by preconceptions which are frequent among the practitioners of science. Either of two philosophies often shapes the interpretation of findings within the rules of science. A typical proponent of the first of these has the habit of operating in a synthetic mode, integrating various levels of knowledge; this is the sort of person who is happiest when formulating general laws and theoretical principles. Psychologists refer to these types as "levelers." They are concerned with what happens in the majority of instances, rather than with tracking down the reasons for the rare exceptions. The second group are "sharpeners," individuals who make fine distinctions and are ever on the lookout for anomalies and violations of scientific doctrine. These types are happiest when they can uncover weaknesses in an accepted way of looking at things. Both levelers and sharpeners are mutually respected and valued members of the scientific community. When confronted with the challenge of explaining a phenomenon such as UFOs, adherents to these two philosophical positions approach matters in different ways.

The leveler takes special heed of the preponderance of incidents accounted for by natural celestial events. Since most UFO reports fall into this category, and since many of the remainder can be attributed to pranks, hoaxes, or the vagaries of the human senses, the leveler concludes that any remaining puzzles could be explained in the same way, once all the relevant facts were known. If 95 percent of the time an airtight explanation exists for a natural phenomenon, it is not worth the effort to ferret out the conditions responsible for the recalcitrant 5 percent. In a field as murky as UFO research, one would expect to face unsolved riddles at least that often. The view is that these apparent anomalies would fall in line nicely if it were possible to identify all the relevant physical and psychological factors involved.

The sharpener takes quite another stance on these matters. This person is more interested in the anomalous 5 percent than in the 95 percent whose explanation is not at issue. The sharpener's argument might proceed with assumptions and end with a question; typically, it might go like this: "All right, let's assume that 90 percent of the reports would never have been made if the observer were aware of some elementary facts of astronomy, for example, the visual movement of the moon, planets, and meteorites. Let's assume as well that 3 percent of the reports are hoaxes—for example, lights in plastic garment bags, staged proof of landings—and that an additional 2 percent are the fabrications of people with serious personality defects. Accepting all this as true, we are still left with a 5 percent residue that demands a hearing." At this juncture the sharpener is open to all manner of suggestions, but the validity of each must be checked by some objective means. Further, this individual may challenge us by asking, "Isn't it plausible that extraterrestrial visitors precipitated a tiny fraction of these incidents? At least this possibility should not be discarded in haste, simply because we want to accommodate all UFO reports under the umbrella of a single theory."

Whether one sides with the levelers or the sharpeners in this debate, it is obvious that we are addressing a point of scientific style, and not one of scientific logic. Both approaches can be considered orthodox. Scientists' interpretations of sightings are based on the same psychological values that guide their interpretation of any scientific evidence. Levelers most likely would deny the validity of UFO sightings; sharpeners simply would leave the whole question open, but neither could be considered strong believers in the extraterrestrial hypothesis.

Scientists, engineers, political critics, and ordinary citizens are each conditioned by their previous experiences and professional training to look at unusual events from their unique standpoint. The perceived meaning of events depends ultimately on the intelligence and social values of the perceiver. The question is whether the hypotheses formulated by these diverse individuals tell us much about UFOs, or whether their professed attitudes are no more than reflections of personal biases. In a field of great uncertainty, such as UFO research, the latter alternative should be afforded careful attention. My own view on these matters is admittedly colored by a social science perspective, but it may still provide coherence to the welter of claims and counterclaims whose truth or falsity continues to elude objective assessment. So let me expand a little on this theme and suggest a psychological theory that draws more upon the results of the experimental laboratory than it does on the intuitions of physical scientists and political philosophers.

Judging from the Gallup survey I surmise that several million people in the United States alone have seen aerial antics that should be placed in the "strange" category in the sense that they appear to have had no ostensible physical cause. It is obvious that the majority of these cases represent perceptions of actual occurrences. *Most people claiming to have seen UFOs are telling the truth:* They saw something exceptional in the sky, and from their vantage point, what they saw was inexplicable. To conclude, as some scientists have, that thousands of individuals have been betrayed by their senses, which seem to function just fine under most circumstances, is a view more unorthodox than the one they are anxious to debunk. To conclude, as others have, that a great many UFO reports are pranks staged by individuals in search of public recognition or financial gain is equally suspect, since this hypothesis overestimates the care and effort people are willing to expend in return for minor rewards. The enjoyment of fooling a few friends or of luring gullible tourists to spend money in the old hometown hardly would justify the elaborate planning required to pull off a successful UFO sham; most such stage shows are directed and acted by amateurs and are quickly unmasked for what they are. Yes, some charlatans certainly have succeeded in tricking the public for extended periods of time, but these successes do not number in the thousands.

Although in my judgment most UFO reports are based on genuine sensory experiences, it does not follow that the interpretation of what was seen mimics reality as defined by physical measurements. And why should it? Ordinary human perception always relies on the stability of a familiar visual world, but our senses can be fooled. Without the assurance of repetition in what we see and experience, everyday living would collapse in disarray. So making sense out of the unfamiliar always requires that one construct a meaningful bridge to what is familiar.

A celestial example of how past experience affects visual perception is the so-called Moon illusion, which has been a topic of delight and study for at least a thousand years. On a clear night the full Moon at the horizon appears exceptionally large, and its apparent size decreases noticeably as it ascends to higher elevations during the course of the evening. The change in perceived extent varies between 15 percent and 100 percent for different observers, but just about everyone notices the change, once the phenomenon is brought to his or her attention. The effect is definitely a perceptual illusion, not dependent on the actual distance to the Moon, which is essentially constant at all elevations. Nor is it due to different atmospheric conditions present in the horizon and zenith skies. These variables cannot be crucial, because the measured size of the Moon's image in a photograph taken from a fixed station on the ground is the same for all altitudes above the horizon.

Consensus has not yet been reached on the best explanation of the Moon illusion, but some of the relevant factors are known, and these bear on attempts to understand reports of UFOs. The principal factors are the physical referents used in estimating objects in the horizon and zenith skies. When the Moon appears at the horizon it is compared in size, distance, and shape with familiar objects on the ground. For instance, the horizon Moon may be seen as a luminous disk, approximately the size of a house or tree seen just below it on the ground. As the Moon rises, observers have more difficulty simultaneously seeing it and the terrain, and so the Moon is more likely to be compared in size with the great expanse of the night sky. Against that large, uniform space it looks relatively tiny. Even when the Moon is straight overhead, a person on the ground may use known referents to gauge its size and distance. Someone might say something like: "The Moon appears to be the size of that car parked over there," or "It looks like a dime held at arm's length."

Mark Wagner and I have conducted several experiments on the Moon illusion, the results of which imply that people have no idea at all about the physical size and distance of objects in the night sky, except insofar as these objects can be related in some way to objects on the ground. The UFO critic and aeronautical journalist Philip J. Klass comes to the same conclusion on the basis of his careful study of the most baffling UFO cases, baffling because they are not readily placed within the accepted framework of physics and engineering. One of his central UFOlogical principles states: "No human observer, including experienced flight crews, can accurately estimate either the distance/altitude or the size of an unfamiliar object in the sky, unless it is in very close proximity to a familiar object whose size or altitude is known" (*UFOs Explained*, p. 57). The experimental findings that Wagner and I have discovered are in total agreement with this principle.

When persons who have seen a UFO have time to reflect on what occurred, they are likely to give incorrect estimates of the object's most prominent features: color, distance, size, and shape. They will, however, use familiar landmarks to anchor their experience, just as a person viewing the Moon perceives its properties within a familiar context provided by objects on the ground. If still later—say, the following day—someone were to ask the UFO witness to attach a label to what was experienced, a description would be offered that made good sense in the observer's familiar environment. Representative comments of our South Shore couple might have been: "The UFO looked like a tilted dime at a distance of one hundred feet," or "It was a bright point near the horizon, maybe five miles away," or perhaps, "It had all the features of a wingless aircraft; for a moment we thought there were portholes along the fuselage."

When these pronouncements are made public, a witness then might be told brusquely by a local skeptic that he or she saw the flashing light of a police helicopter, or the rising planet Venus, or the lights of a commercial airliner. Although these proposals sound vaguely rational, by now the witness is persuaded that physical explanations can be safely ruled out. Once committed psychologically to a personal opinion, no matter how silly it might appear to an outsider, people find it very difficult to entertain the blander theories of "experts." Nobody enjoys being ridiculed or called a fool, and in most people's eyes one would be a fool to mistake a police helicopter for a craft from outer space, or to commit the more glaring error of thinking the harvest Moon seen through a hazy sky was an alien spaceship bent on following one home from a dinner party. When faced with other interpretations, it is far easier to cling to an initial impression, especially since there seems little chance of being proved wrong. The unidentified object in question will have long since disappeared by the time someone else gets around to looking for it.

It has been noted by Air Force scientists that a large proportion of UFO sightings, perhaps as many as 90 percent, are of normal astronomical phenomena, which can be quite spectacular in their own right. Most certainly, UFO witnesses are prisoners of their unique understanding of the physical world around them. But the UFO observer is not alone behind the walls of past experience within which imagination is allowed to roam free. Although the nature of the confinement is different for engineers and astronomers, the reins on their imaginations are just as strong as those limiting the inferences of the "naive" observer of the sky.

These limits are definitely evident in the engineering proposals, noted earlier, to send probes to monitor the radio activity of intelligent life on other planets. However we judge our capabilities for initiating contact on an interstellar scale, we assume that these are a subset of the options available to others. We consider sending messenger probes; therefore "they" will send probes. We rely heavily on radio communication; therefore "they" will rely heavily on radio. We might well try to make contact by repeating radio and TV transmissions;

therefore "they" might signal their presence in the same way. Moreover, we unconsciously accept the tenet that all this technical machinery will be propelled into space for the express purpose of enlightening ourselves and the receiving civilization about the physical laws governing the universe.

Scientific discussions of potential message content eventually get around to assuming that introductory courses on the cosmos, held by alien instructors, will address issues in physics, chemistry, and mathematics. This scientific chauvinism arises quite naturally because those are the topics most valued by the scientists who want to launch probes from this planet to perform similar duties in outer space. The argument for this position is weaker once we back off from considering physics and mathematics, and so we seldom find scientists going beyond that point. If a visiting probe can help us surmount obstacles blocking a thorough appreciation of physical laws, then later this same friendly probe, as programmed by its alien engineer, supposedly will deem us a worthy recipient of information about cosmic biology, social science, and the arts. Who is to say, however, that music, art, and social considerations will not be at the top of its agenda?

There is no telling whether alien engineers manage their society's physical resources. If an organism of pacifist leanings were to enter into the business of designing interstellar probes, the story might have quite another twist. In the first place, a representative of universal peace might decide that it is better for the sanity of the Galaxy if the probe remains grounded, forever if necessary, or at least until guarantees are forthcoming that the target species has learned to live in harmony with members of its own kind. In this eventuality there would be no imperative to publicize the basic laws of the universe, unless a civilization could demonstrate its resolve and ability to apply the elementary laws at its command sensibly, without despoiling the local region of the universe over which it has some control. If the pacifists, and not the engineers, are in charge of alien societies, we may never hear from them.

The Earth-bound pacifist, engineer, and average citizen each seems to express a "need" for psychological symmetry: We attribute to others the form and level of knowledge, goals, and motivations that we ourselves possess. It is not as though one had a conscious choice in this matter. The genetic and psychological consequences of being human cannot be transcended, for example, by the accumulation of scientific knowledge. Unique learning experiences, scientific and otherwise, shape only the manner in which this human perspective is expressed.

REFERENCES AND FURTHER READINGS

Baird, J. C. The Moon Illusion: II. A Reference Theory. *Journal of Experimental Psychology: General*, 1982, *111*,304–315.

Baird, J. C., & Wagner, M. The Moon Illusion: I. How High is the Sky? *Journal of Experimental Psychology: General*, 1982, *111*, 296–303.

Bracewell, R. N. *The Galactic Club: Intelligent Life in Outer Space.* San Francisco: San Francisco Book Co., 1976.

Freitas, R. A., Jr. Interstellar Probes: A New Approach to SETI. *Journal of the British Interplanetary Society*, 1980, *33*, 95–100.

Hart, M. H., & Zuckerman, B. (Eds.) *Extraterrestrials: Where Are They?* New York: Pergamon, 1982.

Hendry, A. *The UFO Handbook: A Guide to Investigating, Evaluating and Reporting UFO Sightings.* Garden City, N.Y.: Doubleday, 1979.

Jones, E. M. Discrete Calculations of Interstellar Migration and Settlement. *Icarus*, 1981, *46*, 328–336.

Klass, P. J. *UFOs: The Public Deceived.* Buffalo, N.Y.: Prometheus, 1983.

Klass, P. J. *UFOs Explained.* New York: Random House, Vintage, 1976.

Regis, E., Jr. (Ed.) *Extraterrestrials: Science and Alien Intelligence.* Cambridge: Cambridge University Press, 1985.

Sagan, C., & Newman, W. I. "The Solipsist Approach to Extraterrestrial Intelligence. *Quarterly Journal of the Royal Astronomical Society*, 1983, *24*, 113–121.

Sagan, C., & Page, T. (Eds.) *UFO's: A Scientific Debate.* New York: Norton, 1972.

Steiger, B. (Ed.) *Project Blue Book: The Top Secret UFO Findings Revealed.* New York: Ballantine, 1976.

Story, R. D. *Sightings: UFOs and the Limits of Science.* New York: Quill, 1982.

Tipler, F. J. Additional Remarks on Extraterrestrial Intelligence. *Quarterly Journal of the Royal Astronomical Society*, 1981, *22*, 279–292.

Tipler, F. J. Extraterrestrial Beings Do Not Exist. *Quarterly Journal of the Royal Astronomical Society*, 1980, *21*, 267–281.

Vallee, J. *Messengers of Deception: UFO Contacts and Cults.* Berkeley, Calif.: And/Or Press, 1979.

CHAPTER 4

FUTURE SPACE COLONIES

A tangible illustration of how difficult it is to overcome the frailties of being human is apparent in engineering proposals to build large-scale, habitable colonies in outer space. Although some scientists feel that society's most recalcitrant problems will be alleviated or surmounted altogether by moving into outer space, social science makes us wary of drawing this optimistic conclusion. It is more likely that all the social ills seen here will simply be transported into space.

Over a decade ago my Dartmouth colleagues Donella and Dennis Meadows summarized the results of a computer model intended to simulate the implications of expanding world population and industrialization, coupled with further depletion of nonrenewable resources—coal, oil, and gas. The conclusions of the model do not augur well for the future. Without the prompt imposition of constraints on the exponential growth of population and commercial technology, the model says in effect that environmental pollution and widespread famine will have a catastrophic impact on the style and quality of life on this planet. This dire consequence could arrive quickly, maybe within the next hundred years.

In response to this gloomy forecast, the Meadowses and their collaborators suggest remedial steps to avert an impending disaster. Global equilibrium of people and resources can be reached, they surmise, by stabilizing the world's population at its present level and by restricting industrial expansion in a manner consistent with the fundamental human needs for adequate food, shelter, and social support.

Acceptance of this "soft" path to global equilibrium necessitates a turnabout in the philosophy many see at the root of present plans to improve social conditions and enhance the chances for long-term survival through the acceleration of technological progress. For this reason, the contentions made in the Meadowses' book, *The Limits to Growth,* have been debated both by individuals who welcome its conclusions and by those who wish to avoid having to fasten a lid on the financial interests of big business and on the continued growth of the world's population.

The finite limits noted by the Meadowses, and incidentally by the "small is beautiful" movement, refer to the current situation on Earth. The options proposed to alleviate the social impact of these limits involve changes in the way humans customarily perceive their niche in the environment at large. Namely, it seems that we must curb population and work harder to preserve physical resources. To some, these "conservative" attitudes are oppressive and patently at odds with the "normal" human instinct to widen horizons, subjugate the forces of nature, and directly control the destiny of individuals and societies.

Whether this view arises from instinct or learning, it nonetheless reflects a "space" value orientation which can be seen in scientists and nonscientists alike. These individuals are made nervous by the thought that their current life-style may be threatened, and in order to extricate themselves from a worsening situation on Earth, they turn to space. They hope colonization of space will satisfy the drive of human acquisitiveness, while simultaneously improving the quality of life on Earth by reducing the population crunch.

The idea is that a practical way to reverse the gradual dissolution of society is to colonize territory far removed from Earth: outer space, the planets, moons, asteroids, and even more remote corners of the Galaxy. According to this notion, there are plenty of untapped resources in outer space, and it is our moral duty to utilize them as best we can to satisfy the pressing social needs of the day.

The very existence of habitats in outer space would extend the reach and influence of the species in a physical sense. Launching the required material, machinery, and people into orbit around the Earth to establish a viable colony would be an engineering project of colossal proportions, a modern version of the effort required to erect the Great Pyramid of Egypt. A successful outcome certainly would be applauded; failure would mean considerable financial loss for the governments or private organizations that backed such an enterprise—the cost to build a modest colony is estimated to be at least 1 billion dollars.

The psychological reasons for investing in the colonization of space may be the very ones that drove people to build the pyramids. The Pharaohs of ancient Egypt fought mortality through their meticulous concern with the physical and social circumstances following their death. Among the very wealthy, the fashionable trend of 2000 B.C. was to have one's body wrapped like an onion in layers of clothing to prevent tampering by future generations, while still providing all the comforts of home inside an impenetrable stone mausoleum. The spacefarers of today view the exportation of humanity into outer space as the surefire way to achieve immortality for the species as a whole, if perhaps not for the individual. Instead of securing themselves behind stone walls, however, the space colonists would seek immortality by leaving Earth just as fast as technology would allow. The initial impetus for moving into outer space might be overcrowding, the gradual loss of natural resources, or even some impending cosmological disaster, such as collision with an asteroid or the explosion of a nearby star—a scenario elaborated upon recently by M. G. DeSan.

In books by physicists Gerard K. O'Neill, Eric Chaisson, T. A. Heppenheimer, and James Trefil the social and political benefits of space colonies are positively reviewed. Near the top of their lists is the claim that a scattering of our kind through a substantial volume of the universe—getting us off the Earth—would help make humans invulnerable to local misfortunes; that is, as a species we would become "unkillable." The need to plan carefully for a productive future in both a personal and a societal sense is among the chief motivations for supporting space colonies, whether built and operated in empty space (O'Neill's model) or erected on other planets and solid bodies of the Solar System (Chaisson's model). In either event, the idea would be to use these early colonies as base camps for more ambitious forays into space.

Another declared reason for colonization is to allow humans to reproduce at a rate that presently taxes the capacity of the planet to feed, clothe, and shelter its inhabitants, while not incurring any of the environmental costs that accompany such a laissez-faire policy toward population growth. Earth simply cannot handle many more of us. But the population explosion is no longer a crucial issue if one thinks of the Solar System, or the Galaxy, as an appropriate and hospitable setting for fulfilling human aspirations. There, the unoccupied space is essentially infinite.

According to proponents of space colonization, this advancing wave of humanity will be catapulted skyward by economic considerations as well. We are constantly on the lookout for new energy sources, and this pursuit translates readily into projects to secure power from the nearest dominant source, the Sun. If power satellites (powersats) could be boosted into orbital positions fixed in respect to the Earth's surface, well above the interference of the atmosphere, it would be possible to absorb and store energy from the Sun on a twenty-four-hour basis every single day of the year. This captured power then could be converted into microwaves, beamed to the ground, and received by banks of special "rectennas." Once there, the energy could be funneled into existing power lines for commercial and residential use.

To build powersats big enough to justify the expense, it would be essential to have materials and human expertise at the construction site. The necessary resources, it is said, could be mined from the Moon or from the asteroid belt and hurled aloft with pinpoint accuracy to a "catcher" in space. A nearby factory would extract natural elements and fashion them into building components, which in turn would be transported to the place where the power satellite was to be assembled.

The workers on this project would have to eat, sleep, and be merry on occasion, and hence they would require a permanent living arrangement. Beginning with a modest space shack (handyman's special) hovering near the factory, the accommodations of the work force might have to keep pace with an economic venture of increasing complexity and expense. At some juncture in the project it would be financially prudent to invest in a more stable home for the workers and their families and friends: No one wants to stay in outer space very long without access to basic social amenities. It would cost a good deal of money to go on vacation if this meant purchasing a round-trip ticket to Earth and back. To maintain worker efficiency and community order it would be especially important to keep an isolated team of workers in a healthy psychological state, as military organizations have learned on many occasions. This goal would prove easier to attain if key commodities and social amenities could be readily obtained in outer space.

The physical features of these colonies, as currently depicted on the engineer's drawing board, have been outlined in fair detail by O'Neill, Heppenheimer, and Trefil. They discuss a variety of shapes, ranging from spheres and cylinders to doughnuts of notable size (one to twenty miles). Eventually, these floating habitats might house hundreds, thousands, and even millions of people. The economics of the enterprise demand that we make many of the structural elements in the space factories from the same raw materials used to construct the power stations. In some ways the actual assembly of parts would be easier than on Earth. Because of the reduced pull of gravity, heavy pieces of equipment and material could be transported and pushed around with comparatively little effort.

The subjective illusion of Earth's gravity would be simulated by rotating the entire colony. The centrifugal force created thereby would lightly press the inhabitants against the inside walls of the enclosure. Without the benefit of artificial gravity the residents would drift about in a state of weightlessness. Although the novelty of this condition might be amusing for awhile, it is not the most comfortable way to accomplish even simple tasks, and it would probably become intolerable over the course of an extended tour of duty; admittedly, this is speculation that can only be validated through experience. The force of gravity would decline as a person moved away from the walls toward the center of the colony, and so there would always be the opportunity to work and play in zero gravity.

The scientific know-how is here right this minute to build a viable colony of the sort imagined by colony advocates. They delineate not only the engineering particulars but also the means by which weather could be created, food produced, and people enticed to leave home for the excitement of the high frontier. Since the daily life in a space colony would be something like being on an island, O'Neill refers to his early prototype as "Island One."

Because the physical conditions inside Island One could be manipulated at the discretion of the residents, they could obtain any weather pattern they wished. A likely candidate is a mild climate similar to that of Palo Alto, California, or the better days in Miami Beach, Florida. The harsher climes of Thule, Greenland, and Point Barrow, Alaska, are not receiving equal attention. There is no special reason to import the rigors of winter or to deal with radical swings in temperature; no real use for clouds, rain, and storms, except perhaps to furnish aesthetic variety (an important consideration for New Englanders). Initially, water, plants, and livestock would have to be brought up from Earth, but in a perfect ecosystem, water would not be lost and growth and regeneration of plants and animals should proceed normally. At present, however, the only ecosystem of this sort that we know will work for an extended period is Earth itself. Biological experiments are now under way to see if the continuous cycle of plant and animal life can be sustained on the micro scale, but until it is possible the colony would have to be restocked frequently with essential biochemical commodities.

Arable tracts of land would be set aside within or near the colony for growing fruits and vegetables year round. Because of the constant solar exposure, the crop yields should be spectacular. In the larger colonies it also would be possible to breed and raise livestock—rabbits, chickens, Thanksgiving turkeys, and the like—but as yet we have no proof that mammals in particular will reproduce themselves in the unusual conditions of a space colony. Once a colony is running smoothly, however, habitual meat eaters would be satisfied; they would not be left dreaming of their favorite meat dish on a dining-room table twenty-two thousand miles away. Conversely, dedicated vegetarians would find themselves in paradise among a plentiful supply of common and exotic fruits and vegetables.

The social agenda is to enrich the colonists' leisure time with a full complement of plays, concerts, nature excursions, and sporting events; and people could always enjoy the novelties of sex in zero gravity. Overall, the day-to-day community life would closely resemble life in a small university town—say, Hanover, New Hampshire, but refurbished with a climate imported from southern California.

What sort of person would emigrate to such a place? An inkling of the personality type who would find Island One attractive is captured by the intrepid slogan of New Hampshire: "Live Free or Die." According to O'Neill, the early pioneers would need to be hardy souls, driven to high standards of excellence, but also of a restless, inquisitive nature, open to new challenges and anxious to test their mettle against the dangers that would hamper the founding of a beachhead in space. Most of all, they would treasure the personal freedom to live as they please. These pioneers' value orientations would be, according to the definition of the social psychologist/anthropologist Florence Kluckhohn, quintessentially American.

The space pioneers also would have to maintain and enlarge upon the industrial activity that supports the "good life" of the colony, and this obligation to Earth-bound concerns could curtail activities of a more playful sort. The work ethic would be everywhere evident, regardless of the religious affiliations or ethnic or national origins of the colonists. Indeed, with an expected increase in the number and scope of colonies as the years pass, Heppenheimer sees endless opportunities for unique communities; for example, one could witness a revival of subcultures that were affected negatively by the spread of technology, cultures such as the Indian tribes of the Americas and the aboriginal peoples of Australia. All self-defined groups would have the opportunity to protect their cultural heritage and continue to evolve in new directions quite independently of how others around them chose to live, because each community could spell out the social rules for its own private colony.

Far above the physical limits of Earth, the space-islanders would be in an ideal position to tap the inexhaustible resources of the Solar System, without incurring the costs reviewed in *The Limits to Growth*. People could have as many children as they wished and, somewhat like the beaver, send their progeny off to establish their own colonies, once it became too crowded at home. Individuals would determine their personal fortunes to an extent unheard of in terrestrial societies. In short, the immensity of outer space would permit all manner of living arrangements, well insulated from the effects of unwanted waste—discarded into space—generated by the colonies and their associated factories.

Double planting, adherence to modern agricultural practice, and exceptional growing conditions would make each community largely self-sufficient in food production. There would be no crippling food shortages to detract from the residents' enjoyment of their island utopia.

According to O'Neill, life in space also would be much safer than on Earth. Before being certified for travel, the emigrants would be subjected to batteries of psychological tests to ascertain their suitability for working and living in space. Sociopaths would not be granted entry visas. Second, from a military standpoint, O'Neill reasons that the colonies would not make convenient posts from which to aggress against fellow colonists or against people on Earth. The very nature of the colonies would make them easily vulnerable to physical attack, and this should encourage mutual respect on all sides. This optimistic scenario was set forth in 1977, before President Reagan's controversial Space Defense Initiative (SDI) was under serious consideration!

If the external shell of a colony were ever punctured or split open, the vital oxygen would gradually slip away into the vacuum of outer space, leaving the hapless occupants at the mercy of the physical elements. But since all colonies would be equally assailable, "responsible" leaders would think twice before risking a retaliatory strike. It seems unlikely that they would be hostile toward their neighbors under these vulnerable conditions. Because it would take a day or two for military planes and missiles from a colony to make the twenty-two-thousand-mile trip to Earth, it is also unlikely, by O'Neill's reasoning in 1977, that colonies would attempt to attack Earth from battle stations on high. Today's stark political realities regarding the militaristic uses of outer space highlight the naiveté of these social science predictions, made by a physical scientist.

The scientist's optimistic outlook for the future rests securely on present knowledge of engineering and physics, but what social science and history teach us about human nature is that not much will change in the human state by moving into space. If a government were willing to spend the funds, such a colony could be operational within a decade. The opportunity is there to be considered and translated into practice; the question remaining is whether this bold step into space will be matched by an improvement in the human condition on Earth or in space. I for one don't think so.

Down through the ages people have exhibited a knowledge of engineering that has baffled succeeding generations. Whether the society at large was in war or peace, in famine or plenty, oppressed or free, the ancient engineers went about the business of designing and building structures to meet the practical, religious, and aesthetic needs of their times. The current plan to deploy space colonies is yet another phase in this long and honorable tradition of faithful, apolitical service to society.

Because significant numbers of people believe that the evolution of civilization is one of steady upward progress, the physical and intellectual limits of the past appear greater than they are today, and much greater than they will be in the future. But the evolutionary increments in civilization's advance over the last four thousand years are in fact smaller than we might suppose. Moreover, the steps along a scale of intellectual power are less noticeable than they are along a scale of technology. While it is within the realm of possibility to think that engineers responsible for the Egyptian Pyramids also could have designed an elevator of the counterweight variety—because they were smart enough to do so—it is quite another matter to think that they had the technical skill to thrust a satellite twenty-two thousand miles into permanent orbit around the Earth. Until very recently, this task was absolutely impossible, not because people living four thousand years ago were stupider than us, but rather because they hadn't developed the necessary physical technology.

A person on site to observe the raising of the Pyramids would receive a practical education on the physical laws allowing the transport of large blocks of stone along the ground and upward against the pull of gravity. If this person were somehow whisked through time to the present era, he or she would be quick to understand the principles governing the common elevator, for example. A physicist with a flair for teaching might even be able to show this person why orbiting space satellites create a problem for engineering that is like the one faced in building the Pyramids. I doubt whether the intellectual capacity of humans has changed in marked ways during the past four thousand years. Biological evolution of the genetic basis of all facets of human intelligence moves too slowly for us to notice dramatic shifts between then and now.

If this person from the past were told, however, that huge metal spheres have already been sent into orbit around the Earth, he or she would be incredulous. The sheer possibility of space travel is still amazing to most of us, even though, theoretically, the possibility has been contemplated for some time. After all, children and playful adults have always envied the flight of birds and have observed what happens when stones are tossed into the air. I would guess that within a few weeks of arrival on the modern scene, the Egyptian visitor would consider the Soviet Soyuz Space Station with about the same awe an American might feel when viewing the Great Pyramid. The almost magical character of both accomplishments would open most minds, American or Egyptian, to a willingness at least to entertain explanations along the lines expounded by writers such as Erich von Däniken. Mysterious, powerful gods from on high might lay legitimate claim to these engineering marvels, whether they occurred in 1987 B.C. or in A.D. 1987.

To many people the next century will mark a turning point in technological development, as the physical constraints of Earth are shed and the exploitation of the nearly infinite resources of the Solar System and other stars gets into full swing. The stated motives for emigrating into space are numerous and complex, but they often include the reason that overcoming physical limits necessarily implies a parallel victory over social and psychological limits. The major space programs are nominally seen as a means to achieve a better quality of life for future generations, here as well as in space. It is interesting to sample such articles of faith from individuals with very different professional backgrounds, but with a shared interest in mining the resources of outer space as a means to extend the influence of humanity. They each convey the same message as they praise the advantages of chasing after the "good life" in outer space. I have selected excerpts from the publications of three prominent individuals: Edmund G. (Jerry) Brown, a forward-looking politician and former governor of California; Gerard K. O'Neill, an experimental physicist who teaches at Princeton University; and Erich von Däniken, the controversial writer who specialized in speculations about the origins of ancient civilizations.

In commenting on our evolutionary potential as a species, Governor Brown says:

We've got to keep on going; we have to keep on pushing, because that is the human impulse. Instead of fighting it or ignoring it, we ought to develop it and respect it, encourage it and celebrate it. That's why we're here: because the potential of this state and of this country and of this species has just begun to be tapped. It's just a matter of courage; it's a matter of investment, of work, of collective effort, of common purpose. That's been the destiny of California, of America, and it's going to be the destiny of this world as those of us on this planet work together to push back the new frontier which is the everlasting frontier: space, the universe itself. [In Geis & Florin, *Moving into Space*, p. 10]

Professor O'Neill adds a dash of optimism about the potential value of space colonies for improving society:

More important than material issues, I think there is reason to hope that the opening of a new, high frontier will challenge the best that is in us, that the new lands waiting to be built in space will give us new freedom to search for better governments, social systems, and ways of life, and that our children may thereby find a world richer in opportunity by our efforts during the decades ahead. [*The High Frontier* (1978 ed.), p. 274]

The same upbeat attitude is cast in a more imperative form by von Däniken:

So it will be man's ultimate insight to realize that his justification for existence to date and all his struggles to advance really consisted in learning from the past in order to make himself ready for contact with the existence in space. Once that happens, the shrewdest, most die-hard individualist must see that the whole human task consists in colonizing the universe and that man's whole spiritual duty lies in perpetuating all his efforts and practical experience. [*Chariots of the Gods?* p. 95]

Despite marked differences in their professional training and social background, these three writers rally round the same value orientation and argue that space research is a valid and necessary pursuit. The chief reason for colonizing space, they claim, is that humans have a moral obligation to explore and exploit as much of the physical universe as is practical. By the time Earth's physical resources have dried up, we should be mining the jewels that await us in the rest of the Solar System; and looking further down the road, we should fly out and stake claim to the material wealth to be found in our region of the Galaxy. It is not obvious how we should treat any aliens we meet along this journey into space, especially those who might try to block or impede our progress. Despite our high-sounding reasons for embarking on the colonization of space, the use of physical force to get our way will probably be the course of choice, because it has always been this way in the past.

The notion of the human species as a beneficent, autocratic force in the universe is upgraded to scientific status by the Russian physicist N. S. Kardashev. He classifies hypothetical civilizations by their ability to harness energy sources of different magnitude in the service of communication. There are three types: (1) a civilization that controls resources equivalent to the energy potential of Earth, (2) a civilization that controls resources equivalent to the amount available from its parent star, (3) a civilization that controls power equivalent to the energy resources of an entire galaxy. Of course, since we are in the ethereal realm of theory, Kardashev's classes could be extended to include civilizations that tame the energy of a cluster of galaxies or some greater fraction of energy in the universe.

As we climb out of Earth's tunnel of gravity and sever the terrestrial bonds restraining population size and food production, new horizons challenge the ingenuity of a bright and energetic segment of society which sees its duty as mastering an ever-larger proportion of the known universe. Speaking as a social scientist, however, let me reiterate that I think it doubtful whether this increased control over physical resources will be matched either by increased wisdom or by improvement in the quality of human life. An illuminating example of why doubts linger on this issue is found in the statements of those colony advocates who are fond of sketching an analogy between current plans to migrate into space and the earlier settlement of North America.

In comparing space settlers with Euro-Americans who have steadily driven westward over the last two centuries, O'Neill notes that the living conditions in space will be difficult but not harsher than those encountered by American pioneers. In addition, he says, the spacefarers will not have "hostile Indians" to hinder their progress. Heppenheimer mentions American Indians in a different context. Because of the freedom allowed in space for alternative life-styles, he suggests that Indian nations, such as the Arapaho or the Cherokee, may welcome the opportunity provided in space to revitalize their culture by establishing a self-sufficient colony that restores the customs and ways of their ancestors.

While both O'Neill and Heppenheimer are certainly well intentioned, the irony in their proposals is hard to ignore. The Euro-American settlement of the West was a case of one social group subjugating another by force, pure and simple. Aliens beware! The indigenous population encountered by the pioneers were protecting their land, crops, homes, and families. They were "hostile" only in the sense that all people under similar pressure will fight to defend their traditions and territory from outside invasion.

To the Native Americans, land is especially sacred, and today it is the particular land of their ancestors they would dearly love to recover and preserve for future generations. Circling the Earth in a mammoth space station would hardly qualify as a promising spot from which to revive and pay homage to the traditions of their forebears. The native peoples who coexisted with the natural environment on equal terms for thousands of years before the abrupt arrival of the Europeans would be disturbed enough to see their nation confined to government reservations, never mind banished to outer space.

Consider the example of the Cherokee, who have a proud tradition of self-government. Their reaction to the U.S. State Department's offer of a private space colony would probably range from cautious skepticism to unbridled anger. This "goodwill" gesture might well be interpreted as the first of a new string of promises, whose disguised goal is to rid the North American continent once and for all of its original settlers.

For these reasons, an Indian reservation in space is probably not high on a list of Native American social goals. For these people Kardashev's three grades of civilization could well appear as just another example of the domineering attitude of industrialized nations, and their continued desire to seal the fate of nations who place less emphasis on the value of military-industrial power.

Nobody of course will be forced to emigrate to space unwillingly. Those who choose to do so, however, need not worry that life there will deviate in any noticeable way from what they have been accustomed to on Earth. A change in the external environment will have little or no effect on the social and psychological well-being of the inhabitants living under the Earth-like conditions inside. In addition to the security afforded by ample food supplies, warm shelters, and solid positions in the economic marketplace, the settlers can be assured that all the trappings of human culture will accompany them into space.

On a typical day in O'Neill's Island One, the breadwinner, most likely the man, will buzz off to work on the power satellite and return in the evening. Except in the most progressive colonies, the woman will stay at home and tend the family vegetable garden, while the younger space cadets attend school at Sky High. When the family occasionally frees some time to reflect on the pressing issues in their lives, they may discuss job security, government interference in private affairs, family relations, and the ever-present threat of war among the nation colonies. The settlers may also discuss whether they can afford to live in the newest Space Condo, whether tomorrow's TV soap opera will be exciting, and whether it is proper for the neighbors' children to use the public beach for nude sunfloating in zero gravity. In fairness to the physicists, at least one among them, James Trefil, paints a more up-to-date Western image of suburban existence in the colony. He depicts the wife as a contributing member of the work force (for example, a plant biologist) and the husband as a writer who is relegated to the home front.

Some attention must also be devoted in colonies to the perennial thorn in the side of every community—social misfits: those who refuse to work, those who rob and assault their fellow colonists or try illegally to disrupt the functioning of the official government. No amount of psychological testing—O'Neill's arguments notwithstanding—will prevent the emigration of sociopaths into space. Moreover, if couples are able to mate and raise children in zero gravity, the settlement itself will be the strongest determinant of the social behavior of the growing child. We cannot guess what that will entail, but vandalism and crime are a nuisance wherever large groups congregate, even in the most insulated university towns, although crime rates are lower there than in less homogeneous communities.

Human frailties will undoubtedly accompany us into space. Could it be otherwise? Emigration to space means emigration of the whole social fabric of Earth; nothing of real significance in the life and attitudes of human beings can be left on the launch pad. It is misleading to use the assumed improvement of the human state as the reason for moving into space. Despite the good intentions of engineers and physicists to rid society of its social blemishes, the real motivation for space colonies probably will be the economic and political concerns of the people controlling the purse strings for such enterprises. Unfortunately, many of these people have not distinguished themselves as champions of social dignity, equity, and welfare for all inhabitants of the globe.

It has all happened many times before. The westward trek of American pioneers established the dominance of a single culture over physical real estate, but who could defend the position that humanity thereby benefited in any other way? We seem to have learned little about the positive side of human nature in the face of adversity; nor have we gained any special insight into the psychological forces determining attitudes, feelings, and behavior toward the physical environment and our fellow human beings.

If we do not rush headlong to destruction in the next century or two, it seems almost certain the scenarios sketched by the designers of space emigration will become reality, at least in their broadest strokes. It is also apparent, although physical scientists who write about the wonders of space colonies imply something quite different, that such novel environments will not alter the full expression of the strengths and faults of human character. On the other hand, a serendipitous result of space colonies may be to increase the chances of meeting other beings from other worlds. If aliens have not actually visited Earth, we could be the first one on the block to migrate from a home planet and thereby reach out to other civilizations located elsewhere in the Galaxy. A successful colony that served as a base camp for more distant excursions into outer space would help convert beliefs about extraterrestrials from the realm of the outrageous into that of the possible. The dissemination of human culture may go on for millions of years, however, before we ever encounter an alien species of similar interests and intelligence. Some space scientists actually feel that we could well be the first civilization in our galaxy with the knowledge and technology necessary to visit other star systems. The implications of this possibility were reviewed recently by Alan Bond and Anthony Martin.

In the year A.D. 6000 a space tourist may look back on the history of human civilization through the lens of an early Island One structure. As the tourist stares at this hollow dinosaur of aluminum and glass, a series of nagging questions may persist. How did the people of such a primitive society lift materials into orbit and build a viable colony of such massive dimensions? How did they mine the Moon and asteroids with such archaic equipment and minimal scientific knowledge? Someone might even suppose that these early humans were handed engineering instructions on a silver platter by another charitable species possessing a superior intelligence—much in the manner proposed by von Däniken to explain the construction of the Pyramids and other monuments of the past.

REFERENCES AND FURTHER READINGS

Bond, A., & Martin, A. R. A Conservative Estimate of the Number of Habitable Planets in the Galaxy. *Journal of the British Interplanetary Society,* 1980, *33,* 101–106.

Bova, B. *The High Road.* New York: Pocket, 1983.

Calisher, H. *Mysteries of Motion.* Garden City, N.Y.: Doubleday, 1983.

Chaisson, E. *Cosmic Dawn: The Origins of Matter and Life.* Boston: Little, Brown, 1981.

Crosby, A. W., Jr. *The Columbian Exchange: Biological and Cultural Consequences of 1492.* Westport, Conn.: Greenwood, 1972.

DeSan, M. G. The Ultimate Destiny of an Intelligent Species—Everlasting Nomadic Life in the Galaxy. *Journal of the British Interplanetary Society,* 1981, *34,* 219–237.

Geis, L., & Florin, F. (Eds.) *Moving into Space.* New York: Harper & Row, 1980.

Heppenheimer, T. A. *Colonies in Space.* New York: Warner, 1977.

Heppenheimer, T. A. *Toward Distant Suns.* New York: Fawcett Columbine, 1979.

Kardashev, N. S. Transmission of Information by Extraterrestrial Civilizations. In Goldsmith, D. (Ed.), *The Quest for Extraterrestrial Life: A book of Readings,* pp. 136–139. Mill Valley, Calif.: University Science Books, 1980.

Kluckhohn, F. R. Dominant and variant value orientation. In C. Kluckhohn & H. A. Murray (Eds.), *Personality in Nature, Society, and Culture,* pp. 342–357. 2nd ed. New York: Knopf, 1953.

Macvey, J. W. *Colonizing Other Worlds: A Field Manual.* Briarcliff Manor, N.Y.: Stein & Day, 1984.

Meadows, D. H.; Meadows, D. C.; Randers, J.; & Behrens, W. W. III. *The Limits to Growth.* New York: Signet, 1974.

O'Neill, G. K. *The High Frontier: Human Colonies in Space.* New York: Morrow, 1977; Bantam, 1978.

O'Neill, G. K. *2081: A Hopeful View of the Human Future.* New York: Simon
    & Schuster, 1981.
Trefil, J. S. *Living in Space.* New York: Scribner, 1981.
Von Däniken, E. *Chariots of the Gods?* New York: Putnam, 1969.
Washburn, W. E. *The Indian in America.* New York: Harper & Row, 1975.

CHAPTER 5

RADIO TELESCOPES AND SETI

Although we are currently exploring a host of methods that may eventually lead to contact with intelligent life in outer space, only the radio astronomers and engineers have the political and financial clout needed to conduct viable searches. Their fledgling programs use but a tiny fraction of the funds allocated to astronomy worldwide, but this commitment should expand in the years to come, as the potential payoff of alien communication dawns on more and more people. As noted earlier, the success of this venture would have lasting implications for all life on this planet, though at this point we can't foretell whether the impact would be positive or negative. Therefore, it would seem socially prudent to examine and evaluate the astronomer's approach from multiple directions; my own bias is to view these matters through the eyes of social science.

A human component, often implicit, is apparent in the proposals to use radio telescopes to detect signals from sources outside the Solar System. In fact, the reasons given to justify this search are amazingly similar to the reasons one could use to motivate the search for people on Earth with extrasensory perception (ESP)—a topic for the psychologist. Both the search for ESP and the search for extraterrestrial intelligence (SETI), as possibly revealed by long-distance radio activity, are based on sheer faith as well as on scientific argument, and so far, neither has proved successful. The parallels between the two approaches help us anticipate and avoid difficulties in seeking out alien beings with kindred interests. There are important differences as well that will not be discussed. The interesting point here is that psychic phenomena are usually investigated and accepted by individuals characterized as nonscientists, while physical scientists are most likely to pursue their goals by means of the radio telescope. Whereas the methods of ESP researchers are supposed to tap means of communication that have never proved effective for solving any problem, the methods of SETI do in fact work in the modern study of astronomical phenomena.

Nonetheless, informal conversation with friends, neighbors, and acquaintances leaves a vivid impression that many people believe that extrasensory perception is a viable means to receive and understand the thoughts of others. Despite this widespread acceptance, it is hard to define ESP unambiguously. As a standard for comparison, we must turn to the principles of ordinary perception, the normal process by which we gain knowledge about the world through the senses. The perception of the outside environment depends on a number of factors: the type of objects "out there"; the sensitivity of one's eyes, ears, and so forth; and the nature of one's past experience. The relative contributions of the outside stimulus and the internal mental state depend on the situation, but in all cases there is some apprehension and awareness of an object or event out there in the physical environment, if we are truly dealing with direct perception.

There are times when the object is not directly there, and yet the perceiver's experience is similar, or perhaps even identical, to the occasions when it is. Dreams are a good example; imagining a familiar scene is another. The ability to imagine a childhood view of Main Street in the old hometown, mom's smiling face, and the color of a friend's hair surely draws upon memories laid down originally by direct perception. This mental imagery is not a form of extrasensory perception because it is based on recall of actual "percepts." Dreams also fail to qualify. Notwithstanding their possible value in targeting psychological disorders—a debatable point—most dreams bear only a passing resemblance to actual happenings in the external world. So neither imagery nor dreams qualify as extrasensory perception, and neither was considered when the late J. B. Rhine defined psychic power as awareness of objects, events, or thoughts of another person without the aid of the senses. Two common examples of what Rhine did mean are mental telepathy and clairvoyance.

Mental telepathy occurs when a "percipient" can tell what an "agent" or sender is thinking, without the aid of normal communication or contact of any kind; that is, no information is obtained by the usual sensory paths to knowledge about the world. Clairvoyance implies a percipient who is aware of an event without the benefit of another person assuming the role of sender. So two people, percipient and sender, are needed to demonstrate telepathy, but a single individual can exhibit clairvoyance. Proof of either phenomenon means that the percipient's verbal reports about events, thoughts, or objects correspond to what actually took place. On the surface at least, telepathy and clairvoyance are relevant to communication of any kind, including that between organisms residing on different planets.

A garden-variety example of telepathy is this: Suppose two friends are separated by physical barriers—say, one is in a New York apartment and the other in a Moscow train station. The New Yorker has a deck of well-shuffled playing cards and proceeds to turn them over one per minute until the faces of all fifty-two have been exposed. Simultaneously, the Muscovite attempts to "call" the identity of the cards, in order. With synchronized watches, the Muscovite calls each card during the sixty seconds the New Yorker is looking at it. Later, at an international conference on ESP, they compare notes and determine the number of correct identifications. If the score exceeds that expected by chance, mental telepathy has presumably been implicated, assuming of course that the test was not rigged to deceive, or that the percipient was not just plain lucky.

Now suppose the New Yorker is replaced by a fancy computer, equipped with an automatic card-randomizer and flipper. The experiment is repeated, and if the Muscovite still scores better than chance, clairvoyance has occurred. Nobody claims that telepathy and clairvoyance are everyday occurrences, although they exemplify mental abilities everyone uses to predict and prepare for future events. The great appeal of psychic stories, regularly chronicled in the sensational news tabloids, is their similarity to events experienced by the average person every now and then. Most people do not feel that they command supernatural powers, but the glimmer of untapped mental energy is ignited by the bold statements of such power in others. And of course only the successes are reviewed in the media and later recalled by the reader. The failure of extrasensory perception on a specific occasion is not very newsworthy.

Each of us apparently engages in mind reading with positive results once in a while. Consider a couple deciding to celebrate their fiftieth wedding anniversary by dining out. Following several minutes of deliberation, both express the same choice of restaurant. Is this mere coincidence or mind reading? After they have arrived at the restaurant and been seated at a table, the cocktail waitress comes by and the woman orders drinks for two without consulting her husband. He doesn't look especially stunned; she ordered exactly what he wanted that night. Without conversing any further, they glance over the menu, and then, while the woman gets up to admire the wall tapestries, the waiter takes the dinner order. The man orders for both without consulting his spouse. Upon returning to the table she isn't at all upset by his selection, since he ordered her favorite entree, as he probably has done numerous times before.

The "mind reading" going on here is not all that mysterious. After fifty years of shared experiences the man and woman have learned to anticipate the desires of their partners in a great variety of social contexts. There may be only two exclusive restaurants in town, and they may have patronized one the week before, so that it was quite natural to choose the second establishment this time. Perhaps they never frequent the same place twice in succession, or maybe the food was poor the last time they went to the other choice. Similar facts about their partner's drink and food habits would be readily acquired over their years of intimate association. In a sense the couple is telepathic when it comes to predicting each other's thoughts on a great many issues, from politics to food, from automobiles to vacation spots. This is not to say that all golden-anniversary couples act and think in unison on all issues, but friends' preferences certainly are easier to guess than those of strangers.

What is unique about claims of extrasensory perception, therefore, is not that people are able to guess the thoughts of others, but rather that they are able to do so on the basis of very meager clues. If the deck of cards is thoroughly shuffled, there is no apparent way the Muscovite's knowledge of card games or extensive friendship with the New Yorker should help one bit; and if the two are not in collusion, there is no reason why their tenuous link in the test should have any bearing on the outcome.

Under even the best of conditions, ESP experiences must be very rare. We think that the number of people with such exceptional abilities is vanishingly small, and to find these folks would require a prodigious amount of searching. In order to motivate a search we would have to examine an array of social and personality factors noted by psychic researchers as relevant to the demonstration of supernormal powers. Chief among these are said to be a person's age, degree of social naiveté, responsiveness, and strength of belief in ESP. If narrow bands of acceptance surround optimal levels of each factor, psychics must be a tiny subset of the world population.

I don't know whether psychics exist or not—my feeling is that they don't—but I do know that none of the thousands of publicized cases has ever been accepted by mainstream social science. On the other hand, paranormal research continues to flourish. Journals are devoted to the publication of experiments and theories dealing with "psychic" phenomena; conferences are held; and so on. So while most social scientists eschew any affiliation with this research, the work is sustained and the general public believes in the potential payoff of an ongoing investigation. As will be evident momentarily, scientists who attempt to gauge the number of civilizations in the Galaxy with the technical potential and desire to communicate on interstellar scales may not be much better off at this stage than are ESP researchers.

Since the refinement of the radio telescope over forty years ago, astronomers have discovered a whole array of extraterrestrial objects that could not be seen by the optical telescope. Because of these successes, a few of the more courageous souls in the astrophysical community have raised the provocative notion that intelligent life in other parts of the universe has taken to beaming radio messages we might do well to receive and decipher. Alternatively, we may be able to eavesdrop on civilizations by monitoring radio activity that they are inadvertently leaking into outer space. The strategy for rationalizing this fascination with extraterrestrial intelligence has more than a passing similarity to the strategy that might be used for finding individuals with the power of extrasensory perception. I think it is not idle to ask whether the search for extraterrestrial intelligence is similar to the mind reading of the golden-anniversary couple—that is, is based squarely on scientific clues—or matches more faithfully the situation of the Muscovite attempting to call the faces of playing cards in a New York apartment six thousand miles away—that is, an exercise of dubious validity.

The central assumption of SETI is that we will be able to communicate with another species whose technological capabilities and level of gregariousness are something like our own. That is, we must "know" this species well enough to expect it to behave as we do. Not that we dare predict its selections from a dinner menu, but at the very least we must think alike in trusting the radio telescope as a preferred mode for exchanging interstellar messages. We are looking for an intelligence with interests in science and with a value orientation that includes curiosity about what goes on in outer space. What is it, then, about the radio telescope that makes some physicists so sure that it will be the instrument of choice among communicating civilizations?

To answer this question we must first review a few facts about the physical nature of light. Visible light, traveling at the all-time record of 186,000 miles per second, represents only a small fraction of the electromagnetic spectrum, spanning the scale from the very short gamma rays to the thousand-meter waves of AM radio. Whatever part of the spectrum we care to examine, we find "light" waves traversing the great empty expanses of outer space at a constant speed.

Optical telescopes were built to accommodate and extend the resolving power of the human eye, which experiences colored light in the region bounded by violet and red, corresponding to physical wavelengths of four hundred and seven hundred nanometers (one nanometer equals one-billionth of a meter). Human perceptual experience is triggered by extremely short wavelengths of light. Modern astronomy, with its new radio antennas and satellite telescopes, operating above the Earth's occluding atmosphere, has greatly extended the cosmic skyscape to include infrared, microwave, and radio waves, which are all longer than visible wavelengths, and the ultraviolet, X rays, and gamma rays, which are all shorter than visible wavelengths.

Though conceding the wisdom of looking for signals embedded in all parts of the electromagnetic spectrum, astronomers have focused on the microwave region as the most likely source of signals. The scientific study of these waves, at the lower end of the radio spectrum, is fairly recent. Radio and television are an integral part of twentieth-century life, but one hundred years ago very little was known about these matters. Radio waves were first identified by the German Heinrich Hertz in 1888 and were then converted to practical use by the Italian Guglielmo Marconi in 1895. Such waves range from three millimeters to three thousand meters in length, and when emanating from natural extraterrestrial sources (chemical reactions in stars and the interstellar medium), they constitute a new and exciting topic of study for modern astronomy.

The birth of radio astronomy is usually traced to the early 1930s, when Karl Jansky of Bell Telephone Laboratories successfully recorded emissions from the center of the Milky Way. The implications of these remarkable findings were initially pursued by a radio engineer and amateur astronomer, Grote Reber, who personally built a thirty-foot dish in his backyard. The citizens in his hometown of Wheaton, Illinois, must have been somewhat puzzled and perhaps even a little concerned about Reber's mental balance. Their puzzlement was natural, but happily, their concern was unwarranted. Reber was a pioneer in the field and is credited with producing the first radio map of the Milky Way—based on reception at a wavelength of 1.87 meters.

Large-scale radio astronomy received an unscheduled boost during the Second World War in England, after J. S. Hey decided that at least some of the reception difficulties encountered by radar operators were not due to jamming by a human protagonist. Rather, he concluded that the Sun itself was a source of interfering radio emission. After the war, Hey helped found several research facilities for the systematic exploration of the radio universe.

Nowadays the telescopes devoted to this task are large by optical standards. The Soviet Union has erected several 22-meter dishes to receive waves in the millimeter range, and the United States supports work employing the 305-meter Arecibo dish nestled in a natural valley in Puerto Rico; it is the largest telescope in the world. With these massive structures, along with more ingenious designs involving synchronous operation of an array of smaller dishes, the world has been treated to a continuous string of discoveries about the detailed nature of outer space: radio stars, radio galaxies, huge gaseous clouds of intense activity, strange pulsing stars, and super-energetic distant radio sources.

The new cosmic skyscape unveiled by the radio telescope is much deeper and more varied than ever believed possible on the basis of observations with even the most sophisticated optical telescopes. The latter are by no means out of business, but the promise of the new astronomy seems to rest firmly with radio. This optimistic spirit is captured by J. S. Hey, who states confidently, "It is radio astronomy with its penetrability, its wealth and variety of data, that offers most scope for future advance and breakthrough in our knowledge" (*The Evolution of Radio Astronomy*, p. 147). When measured against the competition for contacting extraterrestrial intelligence—for example, space probes or colonization—the radio telescope is considered by many astronomers to be our best choice. It can receive signals transmitted over immense interstellar distances, it is less expensive than sending spacecraft, and it relies upon the fastest mode of travel we know: electromagnetic waves.

It was this promise that led two physicists, Philip Morrison and Giuseppe Cocconi, to suggest in 1959 that radio telescopes be directed at nearby stars in the hope of recording signals at the twenty-one-centimeter wavelength—the radio emission line of neutral hydrogen, by far the most prevalent element in the universe. Although no serious searches have looked *only* at that particular wavelength, the immediate region around twenty-one centimeters has received disproportionate attention in the searches to date (see reviews by Eugene F. Mallove and Jill Tarter).

The Morrison-Cocconi proposal was brought nearer to reality during the 1961 meeting of a small, select group at the United States National Observatory in Green Bank, West Virginia. The most widely cited justification for SETI emerged from this conference, primarily through the suasive arguments of two renowned astronomers, Frank Drake and Carl Sagan. The so-called Drake equation is a formula used to estimate roughly the number of civilizations in the Galaxy with the technical expertise and desire to communicate with their distant neighbors. Because of its key role in motivating governments to spend hard cash, as well as its potential scientific payoff, the philosophy behind the Drake equation has been examined inside and out, and each of its terms has been scrutinized in the light of all pertinent data. Therefore, in order to provide a social science analysis of the SETI enterprise, we must first consider the major physical assumptions of the Drake equation.

Several versions are around, but I will concentrate on the recent treatments by Carl Sagan in his book *Cosmos* and by Donald Goldsmith and Tobias Owen in *The Search for Life in the Universe*. The general equation takes a simple form in the service of estimating the prevalence of extraterrestrial intelligence:

$$\text{ETI} = S \times f(s) \times n(h) \times f(l) \times f(i) \times f(c) \times f(L),$$

where S is the number of stars in the Milky Way Galaxy. The constituent terms act as filters that pare down the initially large value of S:

$f(s)$, the fraction of stars with the necessary life span;

$n(h)$, the number of planets in a system falling within a continuously habitable zone;

$f(l)$, the fraction of planets on which life arises;

$f(i)$, the fraction of inhabited planets where intelligent life develops;

$f(c)$, the fraction of inhabited planets where intelligent life develops a technical civilization;

$f(L)$, the fraction of a planetary lifetime marked by advanced technology.

A good deal of detective work is necessary to pin numerical values on each factor. The number of stars in the Galaxy elicits the most agreement; it is said to fall between 10 and 400 billion. Approaching the formula in an expansive mood, let's set S equal to 400 billion. If we next assume that a star must survive at least 5 billion years for intelligent life to gain a foothold—it took life on Earth almost 4 billion to make it this far—an estimate for $f(s)$ can be made. As many as half of the "good" stars pass this longevity test, so we let $f(s)$ equal .5. There are some astronomical data to support this choice, although they are weaker than the empirical data on the number of stars in the Galaxy. In any event, multiplying .5 times 400 billion reduces the pool to 200 billion.

The next term, the average number of planets per star, is more problematic. Astronomers are on the threshold of being able to detect planets orbiting their parent stars, and a space telescope operating in the infrared region has recently detected what appears to be the initial stages of planetary formation around several stars. As of this writing, however, there are no conclusive data to the effect that other stars have companion planets. Since the Sun is considered an average star, nothing special in the cosmic panorama, we can use the extensive information about it to estimate the number of planets for other suns. We know of nine planets in the Solar System, but for ease of calculation let's take the liberty of rounding upward and let $n(h)$ equal 10; who knows, there may be another planet circling out there beyond Neptune and Pluto. Introducing this term actually increases the running total to 10 times 200 billion = 2,000 billion, but this is a temporary enrichment.

The fraction of planets on which life arises can only be based on what is known of the Solar System. Neither Mercury nor Venus appears hospitable for life; Mars is marginal. Some strange life forms might thrive in the gaseous clouds of Jupiter or perhaps on the surface of Saturn's giant moon, Titan. We are certain about only one case, Earth. So that suggests an estimate of one in ten planets as suitable for life. According to technical arguments made by Goldsmith and Owen, only one in four planetary systems may have a continually habitable zone where life could thrive. Accepting this estimate, we assume $n(h)$ = 1/4 × 1/10 = .025, and multiplying this outcome by the potential planets yields .025 × 2,000 billion = 50 billion.

Space chemistry reveals that many essential elements of life abound in the gaseous clouds of the interstellar medium and in meteorites that occasionally manage to weather the blistering trip through the Earth's atmosphere. In addition, the molecular constituents of life can be readily created in laboratory experiments simulating the prebiotic environment of the primitive Earth. On the basis of this evidence we estimate the fraction of planets on which intelligent life has actually evolved as .5. As the next step, .5 × 50 billion = 25 billion.

On each of the planets where life arises the stresses of the environment should presage the onset of natural selection and the multiplication of life's forms. The various forms on other planets may be wildly different in physical and biological appearance from human beings, as well as from each other, but through the pressures of Darwinian evolution we expect some fraction of them to sustain a civilization capable and desirous of communicating on an interstellar scale. Suppose this technical expertise is achieved by half the candidates, then *f(c)* = .5 and the field of interest shrinks to .5 × 25 billion = 12.5 billion.

At this point it is instructive to reflect for a moment on the observation that the four terms just reviewed are based on no hard facts outside our experience with Earth and the Solar System. Nonetheless, physicists have arrived at numbers for each term and have rationalized this procedure by recourse to the "assumption of mediocrity": Namely, on the cosmic scale we presume that Earth and the Solar System are typical examples found throughout the Galaxy. Comparative results from optical astronomy make this assumption likely for the Sun, but its validity for planets can be known only after closer study of other star systems.

The last term in the equation is the most vital, yet here we cannot even find an ally in the assumption of mediocrity. How can we ever predict the lifetime of a technological civilization when the only example is ourselves? Communication by radio telescope has been possible for only forty years. This is a mere blink of the eye in the cosmic time frame of the Galaxy's 10 billion years of existence. In the worst possible case, forty years is all we can expect before a civilization loses the verve to strike out on its own, or inadvertently self-destructs, or succumbs to natural disaster. Then the number of civilizations at or beyond our technological level might well be close to zero. On a more encouraging note, if a civilization were able to grow and prosper over a very extended time period, say a billion years, then *f(l)* = 1 billion/10 billion = .1, and the prospects brighten for interstellar contact. That is, .1 × 12.5 billion = 1.25 billion societies at this moment able to exchange pleasantries with fellow members of the Galaxy.

Unless one is blessed with the faculty of precognition, there simply is no objective way to estimate the lifetime of a civilization that has not yet run its full course. It is nonetheless interesting from a social science standpoint to find out how young people, in particular, feel about this matter, because the upcoming generation will decide the fate of SETI for the next half century or so. Several years ago I asked a group of Dartmouth students to predict the human risk associated with nuclear war over time scales beginning in 1982 and stretching into the future to the years 2000, 3000, 4000, and 7000. They were handed a sheet of paper containing the vertical and horizontal axes of an empty graph. The vertical axis was labeled "risk level"; the horizontal axis was labeled "year" and was marked off in equal time intervals starting at 1982 and continuing out to one of the four upper boundaries. A point situated at the middle of the vertical axis signified the hypothetical risk level in 1982. Each student drew a continuous line on the graph to represent a prediction of future risk. Hence, a rising curve indicated increasing risk; a falling curve, decreasing risk. Most students predicted an increase in nuclear risk in the short run, but in many instances the curve slowly stabilized at about the 1982 value. With longer time scales, however, approximately one-third of the students drew a curve that climbed up to a maximum and then crashed to zero.

Since the pattern of results was similar for other types of environmental risks, for example, environmental pollution, nuclear power, and mental disorders, the precipitous drop in the curve most likely reflected "doomsday" predictions. Most of the predicted crashes would occur within the next 5000 years. If we were to base our estimate of a civilization's lifetime on these results, then $5000 \div 10$ billion = .0000005. Multiplying this fraction by 12.5 billion yields a paltry 6,250 civilizations in the whole Galaxy. Now, we are talking about 6,250 needles in a haystack containing billions of straws. It works out to be about one or two civilizations for every 100 million stars. The practical job of finding those unique cases is staggering, comparable in magnitude to that of locating a handful of potential psychics among the U.S. population, with little or no clues to guide the search.

On the other hand, what do undergraduates know about the lifespan of societies? Among an older generation of physicists are some optimists who feel that a lifespan of a million years is a more reasonable figure. If they are right, then $f(L) = 1$ million/10 billion = .0001. This figure produces a more acceptable, optimistic scenario that is summarized by the Drake equation as follows.

$$ETI = 400 \text{ billion} \times .5 \times 10 \times .025 \times .5 \times .5 \times .0001$$
$$= 1.25 \text{ million communicating civilizations in our Galaxy.}$$

Considering that there are as many galaxies in the universe as there are stars in the Milky Way, then we must have plenty of company. Therefore, the task is to find at least one of these special civilizations among every 100,000 stars. This is like contacting a handful of individuals among the entire population of San Francisco or a few hundred in New York City. I don't think many people outside astronomy realize that even under the most favorable conditions, the search is up against tremendous odds. It seems evident that our current technical competence will necessitate a long-term, patient search, unless, through no special effort of our own, we beat the odds and hit the jackpot early.

More pessimistic views of the chances for success have steadily proliferated since the brighter days of Morrison and Cocconi and the Green Bank conference. After examining the most up-to-date evidence for each of the factors in the Drake equation, the astronomers Robert T. Rood and James S. Trefil wrote in 1981: "We have seen that new knowledge has greatly reduced our freedom to choose any numbers we like for terms in the Green Bank [Drake] equation" (*Are We Alone?* p. 120). They go on to review these new data and end up predicting the existence of a tiny number of advanced civilizations in the Galaxy; in fact, they tell us, they would not be surprised to learn that we are the only communicating society among the pool of 400 billion.

Many diverse opinions have been aired about the ultimate feasibility of SETI. In the process, the original intent of the Drake equation sometimes has been distorted by forcing the numbers to be overly precise. At the outset the terms in the equation were seen as general guidelines, "soft" estimates, whose uncertainty increases as we proceed from left to right in the formula, that is, away from the physical factors and toward those of a social science flavor. The strongest term in the formula is the number of stars in the Galaxy, and even here one can't avoid the impression of slackness. The numbers are always in the billions, but whether we should settle on 10, 100, or 400 billion is apparently left to the personal taste of the astronomer.

The middle terms of the equation rely on the assumption of mediocrity, and hence rest heavily on the single examples of Earth and the Solar System. In other domains of science, investigators are usually reluctant to publicize results based on isolated cases. The weakest link of all is the estimate of the lifetime of an advanced civilization, where sober discussion can generate values ranging from one hundred to 1 billion years. The implications of these various estimates for a search program are markedly different and certainly would not encourage the same policy decisions on either the political or the scientific front. In light of all this attention to numbers, we might well inquire how a scientific formula, dressed up in the best quantitative finery, could lead to such disparate conclusions.

The answer seems to lie more with the psychology of the scientist than with the physics of the cosmos. Physicists are comfortable dealing with numbers. They work with them daily and strive to quantify any and all manner of problems. Relying on procedures of physical measurement, they collect numerical data which are substituted for unknowns in equations such as the Drake formula. These equations then are polished, manipulated, and evaluated to uncover or predict deeper truths about the physical universe.

Not all the important problems of the universe lend themselves to the kind of reasoning seen most often in the physical sciences. The broader philosophical issues surrounding SETI may represent such a set of recalcitrant problems. Given the lack of pertinent factual knowledge, can one really say anything meaningful about the life of a civilization founded on the principles of physics? While admitting the absurdity of trying, some physicists have boldly gone ahead anyway. A typical positive attitude is expressed by Goldsmith and Owen in discussing the related issue of sketching out the expected growth of space colonies. They are led to confess, "Confronted once again with questions that we really cannot answer, scientists have managed to produce some definitions and reflections based on our knowledge of physics" (*The Search for Life in the Universe,* p. 360). But how does a physics bereft of relevant facts help us confront the unanswerable?

A related attitude prevails in the ranks of the SETI community. It is almost as if these astronomers have proclaimed, "Look, friends, we really have no idea about how to assign numbers to most of the factors in the Drake equation, but let's carry on as if we did, cross our fingers, and hope for the best." If social science were caught in a comparable sleight of hand, most astronomers and physicists would shudder in disapproval or chuckle at the naiveté of their social science counterparts.

Composing a string of factors into a form that mimics the equations used in the secure branches of science does not automatically confer validity on the SETI enterprise, just as the elaboration of a formula to estimate the number of psychics in the United States would not anoint that effort with social science's stamp of approval.

Despite the illusion of precision, the actual numbers inserted into the Drake equation rest on a shaky underfooting. Psychological considerations help us understand why. Let me illustrate this point first by way of a common anecdote. If you ask a working woman how far it is between her home and job, you are likely to be given a number which suggests that the distance has been noted with some care and precision. People who commute each day by car are especially attuned to this journey. So the woman may say, "17 miles," or "33 kilometers," or "4.5 miles." If you then ask the same woman how far it is between some major cities in the area, the response will be of a decidedly other character. Even if her profession involves extensive travel, she will likely respond with whole integers, such as "50 miles," "100 kilometers," "200 miles," or "500 kilometers." No one is inclined to say, "46 miles" or "482 kilometers." The inherent uncertainty about the distance is revealed by the fact that the first, left-most, digit is significant, but the trailing zeros do not imply precision; and more often than not, the leading digit is either a 1 or a 5. The restricted nature of the numbers actually given tells us immediately that we should interpret them as falling within a cloud of uncertainty: The numbers do not reflect accurate measurement of distance, but only a person's rough subjective impression. This outcome has been verified in laboratory studies Elliot Noma and I have conducted but it isn't necessary here to go over the details.

The relevance for SETI is this: The estimates entered into the Drake equation are supposedly derived from careful theory and experiment. Although the results are often presented in neat tables, the imprint of scientific rigor is tarnished by the character of the numbers themselves. In their 1981 treatment, Rood and Trefil summarize five chapters of discussion on the appropriate set of values for an optimistic, a conservative, or a pessimistic scenario. The numerical entries in their table 1 (p. 122) have two outstanding features. First, they contain only one nonzero digit, and second, this digit is either a 1 or a 5. Specifically, of twenty-four values, there are eight 1s, eight 5s, one 3, and a maverick .15. The five other entries fall under the heading of the pessimistic scenario and are simply labeled "very small." Essentially, the state of the art in regard to the Drake equation consists of three categories to represent probabilities: 0, .5, and 1. Apparently, the available facts permit only three distinctions: Something does, doesn't, or might happen. One can justly ask whether such qualitative groupings have a rightful place in this sort of equation, even if the smallest number is positive (if one of the terms is 0 then the estimated prevalence of ETI goes to 0 as well).

Rood and Trefil have the company of every other astronomer I have read who plugs values into the Drake equation. Looking at the numbers given in a representative set of books, I find that the same casual manner of expressing uncertainty is evident. I have tallied all the numbers used by Goldsmith and Owen, Carl Sagan (*Cosmos*), Ian Ridpath (*Messages from the Stars*), and Rood and Trefil. Out of a total of fifty-seven values, all but six have just one significant digit, and of these fifty-one entries, I count thirty-two 1s, three 2s, one 3, three 4s, eleven 5s, one 6, and no 7s, 8s, or 9s. These gaps in the number scale are just a trifle suspicious and do not compose the stuff out of which mathematical equations are usually formulated. Isn't it rather devious to pretend that these numbers can be sensibly multiplied? The cloud of uncertainty surrounding each of the terms instills no confidence in the final answer.

As a matter of comparison, we can contrast these numbers with those reported for objects about which physicists actually know a good deal. For example, Rood and Trefil present a comprehensive list of the percentages of the most abundant elements in the Sun. The table confidently begins: hydrogen, 75; helium, 23; carbon, .34; nitrogen, .12; oxygen, .83. In a later discussion of the world's mineral reserves, the figures read: aluminum, 1.17 billion tons; chromium, 775 million; copper, 308 million; gold, 353 million; and so on. When judged against the precision implied by these values, significant to three places, the Drake equation would hardly seem more sophisticated than a playful formula arranged along the same lines to justify the search for American psychics.

In the face of equivocal data the true believer turns to intuition and pure feeling. When astronomers discuss the Drake equation, it is often implicit that the numbers are there only to legitimize an emotional feeling about the prevalence of life in the universe. On the one hand, the enumerable candidate stars make it reasonable to conclude that we are not alone. And if there are other societies out there, it would be exciting to make contact and begin sharing our special views of the universe. I strongly expect that this is the dominant opinion of most people who have thought for awhile about the possibility of extraterrestrial intelligence. The erudite arguments leading to the Drake equation and its quantitative details are just faint shadows of a position widely accepted as valid. My guess is many people are already persuaded of the existence of other worlds like ours, populated by sentient creatures, and although it is reassuring to have the blessing of science, whether there is one or a million such civilizations is of little note.

Nonetheless, the onus of definitive proof is left at the doorstep of the engineers and physicists. Belief is one thing, proof another. For scientists, quantitative arguments are absolutely essential to justify the time and expense of a systematic search. Unfortunately, the necessary facts simply are not there to help assess the ultimate wisdom of continuing. Today's scientists must be risk takers to tie their banner to SETI. In the absence of the standard empirical supports, they must reflect and act on their subjective intuition about the relative likelihood of success and failure. In this reliance on personal intuition they join forces with their nonscientific comrades whose value orientations motivate the same belief in the existence of alien intelligence elsewhere in the universe.

It is this recourse to subjective judgment, backed by tenuous facts, that makes it interesting to treat aspects of the search for extrasensory perception as an enterprise parallel to aspects of the search for extraterrestrial intelligence. If there are only a smattering of civilizations in the Galaxy, and they have no special interest in us, then SETI is an exercise in futility. We are no better off than the Muscovite in his attempt to call the order of playing cards in faraway New York. The New Yorker might just as well be a schoolgirl playing with her homemade radio telescope on a planet circling a star in the peripheral arm of a minor galaxy. If this indeed is a fair characterization of reality, there are social consequences attendant on a program that incurs severe economic costs and enlists long-term societal commitments. The dangers are the very ones encountered by people who through the centuries have sought to obtain proofs for ESP. Understanding these perennial efforts may help us avoid or cope with pitfalls that could derail a legitimate search for ETI. These pitfalls include the tendencies to ignore the results of failed experiments, to engage in hoax and trickery, and to omit the repetition of a procedure that once led to a positive discovery. Finding a signal on one isolated occasion is not enough. We will be looking for repeat performances.

The inherent drawbacks of psychic research are well documented, although the more sensational news media frequently trumpet its efficacy and virtues, and most people are acquainted with at least one person who claims to be telepathic or clairvoyant. What neither the media accounts nor the anecdotal reports include is a list of failures. I think this list would be a long one, false claims and errors in personal intuition far outweighing the rare successes.

Given a modest awareness of the world's political sphere, it would not be difficult to predict accurately the general outline of future events. For example, at this juncture in history the prediction of war between two adjacent countries in the Middle East within the next ten years is a safe bet; especially if the prediction can be renewed on a yearly basis and we are not asked to explain the years when the prediction is thankfully disconfirmed.

People do not enjoy publicizing their mistakes. It is doubtful if scientists are somehow immune in this regard. Hence, as SETI ages—gracefully, we hope—there will be a growing tendency to advertise the smallest hint of contact but little pressure to announce failures. At present, while we are still reveling in the excitement of a new venture, public confessions are encouraged, but this tolerance for negative news will steadily evaporate if the program continues to come up empty-handed over an extended period of time. The potential danger, then, is twofold: The scientists' criteria for reporting a "hit" may soften as the failures mount, and the significance afforded a potential hit may exceed its objective value.

Another concern should be the problem of false alarms. By chance alone, the random noise of radio emission from the Galaxy occasionally will take on the look of a genuine signal. To combat the understandable desire to classify this bogus event as meaningful, it will be important to bear in mind that independent verification is the hallmark of experimental science. The history of psychic research is riddled with cases in which a percipient scored well above chance in naming the faces of playing cards in one or two sessions, only to lose this talent in subsequent tests. Often these later sessions were preceded by efforts to eliminate procedural flaws and to include neutral observers in the audience of onlookers. With these superior controls in place, the power of ESP collapses with great regularity. If a claim of alien contact is to be accepted, it must involve an event that is repetitive and publicly verifiable.

The temptation also will be strong to place undue weight on the practical value of the messages. How do we know that any received signals will be relevant to humans? Turning again to the ESP metaphor, even granting the validity of psychic phenomena, those in control of such powers have done nothing to cure any of humanity's social ills: poverty, famine, war, and political oppression. If these people can peer into the future, why don't they warn the rest of us of impending disasters, such as earthquakes, droughts, and plane crashes? Similarly, even if signals from outer space are discovered, they may turn out to be a subject of natural curiosity but completely devoid of any practical value.

The history of psychic research also conjures up the dark specter of fraud and trickery. From the telepathic "mediums" of the last century to their modern television counterparts, magic tricks and downright hoaxes have been an embarrassing sidelight to the honest efforts of social scientists to investigate mental phenomena. The popular seances during the early part of this century usually centered on the astounding feats of female mediums, who presumably could move furniture around by thought alone and communicate with the dead. In many instances, psychologists and magicians, including the great Houdini, explained or exposed the deceit behind these "supernatural" accomplishments.

The opportunity for fraud will be substantial in SETI because of the esoteric nature of the equipment—radio telescopes and computers are an unbeatable combination—and because of the public's sincere wish to receive positive signs from any authoritative source. The only way to avoid being duped is to insist on normal scientific safeguards. We should be especially wary if a scientist reports contact, but no independent verification is provided. At this point we had best remember the history of psychic research as an instructive example of human fallibility.

Yet another parallel between SETI and ESP is in the personality domain: In both areas there are scientists and nonscientists who believe and those who do not. A person may be aware that statements made by ESP enthusiasts are mostly fraudulent but may still declare its ultimate feasibility. This attitude is prevalent as well with respect to other rare events, such as UFO sightings. Even if careful logic and observation can squelch 99 percent of UFO reports, a substantial group of individuals will still believe in the reality of the remaining 1 percent. Similarly, long-term failure to discover signals from outer space cannot be the last word on whether other technical civilizations exist and/or choose to announce their presence. The faith of the believers will help sustain public commitment, despite centuries of disappointment. And this may not be such a bad outcome. After all, a single positive discovery could dramatically alter the scientific and social direction of humanity. During fallow periods, sporadic reports of success can be expected, and some fierce intellectual battles will surely erupt over the fact and fiction of alien life and intelligence.

In the absence of genuine signals that everyone can agree upon, the antagonism between believers and nonbelievers, optimists and pessimists, will persist, since neither side can lose the argument. If no signals are found, there is a virtual standoff; both sides can cling to their positions with no reason to change. If signals are found, the believer can say, "I told you so," and the skeptic can counter with, "I told you the hard facts would settle the matter."

If messages are ever detected in radio waves, a marked increase should occur in arguments to the effect that communication can be achieved quite easily by anyone with the modest funds to purchase his or her own personal radio telescope. In the years following contact, the business community might be marketing backyard telescopes that would put Grote Reber's instrument to shame. Who knows, by then the social science risk takers may even have earned the right to demand public funds to underwrite the search for human psychics.

REFERENCES AND FURTHER READINGS

Asimov, I. *Extraterrestrial Civilizations*. New York: Fawcett Columbine, 1979.

Baird, J. C. Prediction of Environmental Risk Over Very Long Time Scales. *Journal of Environmental Psychology*, 1986, *6*, 233–244.

Baird, J. C., & Noma, E. Psychophysical Study of Numbers: I. Generation of Numerical Responses. *Psychological Research*, 1975, *37*, 281–297.

Baugher, J. F. *On Civilized Stars: The Search for Intelligent Life in Outer Space.* Englewood Cliffs, N.J.: Prentice-Hall, 1985.

Bond, A., & Martin, A. R. A Conservative Estimate of the Number of Habitable Planets in the Galaxy. *Journal of the British Interplanetary Society*, 1980, *33*, 101–106.

Bowyer, S.; Zeitlin, G.; Tarter, J.; Lampton, M.; & Welch, W. J. The Berkeley Parasitic SETI Program. *Icarus*, 1983, *53*, 147–155.

Cocconi, G., and Morrison, P. Searching for Interstellar Communications. *Nature, 184*, 844–846.

Edelson, E. *Who Goes There? The Search for Intelligent Life in the Universe.* Garden City, N.Y.: Doubleday, 1979.

Feinberg, G., & Shapiro, R. *Life Beyond Earth: The Intelligent Earthling's Guide to Life in the Universe.* New York: Morrow, 1980.

Goldsmith, D., & Owen, T. *The Search for Life in the Universe.* Menlo Park, Calif.: Benjamin-Cummings, 1980.

Gudas, F. (Ed.) *Extrasensory Perception*. New York: Scribner, 1961.

Hansel, C. E. M. *ESP and Parapsychology: A Critical Re-evaluation.* Buffalo, N.Y.: Prometheus, 1980.

Heidmann, J. *Extragalactic Adventure: Our Strange Universe.* Cambridge: Cambridge University Press, 1982.

Hey, J. S. *The Evolution of Radio Astronomy.* New York: Science History Publications, 1973.

Horowitz, P. A Search for Ultra-narrowband Signals of Extraterrestrial Origin. *Science*, 1978, *201*, 733–735.

Kippenhahn, R. *100 Billion Suns: The Birth, Life, and Death of the Stars.* Translated from the German by Jean Steinberg. New York: Basic, 1983.

Mallove, E. F. Renaissance in the Search for Galactic Civilizations. *Technology Review*, 1984, *87*, No. 1, 48–54.

Morrison, P.; Billingham, J.; & Wolfe, J. (Eds.) *The Search for Extraterrestrial Intelligence.* Washington, D.C.: NASA, U.S. Government Printing Office No. 033-000-00696-0, 1977.

Regis, E., Jr. (Ed.) *Extraterrestrials: Science and Alien Intelligence.* Cambridge: Cambridge University Press, 1985.

Rhine, J. B. *The Reach of the Mind.* New York: Morrow, 1975.

Rhine, J. B., & Pratt, J. G. *Parapsychology: Frontier Science of the Mind.* Springfield, Ill.: Thomas, 1957.

Ridpath, I. *Messages from the Stars: Communication and Contact with Extraterrestrial Life.* New York: Harper & Row, Colophon, 1979.

Rood, R. T., & Trefil, J. S. *Are We Alone? The Possibility of Extraterrestrial Civilizations.* New York: Scribner, 1981.

Rowan-Robinson, M. *Cosmic Landscape: Voyages Back Along the Photon's Track.* Oxford: Oxford University Press, 1979.

Sagan, C. *The Cosmic Connection: An Extraterrestrial Perspective.* Garden City, N.Y.: Doubleday, 1973.

Sagan, C. *Cosmos.* New York: Random House, 1980.

Sagan, C. *Contact.* New York: Pocket, 1985.

Sagan, C. (Ed.) *Communication with Extraterrestrial Intelligence.* Cambridge, Mass.: MIT Press, 1973.

Schmeidler, G. (Ed.) *Extrasensory Perception.* New York: Atherton, 1969.

Shklovskii, I. S., & Sagan, C. *Intelligent Life in the Universe.* New York: Dell, 1966.

Smith, S. *Understanding ESP.* New York: Grosset & Dunlap, 1968.

Tarter, J. Searching for Extraterrestrials. In E. Regis, Jr. (Ed.), *Extraterrestrials: Science and Alien Intelligence,* pp. 167–199. Cambridge: Cambridge University Press, 1985.

CHAPTER 6

PURSUING ALIEN MINDS

The enduring goal of science is to gain a deep appreciation of the physical laws governing the material universe, the biological laws underlying the existence of life, and the social/psychological laws determining the thoughts, attitudes, and behavior of life's more intricate forms. Because of the successful extension of the principles of physics to include astronomical phenomena, there really is a valid science of astrophysics. The distinguishing features of our particular sun, planet, and moon can be pinned down with greater assurance than ever before, because there are other suns, planets, and satellite moons available for direct comparison. The use of powerful land and satellite telescopes, together with the application of spectographic techniques to analyze patterns of electromagnetic radiation from the stars and the interstellar medium, enables us to learn a good deal about the chemistry of extraterrestrial space, about the relative mass, distance, and velocity of objects in that space—indeed, about the structure of the universe down to the level of the molecule and the atom. When these data are judiciously combined with information from Earth-bound experiments, we can educate ourselves on many of these seemingly inaccessible celestial subjects.

Much less obvious is the means to decide if life exists on other planets in the Solar System or in other regions of the universe. Although laboratory and computer simulations of the onset and evolution of life are possible once the chemical constituents of a planet and its atmosphere are known, for years to come the best way to investigate life on other planets will be for people or robots to go there, carting along the necessary scientific instruments to conduct on-site experiments. The exploration of nearby planets has been under way for only a few decades, but in this short time the findings have spawned the new field of exobiology: the study of life and its biological and chemical prerequisites as they naturally occur beyond the shell of the Earth's atmosphere.

The chief promise of exobiology is the discovery of some life-form thriving in a natural state in a place other than Earth. A thorough understanding of terrestrial biology and biochemistry may not be reached until we have studied examples of life that originated and evolved under radically different geophysical conditions. Even a single example of extraterrestrial life would add deep perspective to theories of terrestrial biology. So to encourage development of exobiology, scientific experiments can be done on Earth and throughout the rest of the Solar System. Conducting on-site experiments to detect life in the vicinity of distant stars or within the interstellar medium is still a hopeful vision of the future.

Space psychology must be content with a more humble agenda. The possibility of learning anything at all about the thoughts and behavior of alien beings is very remote. We must first find them, then establish communication, and finally, engage in a prolonged exchange of ideas. It may take years to acquire even the most rudimentary facts about the psychological and social makeup of an alien being, even if it is of a cooperative disposition. Perhaps for the next few millennia the subject matter of exopsychology will remain in the realm of pure speculation, gaining substance only through the power of imagination possessed by those sentient creatures who currently populate the Earth. Hence, any progress we make in regard to eventual detection of and communication with an alien intellect will come from our efforts to improve our comprehension of people and other organisms on Earth—unless, of course, aliens decide to pay us a visit first, in "person" or by machine proxy. The human potential for successful interactions with aliens can be gauged at least to some extent by the ability of diverse species here to live in harmony with each other. If we cannot understand the various manifestations of life arising within a common biological and physical milieu, it may be nigh on impossible to understand aliens who evolved under very different conditions elsewhere.

An example closer to home concerns the social relations among people. Future interactions between humans and aliens will be modeled, from our side at least, on how humans generally communicate with one another, and the nature of any social interaction depends upon how each party perceives the intelligence, knowledge, and social status of the other.

Nowhere is this more apparent than in the daily socializing between parents and their children. I think this type of interaction offers a concrete illustration of the different ways humans might approach communication with aliens. In particular, adults make assumptions about the capabilities of the child that determine the mode and substance of communication between them, and I believe these same adults might act similarly toward any aliens that crossed their paths in the future. The example is more to the point than one might at first suppose; witness the characterization of aliens in movies as childlike in physical appearance and mental outlook. The example will have to be elaborated further before its implications become apparent in the present context.

Informal observations of the American family suggest that adults make four principal judgments of intelligence about children. Different adults apply different judgments when attempting to communicate with a child between, let us say, the ages of four and twelve. Such a child speaks competently in the native language of the adult, expresses opinions, and requests fulfillment of personal needs. I want to propose that parents have a tendency to consider this child as a miniature adult, as a subordinate being, as a superior being, or as a totally novel organism. Understanding these alternative modes of parent-child interactions helps us anticipate the assumptions people are bound to make about aliens, especially about their ability to converse with us on a plane of mutual competence and interest.

Perhaps the most common assumption is that children are small adults. Until this century, society at large treated the child as a small replica of the adult. The psychologists Deborah Holmes and Frederick Morrison note that a hundred years ago most children did not wear distinctive clothes, were not given special toys or child-sized conveniences (chairs, tables, etc.), and for the most part, even as very young children, were expected to shoulder the same work burden as adults. Although modern society furnishes separate educational and recreational facilities for children and has passed laws prohibiting blatant exploitation of their labor, many parents still view the mental capacity of their offspring as identical in all critical respects to their own. This attitude can inhibit and damage interpersonal communication if a parent and child actually are quite different. An extreme example is when either the child or the parent is mentally retarded but the other fails to admit this fact. It may take years of anguish for both to realize the cause of their confusion and to adjust their feelings and expectations accordingly. More generally, parents may ask more than is possible from their children. In the same way, if aliens are quite different from us, but we assume they are the same, meaningful communication may be impossible.

The premise of mental equivalence across the entire span of age was dominant within psychology until very recently. In the early part of this century the child was thought to have all the adult faculties for rational and moral thought and action. A mature complement of mental equipment was supposedly present in good working order. The role of education, then, was to fill the youthful mind's empty compartments with the appropriate facts for reasoning and acting in socially acceptable ways. According to the psychologists of the period, this learning was accomplished by the conscious or unconscious application of reward and punishment, which had been found effective in shaping the behavior of laboratory animals.

The great experimental psychologist John B. Watson typified this attitude when he wrote in 1924:

Give me a dozen healthy infants, well-formed, and my own specified world to bring them up in and I'll guarantee to take any one of them at random and train him to become any type of specialist I might select—doctor, lawyer, artist, merchant-chief and, yes, even beggar-man and thief, regardless of his talents, penchants, tendencies, abilities, vocations, and race of his ancestors. . . . Please note that when this experiment is made I am to be allowed to specify the way the children are to be brought up and the type of world they have to live in. [*Behaviorism,* p. 82]

The last qualifying remark is a tall order! From this standpoint, to communicate effectively with a child the parent must be sure the youngster draws on the same pool of information about the world. Once a child has mastered the necessary factual material, there should be no special difficulty in proceeding with the give-and-take of rational discourse.

In brief, one class of adults sees the level and style of human reasoning as identical at all ages. We should expect someone from this group to deal with aliens in a like way by assuming that "their" mental processes are essentially the same as ours. The only important differences between aliens and humans would be expected to be the way they were reared and the type of world they inhabited. By this pattern, communication with aliens should follow the standard educational model used in the schools. In particular, once we all master the same scientific principles, communication of ideas should occur quite naturally.

Other parents deal with youngsters' minds as if they were subsets of their own. This is obviously valid in regard to content knowledge, since the child has not had sufficient time to acquire the same knowledge as the adult. According to some psychologists, however, the differences are deeper because the preadolescent does not command all the adult means of reasoning about either the physical environment or the social rules of society. For fifty years the Swiss psychologist Jean Piaget emphasized the discrepancies among the cognitive skills of children of various ages. A famous case in point is the observation that the very young infant lacks "object permanence," being unaware of the continual existence of objects that appear and reappear over short spans of time. The mother nursing the infant today is not recognized by the child as the same person who provided nourishment yesterday or the day before. The older preschooler, though thinking and speaking in ways indicative of the adult mind, is also limited in the ability to formulate and logically express thoughts. The schoolchild has basic intellectual limits, as well, and below the age of seven, for example, still fails to appreciate that certain physical transformations performed on an object in the environment do not alter that object's essential characteristics—for instance, that moving a doll from the chair to the table does not change its color or shape. The classic demonstration of this phenomenon is Piaget's conservation-of-liquid problem, which can be simply posed as follows.

Imagine two clear beakers of identical size and shape, each half-filled with water. When asked, a five-year-old or a nine-year-old will readily admit that the two beakers contain the same amount of water. They look the same as well. Now introduce a third transparent beaker, narrower and taller than either of the first two. While the children watch, pour the liquid from one of the short beakers into the tall one, making sure that they do not think a trick is being played on them. The common outcome is this: Most five-year-olds will argue that there is more water in the tall beaker than there is in the short one, which still contains the original amount—not just that it looks to contain more water, but that indeed it actually does contain more. The nine-year-old queried on the issue shows an understanding of conservation of liquid by stating correctly that the quantities in the short and tall beakers are identical, although the visual appearances of the two may strongly imply otherwise.

According to Piaget, communication between an adult and a child who has not grasped the conservation principle must be of a more restricted kind than can occur with an older child. Intensive training in the adult style of problem solving will not alter this state of affairs until the child is maturationally ready. There is something fundamentally immature about the methods of reasoning used by the youngster. Adults with a desire to interact on equal terms with their child must be patient and willing to wait a few years. Parents who are convinced of this difference between the adult and the child may slip into addressing their offspring as if they were a subordinate life-form—somewhat as one would treat a pet dog or cat, with sensitivity and love, but with an awareness that the intellect of the child is but a subset of that of the adult. I would expect such adults, when considering the alien mind, to proceed in an analogous fashion by assuming that the intellectual processes of the alien are a subset of their own. They would tend to treat aliens, therefore, as they would treat a young child, with a clear realization of their inherent mental limitations. One result of this attitude would be to search out primitive life-forms, as opposed to alien types more akin to humans.

A third possible assumption is discussed by the anthropologist Ashley Montague, who has recently revived a more radical theory about the maturation of the human intellect. He nicely illustrates a rather intriguing attitude about adult-child communication by proposing that the evolution of the human species is moving toward "neoteny," maintenance of juvenile traits into advanced phases of physical development. In developing his argument Montague claims, "As a consequence of the unique evolutionary history of our species, we are designed to fulfill the bountiful promise of the child; to grow and develop as children, rather than into the kind of adults we have been taught to believe we ought to become" (*Growing Young*, p. 117).

Such positive childhood traits include playfulness, open-mindedness, curiosity, honesty, and vivid imagination, many of which wane or disappear as a person ages. By Montague's reasoning, aging causes a dramatic reduction in the ability to cope effectively with new problems. The adult may have considerable information about the world—purely social knowledge about what to expect and do in this or that situation—but in the course of acquiring this information, he or she has often relinquished the creative talents of the child. In this sense, adult capabilities are a subset of those available to the child. This evocative opinion about human development suggests that it is the lack of neotenous qualities in parents that often blocks their attempts to engage in mutually rewarding dialogue with their children. In effect, youth enjoys an intellectual edge over experience.

Although the continued evolution of *Homo sapiens* may well mean the retention of a greater number of neotenous traits into the later stages of life, and hence a closing of the gap between children and adults, this is a biological transition that will be apparent only in future generations. Until then, by this line of argument, the child should be considered a superior, future-oriented version of the adult: more creative, more imaginative, and better able to face and handle unorthodox problems. By such standards, the adult has much to learn from the child. Again, Montague proposes, "The child surpasses the adult by the wealth of his possibilities. In a very real sense infants and children implicitly know a great deal more about many aspects of growing than do adults; adults, therefore, have more to learn from them about these matters than the latter have to learn from adults" (p. 197).

The implications of this thesis for adult-child communication are immense. The individual who has lost the ability to think in the way of the child, the person unable to retain what Gary Zukav refers to as the "beginner's mind," will have more trouble comprehending the child than the child will have comprehending the adult. The social coupling between them is asymmetric. The curious thing is that in almost every instance it is the adult who controls communication while the child follows along as a relatively helpless companion. It is doubtful if this adult human predominance would exist in communications with aliens perceived to be intellectually superior to us. It is more likely that the aliens would control when, where, and how we interacted.

Assuredly, there are those who suppose that aliens possess intellects superior to our own. This supposition implies that we would have difficulty understanding them, although the reverse would not be true. Their superiority might also not be readily apparent, or indicated only by a tolerance and openness typically found in children. Within the context of the search for extraterrestrial intelligence this attitude is usually revealed by references to hypothetical "advanced" civilizations, demonstrated by their superior technology and scientific understanding of the universe. It is assumed that we would view accomplishments of such civilizations, eons ahead of us in technology, as sheer magic.

Finally, I have noticed that some parents are so confused by the strange workings of a young mind that they respond to the child as one might to someone who possesses an entirely foreign set of mental traits. In the classic science fiction story *Childhood's End,* Arthur C. Clarke reminds us that parents may be astonished to realize that the child they are shepherding into adulthood is utterly alien to them, sharing none of their personal motivations, desires, and accepted ways for dealing with what seem to be perennial social issues. In exasperation, the parent asks wistfully, "What logic is there in the actions of a child?" The logic, if there is one, seems to include rules totally foreign to those respected by the adult. The parent who relates to the child in this way has no apparent reason to foster contact on any but the simplest level of life's necessities. The adult seems to believe that one should ignore this odd little creature until it matures enough to take its place in society on adult terms. When applied to aliens, such an attitude would have a stifling effect on attempts to communicate, even though it might represent a realistic approach to the situation.

If the human species is ever fortunate enough to join an extraterrestrial communication network, the quality and nature of the messages exchanged will depend on the assumptions each side makes about the other's level and type of thought processes: What kind of alien mind have we run across? Rather than identifying the communication potential of a society by the amount of physical power at its disposal, as does the physicist Kardashev, we might experience greater success by classifying alien civilizations according to the patterns that I have suggested are applicable to parent-child interactions. I want to be careful here to say that I am not passing judgment on the four approaches just discussed. It is informative to consider these attitudes in the context of space research and just see where they lead.

The strategy for contacting alien life depends critically on our assumptions. If we think the alien mentality is comparable to ours, then it makes good sense to use standard techniques to make contact. We are informed by the physicists that the common denominator for the two civilizations will be the language of science, but if we are mentally similar, the aliens should also appreciate human art and sympathize with our political and social problems; that is, if they are intellectual copies of the human species, we will have more in common than physical science. A rich variety of intelligences is found in the human population, but only one type places heavy weight on scientific thinking. This is of course an oversimplification. Some of the foremost scientists and mathematicians hold poetry and art in high esteem. My point is only that the language of science is not outside the psychological constraints that determine all other modes of human expression.

If we assume that the alien mind is humanlike in all essential respects, we can expect to develop communication in the same way one might teach a foreign language. You may speak only Mandarin and I may speak only Swahili, but we both perceive and cope with the external environment in the same manner; we laugh, cry, and exhibit a common range of human emotions. Just as some people see the child as the intellectual equal of the adult, by this approach we see the alien as the intellectual equal of the human. As will become clearer in later chapters, this attitude currently guides the search for extraterrestrial intelligence and is the first to surface when the nonscientist reflects on the problem of seeking contact: "They" will be like us. Their outward appearance may be a little weird, but deep down where it counts their psychological makeup will be indistinguishable from ours.

I think most laypeople expect the first encounter with aliens to be a meeting of like minds. The commercial films about aliens portray them as essentially human; perhaps they have misshapen appendages, are overly hairy, or otherwise look funny, but they still are beings with recognizable physical and psychological features.

Scientists are not immune to this anthropocentric bias. The Pioneer 10 spacecraft, launched in 1972, is the first human artifact to leave the Solar System. It has a 6- by 9-inch aluminum plate attached to the struts of its radio antenna, and on this plate is engraved a message from planet Earth to sentient beings who might intercept the craft at some future date—say, a hundred thousand years from now. The content of the message was decided upon and brought to reality within a period of three weeks by Carl Sagan, Linda Salzman Sagan, and Frank Drake. The National Aeronautics and Space Administration had to be talked into sending any message at all, and consequently, precious little time remained for consultation with other experts, scientists or nonscientists. The intended visual message anticipates the questions that might arise in any social encounter between total strangers. The idea was to have the plaque answer such expected queries as "What's your name? Where are you from? What do you do?"

In response to the first question the species responsible for sending the plaque is depicted by the outline drawing of a naked man and woman. The rather bland frontal view shows the woman with her hands at her side and the man raising his right hand—supposedly in a sign of universal peace. American social conventions still are revealed in these naked portrayals. The man's hairstyle is decidedly Madison Avenue and his face is hairless. So this part of the message is intended to tell who we are—more or less. Behind the couple is a schematic diagram of the Pioneer spacecraft, whose dimensions would be important in assessing the size of the humans and would give some idea of the sorts of things we like to do: for instance, build and launch spacecraft, complete with technical graffiti.

There also are indications on the plaque of our current position in time and space. A series of circles represents the relative size and distance of the Sun and the nine planets. A solid line begins at planet Earth and traces the trajectory of the spacecraft between Jupiter and Saturn and into outer space, where an arrow points to a small outline of the spacecraft. A more cosmic scenario of where and when Pioneer began its journey is shown on another part of the plaque, where the Sun stands at the origin of fifteen radial lines. One of these lines, the longest, is supposed to point to the center of the Galaxy. The other fourteen lines point toward pulsars, objects in the Galaxy that emit periodic bursts of radio energy, whose frequency runs down gradually over the course of millions of years. If an alien civilization were able to decipher the time units, shown in scientific notation on the plaque, they could locate Pioneer's home base within an envelope of about one thousand stars out of the available pool of several billion in the Milky Way, and possibly narrow the epoch of launch to within several centuries.

A more elaborate synopsis of life on Earth has been affixed to the two Voyager spacecraft, launched in 1977 and destined, like the Pioneer vehicles, to leave the Solar System. Attached to each is a sturdy phonograph record, containing 118 photographs of Earth and its people and habits; ninety minutes of music, ranging in style from Beethoven to Louis Armstrong; and brief greetings in fifty-six languages. The photographs, considered as television pictures, were coded as organized collections of sound frequencies before being recorded. An alien must somehow figure this out if the pictures are to be properly reconstructed. Carl Sagan and his coauthors frankly admit that the messages are directed as much toward humans as they are toward potential alien recipients. If beings from a distant civilization resembling ours happens upon the Voyager craft they should be able to figure out how to play the record, since instructions and stylus are included in the package. Deciphering the instructions may tell them more about us than the record itself. Other alien types, markedly different from ourselves, might be mystified by the content of the message but still able to fathom the type of being that sent such a record by careful examination of the spacecraft itself.

On the other hand, if the aliens we meet someday are subsets of ourselves, the first order of business will be to determine their exact characteristics. Are they a subset in the sense of being composed of the same chemical elements—carbon, oxygen, nitrogen, hydrogen, and phosphorous—but perhaps with a different mix of the critical quantities? Are they a biological subset in the sense that the chimpanzee's genetic blueprint overlaps 99 percent with ours? Are we talking about a subset in the sense in which bacteria are like us because the deoxyribonucleic acid (DNA) molecule is the common linchpin for successive reproduction? Or, as some parents view their infants, are extraterrestrials similar in biological structure but simply not blessed with the same level of intellect? However we choose to answer these questions, one thing remains clear: If extraterrestrials are perceived as a subset of humans, we will certainly want to study them on all scientific fronts, and it will be possible to do so because we will arrange the social conditions to satisfy our own schedule. Even if such aliens can communicate with us, they may have nothing of special value to relate; but if all else fails, we can at least look to them as a means to broaden the scope of terrestrial biology and psychology.

Biology and biochemistry are the chief disciplines seeking out organisms on other planets, but to some biologists the most promising clues about alien life of a primitive sort are found right here on Earth. This idea came first from scientists at the turn of the century who speculated about the origins of life. In 1903 the Swedish chemist Svante Arrhenius elaborated upon the views of the English physicist Lord Kelvin, who had proposed that life arrived here as small "germs" transported by a wayward meteorite. Arrhenius argued for the so-called Panspermia (seeds everywhere) theory which stated that "infection" from another celestial body arose by light exerting pressure on small spores, containing living matter, and thus propelling them into the interstellar medium to their eventual resting place on the surfaces of other planets.

This notion was taken seriously and resurrected lately by the biologists Francis Crick and Leslie Orgel. Their version of the story envisages primitive forms of life being deliberately sent here by an advanced society with the desire to sow the seeds of life throughout the cosmos. Assuming that extraterrestrials act as we do, Crick and Orgel remind us that we now can launch squadrons of unmanned spacecraft into outer space. If a colony of microorganisms were purposefully or otherwise carried along as freight, they might someday reach an uninhabited planet and thus begin another upward spiral of life's development. By invoking the notion of psychological symmetry—they are like us—we might assume that an extraterrestrial culture of 4 billion years ago, similar in technological level to ours, might have wanted to "pollute" its stellar neighborhood biologically in order to perpetuate a good thing: life based on the DNA molecule. What better way to combat the possibility of being wiped out by a freak accident than to dispatch hordes of tiny biological messengers to other planets. In this way at least they would have rendered the building blocks of carbon-based life "unkillable."

Francis Crick has listed some plausible reasons for supposing that bacteria or a near relative would be a logical choice for an interplanetary journey of several thousand years. Bacteria are relatively impervious to the rigors of the low temperatures of interstellar space, can live in a frozen state almost indefinitely, and upon "awakening" can survive with little or no oxygen. Hence, if a cargo of bacteria happened to fall into the primal oceans of the Earth—say, 4 billion years ago—the chemical soup would offer them a welcome environment in which to survive and multiply. Subsequent evolution would gradually lead to the variety of animals seen today.

This theory of Directed Panspermia is consistent with the fact that all life's cells possess the identical genetic code (DNA). The same biological message is found uniformly throughout living things: trees, plants, bacteria, cows, people, and swamp grass. As far as we can tell there are no exceptions. This means that we should look very carefully to see if other biological properties could be traced to extraterrestrial sources. For example, the important biochemical element molybdenum is scarce on Earth but might be abundant on some other planet whose parent star contained a more plentiful supply of this chemical. If life started there and not here, the chemical mix comprising our cells would match more faithfully the nature of their distant home than would the particular chemical constituents of the Earth. Several billion years ago the forces of evolution, through natural selection, would have taken over from the early bacterial colonists and gone on to produce life's subsequent diversity. This is not to say that life exists in a hierarchy of levels within which any species can be measured for its value, worth, or progress. Some modern biologists are quite sensitive on this point. They prefer to see life more as a bush than a tree, without implying that one species is in some way above another. On the other hand, there is no denying that some creatures have a wider set of options for action than do others. Given the psychological makeup of humans, we seriously doubt whether any creature resembling a bacteria through and through could have invented the radio telescope.

At least one manifestation of life has achieved the technological expertise and mental outlook to imagine that many eons ago a thinking being like us had the foresight to colonize other planets with primitive life-forms. These primitive biological forms would have evolved into a species quite similar to the one that sent these messengers in the first place. Some scientists have asked whether we are now ready to do the same and deploy life's banner to even farther regions of the universe. In fact, we are indeed close to embarking on this new adventure.

On July 20, 1976, the first Viking lander touched down softly on Mars and began transmitting pictures back to Earth. In the unlikely event that a largish organism happened to be up and about in the late Martian afternoon, the Viking's lens would have registered its presence and given us the first glimpse of life on another planet. This extraordinary event did not transpire. The scene that day was of a rocky orange red landscape, quite barren, totally devoid of visible signs of plants and animals of any kind. If in the near future a mobile organism does catch Viking's eye, its presence will be beamed to Earth, where someone may or may not be around to notice. Until this event occurs there will be no evidence of creatures on Mars resembling us in size and order of complexity, no aliens of any type tromping about the landscape in the vicinity of the stationary lander.

The principle Viking tests for life on Mars, however, were modest in scope. Eight days after touchdown a mechanical arm reached out, scooped up some Martian soil, and let it filter down into compartments where biological experiments automatically tested the hypothesis that primitive forms of life existed under the desertlike conditions. The scientific instruments in the so-called biology package worked fairly smoothly, and data promptly began to accumulate that could have resolved one of humanity's long-standing questions: "Is there life on Mars?" After a period of initial uncertainty, it became clear that just about all the incoming results could be due to chemical reactions which in some instances mimicked biological processes remarkably well. Very little ambiguity remains today. Laboratory simulations done on Earth since 1976 have led biologists to conclude that no positive indications of life on Mars have been obtained. Not that such indications might not be forthcoming in the future—this must remain an open question—but we have no basis at the moment to assume the existence of life-forms in the location where we were most hopeful of finding them.

The search for life on Mars was primarily directed by biologists and geologists who expected to find organisms of a lower order—lower in the behavioral sense just noted. After all, this is the form of life they are trained to discover and study. Their deep-seated assumptions about the nature of alien life determined and limited the types of experiments considered worth doing. According to the account of Henry Cooper, Jr., the expedition planners devoted much less effort to the analysis of pictures that might have offered further clues to the existence of more active life-forms. Future landings and searches controlled by scientists of similar persuasion can be expected to reflect a low commitment to the search for life-forms that we might on psychological grounds assign to "higher" categories of complexity and intellectual competence. One low-cost experiment to reverse this trend would be to have the lander attract attention to itself by broadcasting a variety of powerful radio, light, and audio beacons. A roving alien might be curious about the source of the clamor, approach the lander, and thereby be noted by on-board cameras and tape recorders.

Humans are in the habit of making evaluative judgments on just about any conceivable topic. Intelligence level is no exception. Despite the biologist's view that all life-forms should be valued equally, if the extraterrestrials we meet someday are perceived by us to occupy a superior rung on the ladder of life, then we will be the eager student, never the patronizing teacher, and perhaps there is much to be gained from willfully initiating contact under these circumstances. The assumption that "advanced" aliens represent our best bet for contact is most evident in the efforts of scientists attempting to find patterns in radio waves emanating from outer space. Curiously enough, many nonscientists believe that humans with the power of extrasensory perception also represent a superior species. Civilizations capable of sending messages to us will be judged by this group to be our intellectual superiors, just as individuals capable of perceiving events by means outside the recognized sensory channels are considered super-people. In both instances the rest of the world's population can expect to be learning and listening for a long time before expressing any personal philosophy or gaining entry to more esoteric realms of knowledge.

If advanced civilizations exist, but in a wildly alien form, located in effect along very different physical, biological, and psychological dimensions, then all the observation time spent at the most sophisticated telescopes will be for naught. The aliens we seek will be going about their business in an alternate universe we are forever prohibited from learning anything about. Once this truth is realized, there will remain little point in continuing the search, since the target civilization will forever lie outside the scope of human comprehension. If we are children about to cross the threshold of the galactic clubhouse, we will just have to be patient and wait a little longer before joining in on the fun. In our present condition of relative ignorance, we will have to be content with the joys of parallel play with a species whose presence may never be revealed to us.

This level of civilization is, in fact, very likely, according to John A. Ball, who suggests that civilizations millions of years our senior may even now be amusing themselves by watching us grope toward an understanding of the physical universe. He proposes the unorthodox theory that this civilization may wish to remain the anonymous keeper of a natural zoo inhabited by all Earth's flora and fauna—including humans. Of course, if these super-beings are successful at concealing their presence, we will never know whether Ball's theory is correct or not, a result which turns the whole notion into an untestable speculation.

In summary, human assumptions about the alien mind parallel adult assumptions about the child's mind. One type of adult interacts with children differently at different stages of psychological and biological development, while other types do not. A subset of scientists and non-scientists alike makes similar assumptions when considering the possibility of extraterrestrial intelligence. The importance of this observation is that holding firm to one assumption about aliens may reduce the chances of finding aliens who do not fit the expected mold. Exobiologists interested in discovering rudimentary forms of life may completely overlook complex forms that are right under their noses, and physicists concentrating on the detection of advanced civilizations may miss opportunities to find species of a simpler order.

In general, the degree to which humans are willing to entertain alternative premises about the alien mind seems to be linked to how easily the premises can be acted upon. If all civilizations oriented to outer space happen to be radically different from us, then we are flat out of luck and have nothing more to do. Nonetheless, it still might prove cathartic for humans to continue the search for beings of a type radically different from themselves.

The most favorable outcome of a search might be the discovery of aliens who are our psychological equals, comparable in intellectual power and technical competence. This seems to be the expectation of the average person, and if it is accurate, it may prove to be the most productive possibility. Failing this outcome, it probably would be easiest to interact with an organism which was a subset of us (less able technically), although this interchange might not be especially illuminating. The exobiologists' search for life on other planets in the Solar System appears guided by this assumption. Another situation, more perplexing but far more interesting in its probable payoff for the human species, is that our particular forms of intelligence may turn out to be a subset of those found in the civilizations we are trying to contact. The search strategy in this case is passive, in that we should prepare to receive signals rather than send them. We should still encourage direct methods of contact—for example, space satellites and colonies—while keeping open the possibility that we will be contacted first by a technically superior species. This brings us back to what many feel is the most promising way to engage extraterrestrials: seek meaningful patterns in radio waves arriving from outer space and attribute the origin of these patterns to aliens.

But how intelligent must these aliens be in order for us to understand each other? The ensuing chapter frames this issue by noting the chief social values that motivate a special interest, professional or amateur, in outer space. It also establishes a social science platform from which to address the entire question of extraterrestrial intelligence. We must now inquire into the nature of terrestrial intelligence and ask whether it can incorporate alien cases within its definition. Once having laid this groundwork, we will be ready to tackle the more substantive themes concerning the human limits inherent in any effort to communicate with extraterrestrials.

REFERENCES AND FURTHER READINGS

Arrhenius, S. The Propagation of Life in Space. *Die Umschau,* 1903, *7,* 481–482.

Ball, J. A. The Zoo Hypothesis. *Icarus,* 1973, *19,* 347–349.

Billingham, J. (Ed.) *Life in the Universe.* Cambridge, Mass.: MIT Press, 1981.

Clarke, A. C. *Childhood's End.* New York: Ballantine, 1953.

Cooper, H. S. F., Jr. *The Search for Life on Mars: Evolution of an Idea.* New York: Holt, Rinehart & Winston, 1980.

Crick, F. *Life Itself: Its Origin and Nature.* New York: Simon & Schuster, 1981.

Crick, F. H. C., & Orgel, L. E. Directed Panspermia. *Icarus,* 1973, *91,* 341–346.

Goldsmith, D. (Ed.) *The Quest for Extraterrestrial Life: A Book of Readings.* Mill Valley, Calif.: University Science Books, 1980.

Goldsmith, D., & Owen, T. *The Search for Life in the Universe.* Menlo Park, Calif.: Benjamin/Cummings, 1980.

Holmes, D. L., & Morrison, F. J. *The Child: An Introduction to Developmental Psychology.* Monterey, Calif.: Brooks/Cole, 1979.

Kippenhahn, R. *100 Billion Suns: The Birth, Life, and Death of the Stars.* Translated from the German by Jean Steinberg. New York: Basic, 1983.

Mann, A. P. C., & Williams, D. A. A List of Interstellar Molecules. *Nature,* 1980, *283,* 721–725.

Margulis, L., & Sagan, D. *Micro-Cosmos: Four Billion Years of Evolution from our Microbial Ancestors.* New York: Summit, 1986.

Montague, A. *Growing Young.* New York: McGraw-Hill, 1981.

Nikolaev, L. *Space Chemistry.* Translated from the Russian by Y. Nadler. Moscow: Mir, 1976.

Piaget, J. *The Origins of Intelligence in Children.* New York: International Universities Press, 1952.

Piaget, J. *The Construction of Reality in the Child.* New York: Basic, 1954.

Sagan, C.; Drake, F. D.; Druyan, A.; Ferris, T.; Lomberg, J.; & Sagan, L. S. *Murmurs of Earth: The Voyager Interstellar Record.* New York: Ballantine, 1978.

Sagan, C.; Sagan, L. S.; & Drake, F. A Message from Earth. *Science,* 1972, *175,* 881–884.

Watson, J. B. *Behaviorism.* New York: Norton, 1924.

Zukav, G. *The Dancing Wu Li Masters: An Overview of the New Physics.* New York: Morrow, 1979.

CHAPTER 7

INTELLIGENCE
AND VALUE ORIENTATION

People have strong intuitions about the relative intelligence of familiar animals. A bird is seen as smarter than a worm, a dog as smarter than a bird, a chimpanzee as smarter than a dog; and most humans are granted loftier rungs along a ladder of animal intelligence than are the chimpanzees. When we consider intelligence along these lines, we seem to have in mind the rank ordering of an innate, biological capacity for solving problems. Those creatures able to complete difficult tasks in efficient and adaptive ways are seen as more intelligent than those having at their disposal a smaller pool of effective, goal-directed behaviors. The deterministic character of intelligence implies that it is an inherited potential of the brain: The better the brain, the higher the intelligence.

Despite the intuitive appeal of this popular belief, there are good reasons to question its validity. Two matters are especially troublesome: how to measure brain capacity apart from noting an animal's behavior, and how to arrive at a single number to represent the general intelligence in a species. Neither of these questions has received satisfactory answers. An animal's observed behavior is one step removed from the inborn, unseen capacity supposedly directing such behavior; native intelligence in this sense can only be inferred, never directly observed. The second matter pertains to the view of intelligence as a unitary trait. Although many psychologists in the field of mental testing—those who administer IQ tests in schools—feel that intelligence is a single measurable entity, the mood among practitioners is gradually shifting to allow for a more expansive definition. A growing number of experts now claim that intelligence denotes, or can be inferred from, a wide assortment of adaptive or learned behaviors.

There probably isn't a sole overriding intelligence. Rather, a host of independent biological and psychological factors work in concert to produce a constellation of behaviors that are deemed intelligent, and of course, there can be marked differences of opinion about the distinction between intelligent and nonintelligent behavior. Sparkling brilliance apparent to one person may be sheer madness to another. The upshot of all this is that multiple intelligences characterize the social and biological makeup of all species. In the broadest terms, however, these intelligences are manifested as conscious adaptations to the environment.

In the absence of additional facts we must assume that this definition holds as well for aliens, if anything more is to be said. Similarly, I assume that alien motivations regarding contact with other forms of intelligence bear a likeness to our own. So I am squarely taking the stand that "they are like us," but only so far as saying that there is great variety within both human and alien populations. Both assumptions are almost certainly wrong at some level, but they are absolutely necessary in order to say anything specific about what it might be like to communicate with extraterrestrial intelligence. An important task then becomes the description of what is meant by human intelligence and motivation as they relate to the search enterprise.

The idea that intelligence is composed of a number of separate faculties has been a persistent theme in the history of mental testing (see the recent reviews by Robert J. Sternberg). As far back as 1946 one of the discipline's brilliant innovators, Leon Louis Thurstone, clearly stated that intelligence is a multifaceted concept: "Instead of attempting to describe each individual's mental endowment by a single index such as a mental age or an intelligence quotient, it is preferable to describe him in terms of a profile of all the primary factors which are known to be significant" ("Theories of intelligence," p. 110).

Thurstone's perspective has been updated and revitalized by the biologist-paleontologist Stephen Jay Gould and more recently by the psychologist Howard Gardner. Gould takes a hard line against the negative political and educational effects traceable to America's reliance on IQ tests in delineating the opportunities available to its citizens, especially children. He says that the questions in these tests are often biased against the culturally and economically disadvantaged. In particular, Gould challenges the familiar practice of securing an average test score to denote the intellectual level of a child who by common-sense standards would be judged as good at some tasks and poor at others. Taking the average score from a battery of tests as an indication of raw intellectual power fails to capture the spectrum of competences, some high, others low, so visible in the daily activities of children and adults.

Howard Gardner expresses his own indignation about the mistakes of mental testers and then goes on to offer an alternative view of intelligence defined as a set of independent "modular" abilities that can be inferred from biological and behavioral "signs" or "criteria." Evidence for the existence of independent abilities is provided by the documented accomplishments of "idiot savants" and "child prodigies" who show exceptional talent in one realm of the arts or sciences but not in others—musical geniuses, mathematical whizzes, and the like. A unique mental ability is also implicated when brain damage produces a loss of function in one aspect of a person's life but not in others. For example, the ability to speak can be lost while the knack for solving problems is not. Other evidence that reveals the presence of a unique ability is the distinct development of a child's competences through well-ordered stages along the path to maturity. A good example is the unfolding of the child's comprehension and use of language over the period from birth to around the time of puberty. Children in all cultures begin to babble shortly after birth, handle two-word phrases after a year, and speak fluently by age four.

After appraising the evidence for modular abilities, Gardner weaves a convincing case for three overarching classes of intelligence: "object-related," "object-free," and "personal." The object-related forms are reflected in the ability to manipulate objects in the environment, recognize and imagine spatial relations among objects, and reason logically about things and their interrelations. These three intelligences are fittingly labeled "bodily-kinesthetic," "spatial," and "logical-mathematical."

The object-free types mirror competence in the spheres of language and music. The implied free form reminds us that linguistic and musical symbols vary greatly across cultures and need not designate aspects of the physical environment at all. For instance, a piece of electronic music might not conjure up for the listener any concrete referents in the physical world, not even the thought of someone playing a musical instrument, but might just be accepted by that listener as a composition whose purpose is to stimulate interest in the range and complexity of sound that humans can appreciate. Similarly, the poet's art can be enjoyed on the basis of the quality of the rhyme (or rhythm or sound), quite apart from the meaning of the words. Language and music elicit purely aesthetic pleasures in addition to their commonplace roles as media for the transmission of knowledge.

Gardner divides "personal" intelligence into two categories: intrapersonal and interpersonal. Those who are unusually gifted in the intrapersonal domain accurately "read" their emotional states and understand their intellectual strengths and weaknesses, a process which helps them develop and sustain a realistic picture of the inner "self." The interpersonal form implies an ability to use these same skills in social situations—an indication of what is often called human sensitivity or social awareness. The chief difference between the two personal intelligences turns on whether the focus of attention is directed inward to assess private cognitions and feelings or outward to monitor and reflect upon the cognitive and emotional expressions of others.

I doubt if Gardner would delimit these intelligences with sharp borders or even vigorously defend the seven types he discusses. As I see it, whether there are five, seven, or fifty-three different varieties is not the crucial point. What is important is the notion that intelligence should not be evaluated solely from the answers to questions designed to tap one style of problem solving, which in Western cultures means those types relying on language and mathematics. Once the concept of multiple intelligences is accepted, individuals can be more accurately described by noting the relative strengths of their abilities across a range of intelligences.

When we consider the intellectual potential of humans in the context of the search for extraterrestrial intelligence, two general types emerge: those people with an interest in science and those without. I would say the abilities associated with science are slanted toward the object-related areas of mathematical-logical reasoning, apprehension of spatial relations, and bodily-kinesthetic skills. Within physical science a distinction also might be drawn between theoreticians and experimentalists. The theoretical physicist must certainly be adept at mathematics and logic, since they are fundamental to an understanding of modern science, whereas the experimentalist also requires some degree of motor coordination in order to arrange conditions in the laboratory to test theories: Considerable dexterity is often called upon in building apparatus and in applying the rules of electronics and engineering. Both theorists and experimentalists must be proficient pattern recognizers and must have the ability to create and imagine meaningful relations among real and hypothetical objects. The object-free intelligences of language and music are needed less in science, except for translating ideas into a format that is comprehensible to others.

This is the situation, as I see it, in the physical sciences. In some branches of social science—say, anthropology or political science—linguistic facility is more essential than an aptitude for mathematics. It also is generally true that the personal intelligences are more pivotal in social science than in physical science, where their function is usually secondary. Of course, some physical scientists demonstrate a high aptitude for handling social problems outside the area of their professional duties. I presume only that personal intelligences are not an integral part of the abilities these people rely upon to solve scientific problems.

The personal intelligences can unfold quite independently of the object-related forms. How else can we explain the discrepancy between the quality of some scientists' work and their lack of awareness regarding current events of great social import? A scientist might be skillful at devising weapons of military destruction while simultaneously revealing major ignorance about the impact of such work on the long-term survival of the human race. In short, daily experience makes it apparent that a person can be outstanding in one facet of intelligence and underdeveloped in another.

If scientific methods are used in the search for extraterrestrial intelligence, in the construction of space satellites, colonies, or radio telescopes, it is natural to expect that scientific skills will characterize individuals engaged in the development of such techniques. It is also true that these individuals will be less intrigued by the popular topics associated with outer space, typified by an interest in unidentified flying objects, extrasensory perception, and ancient astronauts.

On the other hand, these popular topics will be highly regarded by many whose intellectual strengths show little or no overlap with that of scientists. It would be foolhardy to attempt a sweeping definition of the nonscientist, but some main features might at least be roughly sketched. In the nonscience case the object-related intelligences seem subordinate to the objectless forms of language and music, or else the personal intelligences dominate and shape opinions about space projects and the search for extraterrestrial intelligence. A nonscientific approach is apparent whenever science and mathematics are of lower priority than other modular abilities. The number of possible nonscience types is very large; it would serve no purpose to spell out the details of one subtype. This group as a whole is not likely to engage in the scientific search for extraterrestrial intelligence, but certainly it might be keenly interested in any messages resulting from that search.

The presence of a scientific bias, however, does not guarantee an abiding interest in outer space, and a nonscientist may still be curious about the prospect of communicating with alien life. None of Gardner's classes of intelligence say anything at all about a person's motives for choosing an occupation or avocation; no particular line of work or weekend hobby is linked to a constellation of abilities. Depending on the way a person was raised and educated, an innate predisposition for a career in science may be pushed aside by social goals that take precedence. A person predisposed to think scientifically may in fact end up in the business world, in a health profession, or in one of the trades, perhaps plumbing or carpentry. The same can be said for the nonscientist. An individual's predispositions are one thing, but whether these tendencies are ever translated into behavior is quite another. So in addition to knowing something about intelligences, we must also know something about human motivation and value systems, if we are to assess with any confidence the attitudes held by different people about the costs and benefits of space research and about the strategies under consideration to contact alien intelligence.

A particular sort of intelligence is revealed through the expression of behaviors and attitudes that may or may not be valued by the culture in which they occur. The distinctive traits of the scientist may be highly esteemed in some quarters of society and roundly criticized in another. Similarly, a community's lack of attention to matters scientific may be seen either as a praiseworthy quality or as a lamentable short-coming, depending on the social group passing judgment. According to the anthropologist Florence Kluckhohn, such variation in value orientations is as definite and important as well-known variations in physical and biological phenomena. Although cultures differ in the emphasis placed on different value orientations, the full scope of opinion about the key philosophical problems facing every society is found in each of them.

If motivation is independent of intelligence, a personal commitment to the search for extraterrestrial intelligence is not determined by whether one's outlook on the world is consistent with scientific thought. Both scientific and nonscientific minds may be inquisitive about the details of this unique search enterprise, if their private value orientations guide them along that path. It is just that their methods of search will be different. In this sense, the NASA engineer who sends electronic probes to Mars is a psychological comrade of the plumber who is looking for flying saucers in the skies above the California freeway.

The anthropological field studies of Kluckhohn and her colleagues offer strong support for this contention. She concluded that all peoples at all times must cope with the same limited number of human problems, perhaps only a handful of which are of perennial relevance. The unwritten assumptions about human personality and culture that underlie solutions to these problems define a value profile that is evident in the beliefs and attitudes of most members of the community. These shared problems and the particular solutions arrived at by different cultures also provide a stage from which to address the multiple opinions held about the search for extraterrestrial intelligence, and hence I want to review briefly the key points of Kluckhohn's theory and some of its empirical underpinnings.

The most pertinent study, reported by Kluckhohn and F. L. Strodtbeck, was carried out in the American Southwest some twenty-five years ago and dealt with the value orientations of five small communities, each with a distinct cultural background. Two of the communities were Native American: the pueblo Zuñis who lived on a reservation and an off-reservation community of Navahos. The three other groups were Spanish-Americans, Mormons, and a community founded originally by migrant Texans and Oklahomans. The Kluck-hohn team determined prominent value orientations by asking questions and extracting recurring themes from the answers obtained from members of each community. The questions were formulated to reveal preferences for hypothetical life-styles.

For example, attitudes toward the concept of "time" were determined by relating the following vignette and then asking people to choose the answer that was closest to their opinion or to that of their community. The time orientations given here in parentheses were not shown to the respondents.

Some people were talking about the way children should be brought up. Here are three different ideas.

A (Past) Some people say that children should always be taught well the traditions of the past . . .

B (Present) Some people say that children should be taught some of the old traditions . . . , but it is wrong to insist that they stick to these ways. These people believe that it is necessary for children always to learn about and take on whatever of the new ways will best help them get along in the world of today.

C (Future) Some people do not believe children should be taught much about past traditions . . . at all except as an interesting story of what has gone before. These people believe that the world goes along best when children are taught the things that will make them want to find out for themselves new ways of doing things to replace the old. [*Variations in Value Orientations,* p. 81]

In deciding among the options presented, the respondent stated a preferred orientation for the past, the present, or the future. By posing and noting the answers to many such queries about a variety of personal and societal issues, the researchers were able to draw up a profile of the value orientations that typified the community. The issues being explored had more of a philosophical than a practical twist, but the questions were phrased within the context of a realistic situation that might be met by someone in the course of everyday life. As such, the Kluckhohn results are valuable in shaping our opinions about the sorts of people who are likely to look favorably on efforts to explore outer space and keep open the possibility of contacting extraterrestrial intelligence. People with such attitudes probably hold special values, even though at present we are not really able to know what they are.

The Kluckhohn study assessed attitudes toward five human problems: (1) the relative good and evil inherent in human nature, (2) the relationship between humans and the material world, (3) the concept of "time," (4) the intrinsic value afforded an "activity" dimension, and (5) the social affinity between a people and their neighbors and kin. Each of these problems was framed as a question to which the investigators expected different answers from individuals with different value orientations.

The five Southwest communities each had a dominant set of value orientations, and all were different. For example, the attitude of the Texas-Oklahoma community was stereotypical American, with emphasis placed on individualism, future time, mastery over nature, doing, and the view that human nature is evil but perfectable through hard work. On the other hand, the Spanish-American community placed a premium on the values and ideas that had been handed down from previous generations, stressed the present, felt that people were subjugated to nature, and preferred the being form of activity.

Although a single constellation of values prevailed in a community, all members did not exhibit the same one; in fact, all the various viewpoints found across communities could be identified in some individuals within each. Not even the most insulated community is comprised of a cast of think-alikes! For instance, a typical Spanish-American might be a contented member of the Texas-Oklahoma community, in spite of value orientation; a typical Navaho orientation might still find a niche in the Mormon community; and so on.

If we can extend the Kluckhohn analysis to communities of any size, it means that a complex pattern of value orientations exists within all the various compartments of society. Two major types of value orientation seem especially pertinent to space research and to the search for extraterrestrial intelligence. Put simply, the two types represent those whose values lead them to applaud these ventures and those whose values lead elsewhere.

In the absence of direct study it is impossible to know exactly what a value orientation toward an interest in outer space might look like, but I am willing to propose some candidates derived from Kluckhohn's theory. Such a characterization would probably match the dominant

American view on basic philosophical issues. People who are attracted by the prospects of life in outer space will believe that human nature is innately good, and therefore worth preserving, that humans have a right to exert control over the physical universe, that the human perspective on life should include the future, that one must be willing to act with positive resolve to achieve goals, and that strength of character is a prerequisite for the accomplishment of anything worthwhile. It would be interesting to see whether this list compares favorably with the views expressed by astronauts and cosmonauts who are currently active in the world's space programs.

There are of course innumerable nonspace types of value orientation. My guess is that an extreme nonspace orientation would presume that the human state is innately evil (or some mix of good and evil) and that it is subjugated to nature; people with this orientation remain tightly coupled to the past and are frequently devoted to the cause of maintaining smooth social relations. I don't mean to suggest that a crisp boundary should be drawn between the space and nonspace value orientations, but despite some areas of overlap, major differences seem to remain between them. Empirical studies along the lines followed by Kluckhohn would be needed to pin down any true differences, but for purposes of our argument, I will proceed as if we already know them.

Uncertainty colors any attempt to define a precise intelligence or value type for either an indvidual or a culture, but perhaps we can concur on the broad outline of the cases that matter here. There are two classes: science and nonscience intelligences, space and nonspace value orientations. Assuming that a particular style of intelligence is not always joined to the same value orientation, it follows that there are four possible combinations: (1) nonspace/nonscience, (2) nonspace/science, (3) space/nonscience, and (4) space/science. I refer to these select combinations in a shorthand way as "intellivalues" to highlight the interplay between prevailing intelligences and value orientations found within the same person. An individual's distinguishing intellivalue depends both upon inborn capacities and upon the ongoing influence of life experiences—more specifically, parental upbringing, schooling, and the impact of social and physical variables.

My guess is that the most common intellivalue in the world characterizes someone who approaches problems from a nonscientific standpoint and who shows little or no regard for issues related to outer space. The diversity within this category is enormous, since it would include a whole gamut of occupations, avocations, beliefs, and attitudes. Although I have no hard facts to rely on, my suspicion is that this segment is only marginally aware of the tangible and potential rewards traceable to past or projected ventures into outer space. Most humans on this planet probably have only dim awareness of the fact that a spacecraft has been catapulted beyond the boundaries of the Solar System, that men have walked the face of the Moon and returned with souvenir rocks, or that astronauts have spent months living in the weightless environment of outer space. Alternatively, they may be aware of such claims and not believe a word of them! I might wager further that most of these people have barely heard of flying saucers or space colonies, and certainly nothing at all about radio telescopes. These themes are not counted among their vital concerns. Individuals distinguished by a nonspace/nonscience intellivalue are not the sort who would report a flying saucer or lend moral and financial aid to a nation's scientific excursions into outer space.

Another large and vocal group about which I say very little in this book is represented by the intellivalue of nonspace/science. Those scientists and engineers, of either the professional or the garden variety, who admit to having no interest in the enigmas, scientific or otherwise, of outer space, are worthy members of society for other reasons, but their skills and motives do not stimulate interest in space exploration and the search for extraterrestrial intelligence. Hence, an analysis of this group and the important scientific viewpoint it propounds is not the object of our psychological probes into the dominion of natural science.

This leaves space/nonscience and space/science types as the principal focuses. The person of nonscience intelligence, but with a strong interest in outer space, may be fascinated by the hypothesis of unidentified flying objects and ancient astronauts, and quite taken by the prospect of personally visiting alien communities existing on different planets within and outside the Solar System. In addition, a person of this disposition will surely express curiosity about the technological exploits of the scientific community, insofar as they pertain to outer space. One doesn't have to be a scientist, or think like one, in order to appreciate the goals and accomplishments of scientific programs, and of course not every nonscientist believes in flying saucers.

A scientific interest in outer space is prevalent among the scientists and engineers at the forefront of research in astronomy and space engineering, though it is found only rarely within society as a whole. A still smaller group is also sympathetic to work in some of the outlying precincts of science: the search for extraterrestrial intelligence by means of the radio telescope, electronic monitoring of other stars by space probes, and biological experiments that delve into the possibility of life on other planets. It is this particular intersection of space values and scientific intelligence that motivates those whose work will be examined in upcoming chapters. I won't offer much in the way of a personality analysis of these people—I could not go much further down this road anyway—but rather will concentrate on what they are actually doing, their observed behavior. The discussion centers on the potential difficulties that might result from using the radio telescope to open a window of communication to extraterrestrial civilizations.

A fruitful conversation with alien civilizations probably can't occur unless the intelligence and values of aliens are similar to ours. Since contact with aliens will involve the entire human species, the match will be greater with some people than with others. It is probable, but by no means certain, that initial contact will involve individuals already looking to outer space for answers, because these are the people actively trying to establish communication. For reasons of expediency, from now on I will speak as though this were indeed the case. What about the alien side? Can we speculate at all about the aliens we are likely to encounter? To consider this matter it is helpful to differentiate between extraterrestrial life and extraterrestrial intelligence. The probability of life in outer space may be judged as more common than the existence of intelligent life, and the presence of intelligent life with a desire to communicate with the likes of us may embrace a smaller fraction yet of the available life-forms in the universe.

There is no rational procedure for computing the size of this fraction in the absence of facts. If we are optimistic about the intentions of aliens, however, we can assume that an alien curious about humans would share some of our intellectual abilities and value orientations about a common physical and social environment. This shared context could be the basis for an exchange of information.

We can therefore characterize aliens by the four intellivalues already discussed: nonspace/nonscience, nonspace/science, space/nonscience, and space/science. The relative frequency of each type in the alien population may set upper bounds on the degree of success we can ever hope to achieve through conscious search, however diligently the enterprise is pursued. On the other hand, the view of the majority may be unimportant so long as an active minority is interested in contacting alien civilizations.

An alien society with no desire to send messages to other civilizations in the Galaxy would not be planning to receive helpful signs from the stars. It also would not possess the technical means either to send or to receive messages on a galactic scale. Outsiders' attempts to fraternize with such a society would simply fail. This society might have a healthy and happy citizenry of talented poets, musicians, and philosophers, but on the whole it would have evolved a view of the universe that would be hard to reconcile with human trust in the laws of natural science.

If creatures like these are left alone, we will never hear from them, and if we ever do reach out and make contact, it is doubtful if much progress can be made toward reciprocal understanding. As the initiator of an interaction we would be handicapped by the technical procedures developed on Earth to foster interaction among humans with comparable attitudes toward science and outer space—for example, through the use of mathematical equations and chemical formulas. Obviously, these modes of expression might be hopelessly inadequate when confronting "beings" who have markedly different ideas about their personal goals and destiny, whether these beings are humanlike or alien in their mental outlook. That is, we shouldn't lose sight of the fact that most humans falling into the nonspace/nonscience category are prevented from engaging in any deep conversation about science because they do not understand its technical language. The communication barrier can be expected to be more formidable in the case of aliens.

We also cannot expect to hear from a society dominated by creatures interested in outer space but scientifically illiterate. They would not command the physical resources to journey far from home. Nor would they have the technical expertise required to make contact less intrusively—for example, by means of light or radio signals. Their interest in places beyond the confines of their home star or planet implies that they would be receptive to an outsider's attempts to establish communication, but for us to assume the facilitator role with them would require that we pay an on-site visit.

If this ever did happen, the human spacecraft of the future might come to typify an alien society's idea of an unidentified flying object. If the aliens had not the slightest inkling of scientific principles, however, they might consider human guests as some sort of gods or mythical beings, whose true reasons for coming would always be a mystery. We could imagine such a reaction to space visitors among human communities of today, and in ages past any visitors of this sort would have surely befuddled any and all they met.

We also cannot anticipate hosting visitors or receiving messages from alien cultures who are scientifically inclined but pay no attention to outer space, or who don't believe life is widespread throughout the universe. In this case, too, it would be necessary for us to take the initial steps toward communication, but having done so, we could expect to swap information based on the shared tenets of natural science. The major obstacle in approaching such a culture is that we would first have to arouse its attention. A civilization that doesn't look skyward for scientific facts may prove a poor partner in a conversation, short of our making direct contact through firsthand visits.

The chief targets of any search for extraterrestrial intelligence, therefore, are those alien communities interested in the scientific study of outer space. Whatever their level of development in intelligence and values, these aliens would be intrigued by the prospect of life in other regions of the Galaxy and would be prepared to seek contact through the use of science and technology—just as we are. When contemplating this sort of life-form, the only question is which side will be the first to succeed in contacting the other. Even thinking about such civilizations lifts the spirits of those on Earth with similar desires and aspirations. The thought of a large number of civilizations within the

Galaxy seeking high-level dialogue with other forms of life gives a tremendous impetus to the search efforts conducted on Earth.

While granting that the most promising candidates for contact have a stake in outer space, we can still speculate about the absolute level of intelligence and commitment to space demonstrated by these aliens. They might be perceived as smarter than us, about the same, or stupider. They might be deeply committed to space research, moderately interested, or only mildly engaged. The specific combination of scientific skill and value orientation will ultimately determine who contacts whom. A civilization with superior science and technological skills and a strong commitment to space research is likely to find us before we find it. Contrariwise, a less mature civilization with the same value orientation may be incapable of deploying spacecraft and operating telescopes and might not have a firm commitment to space research of any kind. It is likely we would contact it before it contacted us. Such a civilization might resemble Earth's scientific community of say the year 1600—a short time ago when pictured along a cosmic scale of millions and billions of years.

We should not, however, be too surprised if aliens are nothing like humans, either in the nature of their intelligence or in the social values held most dear. Unfortunately for our search efforts, this possibility is not remote. The potential variety of life-forms, even within the Galaxy, makes it doubtful that many aliens we encounter will be anything at all like us. Communication problems arising because of this mismatch cannot be planned for in advance. We will just have to wait and see.

Having surveyed the multifaceted nature of intelligences and value orientations, we are in a better position to appreciate the deepest problem that plagues attempts to communicate with extraterrestrials. The opportunities for meaningful contact depend mightily on whether the alien civilization is reasonably similar to what I have discussed under the heading of space/science. The aliens in this category that we might meet in the forseeable future are likely to be at least as advanced as us and might be the side that makes the first overtures toward getting together on some plane of discourse. It will be a very long time before humans launch spacecraft on expeditions to significant numbers of neighboring star systems. Once there, we may discover creatures of great diversity, sufficiently deviant in appearance and thought so as to render hopeless any good-faith efforts to establish communication along shared dimensions of experience. Judging from the nature of human experience so far, it seems clear that we will never resolve these issues without trying.

REFERENCES AND FURTHER READINGS

Baird, J. C. Linear Man. *Fields within Fields*, 1974, No. 12, 36–45.

Gardner, H. *Frames of Mind: The Theory of Multiple Intelligences.* New York: Basic, 1983.

Gould, S. J. *The Mismeasure of Man.* New York: Norton, 1981.

Hebb, D. O. *Organization of Behavior.* New York: Wiley, 1949.

Kamin, L. J. *The Science and Politics of I.Q.* Potomac, Md.: Erlbaum, 1974.

Kluckhohn, F. R. Dominant and Variant Value Orientations. In C. Kluckhohn & H. A. Murray (Eds.), *Personality in Nature, Society, and Culture,* pp. 342–357. 2nd ed. New York: Knopf, 1953.

Kluckhohn, F. R., & Strodtbeck, F. L. *Variations in Value Orientations.* Evanston, Ill.: Row, Peterson, 1961.

Sternberg, R. J. Human Intelligence: The Model is the Message. *Science,* 1985, *230,* 1111–1118.

Sternberg, R. J. (Ed.) *Handbook of Human Intelligence.* Cambridge: Cambridge University Press, 1982.

Tang, T. B. Fermi Paradox and C.E.T.I. *Journal of the British Interplanetary Society,* 1982, *35,* 236–240.

Thurstone, L. L. Theories of Intelligence. *Scientific Monthly,* February 1946, 101–112.

Vernon, P. E. *Intelligence: Heredity and Environment.* San Francisco: Freeman, 1979.

CHAPTER 8

ATTRIBUTION: HERE AND ALOFT

The Dominican monk Giordano Bruno was burned at the stake in 1600 for preaching the Copernican view of the Solar System and for proclaiming the existence of innumerable alien worlds that obeyed universal physical laws and were inhabited by beings at least as intelligent and noble as those on Earth. Although Bruno's prosecutors could have presumed that these worlds were governed by the omnipotent God who oversaw activities on Earth, they chose instead to retain the belief in a special relationship between God and humanity, an association leaving no room for competitors, regardless of their level of intelligence or good intentions.

Four hundred years later the major religions extend God's arm to encompass a grander scale, while accepting the legitimate right of science to theorize about the forces of nature initially set in motion by his command. The causes of physical and human affairs now take on a dual flavor; we speculate either about the influence of visible, extrinsic factors or about the invisible, intrinsic control exerted by a higher force. Personal faith dictates the relative weight placed on extrinsic and intrinsic factors in theories about causes of human behavior in both the personal and the political realm.

Although God is seldom mentioned, this duality of attribution is obvious as well when we consider the causes of events pertaining to outer space: satellite probes, unidentified flying objects, ancient astronauts, space colonies, and the search for radio messages. Those pursuing these topics bring to bear a complex mix of ideas and social backgrounds, representing the views of professional scientists and engineers, science fiction writers, and ordinary laypersons. But each person considers both internal and external causes when attempting to explain the phenomena that arise in the course of satisfying natural curiosity about outer space. The particular blend of the two sources depends on the issue and the person. The difference from Bruno's time, aside from the severity with which religions punish deviants, is that we now look to the inner disposition of humans as a causative agent to complement the role of external, physical circumstances. In effect, the psychology of the individual has been substituted for the hypothetical will of God.

When considering the personal motivation of aliens it is altogether natural that the same power of psychological attribution should hold sway. It is tacitly assumed that aliens act in response to internal and external circumstances like those that motivate us. Therefore, even if aliens are thought to exist on a purely hypothetical plane, they are assigned motivational states which presumably could be traced to the external conditions surrounding them or to the internal conditions within them that accompany their particular way of "thinking" about topics of outer space, technology, other beings, and so forth.

In recent years psychologists have learned a good deal about the factors determining the attribution of motives to others. The social psychologist Fritz Heider was among the first to investigate the ways in which people assign causation to explain their own behavior and that of others. He proposed that people assess both the physical environment and personality traits in trying to sort out the reasons for an individual's behavior in any situation. The two kinds of influence are not identical. To appreciate the difference, consider this example: Suppose I notice that a friend has recently broken a lifelong habit of smoking cigarettes. In reflecting on the possible causes for this change in behavior I may focus on the external environment: "She was pressured into quitting by the constant badgering of her family and friends." Alternatively, I may place more emphasis on personal factors: "The taste of cigarettes no longer turned her on."

Each of us is at least marginally aware of the social and physical conditions, external to the individual, that shape human behavior. On the other hand, people tend to zero in on internal personality variables when assigning causal responsibility to others—especially, for some reason, if the behavior in question is negatively valued by society at large. War is a prime example. Every nation in the world has experienced the horror of atrocities committed against its people by aggressors from other nations or at the hands of criminal elements within its own borders. Crimes perpetrated by military personnel are the most frequent examples. The accused parties usually deny responsibility by pointing to extenuating circumstances beyond their control: "My commanding officer ordered me to do it." "I thought those people [the victims] were enemy soldiers disguised as civilians." Meanwhile, the leaders of the offended nation refer to the incurable sickness of the criminal mind, overrepresented among the ranks of the enemy. No leeway is permitted for explaining atrocities as the result of external circumstances beyond the personal control of the individual soldier. The attention of the prosecutor stays riveted on the perceived character defects of the accused: "The situation did not call for this type of overreaction from the soldiers. The satanic elements of the world's population should be prevented from satisfying their demented wishes through the infliction of pain on innocent people." The victimized leaders may also remind the world of their own purity: "None of our citizens would ever do such a dastardly thing. We in the highest echelons of government find it impossible to believe that our troops would behave in the outrageous manner regularly practiced by the enemy."

The truth is that external circumstances are more crucial in affecting human behavior than outside observers commonly give them credit for. One of the key psychological studies showing this to be the case was reported some twenty years ago by the late Stanley Milgram. Imagine for a moment the following scene. Two strangers are brought together and told they will participate in a scientific investigation of learning, involving the administration of electric shock. One is given the role of the learner, the other the role of the teacher. Unbeknownst to the teacher, the learner is actually a member of the experimental team, privy to the purpose of the experiment and quite adept at feigning distress and pain. The teacher thinks he is delivering a shock to the learner every time an incorrect answer is given. The real purpose of the experiment is to determine the extent to which unacceptable social behavior can be directed and maintained by the incessant prompting of an authority figure.

The procedure is deceptive but realistic. The learner is strapped into an electric chair located in a room apart from the teacher. The learner must push one of four levers to indicate the appropriate answer on each trial. The response choice is also depicted on a board of lights facing the teacher, and every time the learner makes an error, an official-looking experimenter tells the beleaguered teacher to activate a switch and hence administer a jolt of electricity. What the teacher does not know is that the wires attached to the learner are inactive, and absolutely no electric current is ever felt. From the standpoint of the teacher, however, on succeeding trials the shock is increased from a starting point of 15 volts on up to a maximum of 450 bolts. These voltages are prominently displayed, and the higher regions of the intensity scale are marked with the ominous phrases "EXTREME SHOCK" and "DANGER: SEVERE SHOCK." It is rather easy to deceive the teacher into thinking the learner is making numerous mistakes, so as to necessitate the delivery of increasingly powerful shocks. As the intensity marches inexorably upward, the learner-actor in the adjacent room first begins to grunt and moan and then asks to be released from the experiment. Still later, he pounds the wall in apparent pain and finally, at the highest intensity of shock, falls silent.

The amazing result of this experiment was that some 60 percent of the teachers complied with the voice of authority and dispensed the maximum shock! The unsuspecting participants were recruited from all walks of life: professionals, business people, and blue-collar workers. If we honestly ask ourselves why they acted as they did we are likely to attach blame to their personal characters by thinking something like: "The experimenter must have chosen a bunch of sickies for the study," or more cynically, "After all, people are basically evil at heart. It's no wonder they pulled the switch on their fellows." Still, not many of us could have predicted the actual results beforehand. In fact, when Milgram asked a group of psychiatrists to predict what percentage of the general population would obey the experimenter and deliver the maximum shock, they painted a flattering picture of human nature, predicting that less than 1 percent—the hard-core psychopaths—would continue to the upper limit, and that most people would quit the study once the intensity reached 150 volts. In other words, they thought that normal adults would not behave with such wanton cruelty, even if they knew it was only a psychology experiment and no one would be really hurt. The psychiatrists were, of course, wide of the mark in this opinion.

That stressful conditions, coupled with unreasonable demands from authority, can overwhelm altruistic feelings—as demonstrated in the Milgram study—is a fact that most people, including experienced psychiatrists, often fail to appreciate. In general, when judging the causes for another's actions we underestimate the impact of the external context. In effect, we discount the influence of social pressures. This is not a conscious decision to emphasize one or the other contributing factor; the attribution is usually unconscious and instantaneous.

After hearing of the Milgram study, the typical person still is likely to interpret nonsocial behavior in terms of personality variables, and it would be the rare individual who would admit that he or she could be goaded into delivering the highest intensities of shock. We hold exalted opinions of ourselves, especially with regard to our ability to view matters objectively and to act morally in the face of immoral demands. Because of the obvious sadism implied by continuing the task, we believe that we could muster enough common decency to simply get up and walk out of the laboratory. That is, we decide that we would surely realize the immorality of the experiment (external conditions) and act accordingly. This is how we see matters before we are placed in the situation.

The motivation behind the other guy's behavior is quite another matter. When interpreting the actions of others, after they occur we tend to overstate the influence of what we perceive to be fixed personality traits. Despite the care with which Milgram sampled the general population, we still have a lingering suspicion that 60 percent of his subjects were just a little sadistic to begin with. We feel that only a serious character defect could underlie such blatant disregard for human welfare. Social psychologists refer to this tendency as the *Fundamental Attribution Error: People overrate psychological causes and underrate external pressures in explaining the behavior of others.* It is a remarkably pervasive judgment error.

When justifying our own behavior, we are apt to mention external circumstances as the controlling force, but we strongly resist applying a similar logic to justify the behavior of others. This tendency doesn't occur just in the laboratory under unusual conditions. It is noticeable in nonthreatening situations as well. Picture a classroom scene in which an astronomy professor asks students to write an essay on the search for extraterrestrial intelligence. The class is split into two groups. Half the students are told to write on the merits of the radio telescope as a search technique, the other half on its disadvantages. The instructor explicitly dictates the gist of the positive and negative arguments to be followed in composing the two essays. Students are given no choice. The completed papers are then read by a third group of students, who are told the exact classroom circumstances under which the essays were written. When these readers are asked to guess the writers' true opinions, independent of what was said in the essay, they tend to think that the essays reflect real views. Those who wrote on behalf of the radio telescope must believe that it is the best approach; those who wrote against it must not—this despite the fact that the position in each essay, pro or con, was dictated by the instructor, and the raters have been so apprised. In trying to understand the actions of others—in this case, the view expressed in an essay—people play down the influence of situational constraints and assess causality instead by reference to individual personality.

Why do we commit the Fundamental Attribution Error with such regularity? The social psychologists Richard Nisbett and Lee Ross suggest that people as actors stand out against the larger backdrop of environmental and social constraints, even though these constraints are chiefly responsible for guiding behavior. The acting individual is a more interesting, salient figure than the pallid, inactive background; and so the outsider concentrates on the dynamic actor and discounts the static environment. On the other hand, as noted, when attributing causality to one's own behavior after the fact, reasons are sought in the world "out there," and the influence of psychological factors is often minimized or disregarded.

Most people strive to attribute valid causes to unusual occurrences experienced in the course of everyday life. In some instances the truth or falsity of an opinion about the underlying causes of these occurrences is secondary to the fact that any explanation is possible at all. It is comforting to come up with plausible reasons for the physical happenings around us, even though these explanations may appear far-fetched to others. It is nonetheless worthwhile to understand the process by which causes are assigned to events, and this is done best by examining specific cases from a little distance.

There are numerous examples of the Fundamental Attribution Error among scientists and nonscientists characterized by an interest in outer space, a subject that excites childlike curiosity while holding the promise of yielding information that may greatly enlarge the reach of human civilization. Being aware of the conditions under which this error generally occurs should sharpen our ability to determine the actual causes of events, and hence to come to a better understanding of one another and the potential influence of external pressures on human behavior.

My first and favorite example concerns the explanations offered to account for the sighting of a UFO—an arresting event, after all, from the standpoint both of the witness and of those who later learn details from the witness's account. But the attributions of causation from the two vantage points are often quite disparate.

Upon first encountering a strange object in the sky the witness scans through memory to find some past episode of a similar nature with which the new experience can be compared. Attributions of causality at this stage typically invoke external agents: The object may have been an airplane, a shooting star, or a bug sprawled against the car windshield. If none of the obvious reasons appears adequate, the witness may label the object "unidentified" or may begin to conjure up more fantastic images about its origin and purpose. For instance, in light of the publicity accorded such cases, the person who would enjoy a bit of notoriety may come to believe that the object was an alien spacecraft sent on a scouting mission to the Solar System or sent by a faraway civilization that plans to colonize Earth and subjugate its inhabitants. In all such attempts to comprehend the cause of the sighting, however, the responsible agent is located somewhere in the external environment. So far as the witness is concerned, an appropriate explanation must refer to physical factors. It does not generally occur to the witness that the sighting was the result of faulty eyesight or that some neural connections in the brain were inoperative at the time. People believe that their eyes and ears perform faithfully to inform them of incidents occurring in the external environment, and certainly no one is particularly anxious to admit that a defective mental state underlies the report of a UFO.

The outside scientist or layperson who is told about a UFO sighting is quick to entertain a radically different opinion about the underlying cause. More than likely, the first thing occurring to the outsider is that the witness is just a little wacky. The outsider might assume that the witness is too naive to recognize familiar objects in the sky, such as shooting stars, police helicopters, and weather balloons, or that the witness is a provocateur and liar or maybe just lacks the intellectual aptitude to live in a society which routinely dismisses reports of alien spacecraft in the night sky. In short, the outsider is prone to attribute the sighting to the inner dispositional traits of the witness and will remain uneasy about hints that extraterrestrial beings are in any way involved. The witness has imagined things, or has faulty eyesight, or is fond of playing jokes on the unsuspecting. It is no wonder, then, that UFO witnesses are looked upon with suspicion by friends and strangers alike. They stand convinced of the external causes of their perceptions; their critics suspect that the actual cause is in their psychological or perceptual makeup, quite independent of what transpired in the environment. The clash of viewpoints will more often than not generate antagonism and frustration, rather than a resolution of the riddle posed by reports. The findings of social psychologists who have studied the Fundamental Attribution Error would lead us to predict exactly that outcome.

The communication barrier between people trying to provide reasons for their own beliefs and people trying to explain the perceptions of others is nowhere clearer than in debates about Erich von Däniken's theory of ancient astronauts, discussed in chapter 2. As far as von Däniken was concerned, his theory was a direct response to the "facts" available for all to see. The impressive stone monuments of the past, such as the pyramids and the Easter Island statues, were undeniable clues that Earth was visited long ago by extraterrestrial voyagers who generously furnished blueprints for the human race to follow in erecting the monuments. The tangible evidence, there for all who cared to pay attention, demanded an interpretation like his. There is no indication in von Däniken's writings that he considered these ideas the least bit biased or bizarre, either in their failure to conform to scientific knowledge or in their flimsy link to reality as defined by archaeologists and other scholars of the regions in question. He gave no credence to alternative theories that might seem equally compelling to a neutral outsider.

On the other hand, when von Däniken stepped forward to meet the opposition, he no longer rested his case on observable, external facts; instead he leveled his barbs straight at the personalities of the critics, portraying his opponents as narrow-minded prigs, inexplicably defensive, and unable to pass informed judgment on unorthodox ideas. In refuting all criticism leveled against him, von Däniken assumed a cloak of high morality, as is apparent in the following excerpt from one of his books: "Occupational blindness appears everywhere, and not only in scientific circles, once disturbing new knowledge is deliberately disregarded. The 'experts' prefer to snatch at the most absurd explanations rather than pay the least attention to anything new, so that they can go on contemplating their own navels in the shrine of inherited knowledge" (*Signs of the Gods*, pp. 239–240). These comments vividly illustrate the general inclination to attribute the behavior and opinions of others to psychological, as contrasted with external, causes.

Interestingly enough, this polemical style is matched in kind by scientists who contest von Däniken's views. The majority of astronomers refuse to acknowledge that his outlandish theories could arise from even the barest shred of objective fact, whereas their own scholarly findings are presented as inescapable conclusions based on the best available methods for ascertaining "the truth."

Stating these conclusions, however, leaves the scientist in yet another quandary. If the theory of ancient astronauts is not founded in reality, then why did von Däniken ever propose it, and more important, why do so many others follow suit, or at least purchase his books in such large numbers? These questions perplex many physical scientists who look to psychology and religion as potential reasons for the puzzling behavior they observe. Their explanations generally refer to the personal, intellectual, or emotional limits of von Däniken himself and/or his supporters. In offering such explanations, of course, these scientists commit the Fundamental Attribution Error.

For example, the noted astrophysicist Carl Sagan discusses the von

Däniken "myth" in the foreword to a book on the topic by Ronald Story. Placing the theory of ancient astronauts on a plane with Superman comics, Sagan argues that the human need for religious salvation is at the root of von Däniken's success: "The popularity of von Däniken must, I think, be theological in origin. Our times are very perilous. The immediate relevance of traditional religions to contemporary problems is not so obvious as was once the case. At just this moment arises the beguiling doctrine that all-powerful, all-knowing, and benevolent creatures have in the past and will one day in the future come out of the sky and save us from ourselves" (*The Space-Gods Revealed*, p. xiii). This is a psychological attribution. Sagan feels that people obviously ignore the physical facts, so they must be resonating instead to an inner call of religion.

A similar discrepancy between the explanations for behavior given by an actor and by a bystander occurs in the controversy over the wisdom of launching satellite probes and establishing space colonies. When scientists ruminate about these projects, their avowed motivation for doing so is traced solely to external demands, perhaps because the feasibility of launches must be pleaded on grounds acceptable to the politicians who control the underwriting of such projects. The rest of us are led to believe that the motives for the pursuit of space research have nothing to do with the personal emotions and preferences of the scientist. The anticipated deployment of space satellites is linked with the perceived need for an efficient worldwide communication network, the recognized value of accurate weather prediction, or the desire for foolproof methods of military surveillance and national defense. Similarly, the globe's pressing energy needs encourage us to assemble power stations above the atmosphere or on the Moon and, subsequently, to build orbiting homes for the people who must work there. We are reminded that the economic and engineering barriers facing space programs would be greatly reduced through the construction of habitable colonies. This outcome, too, is seen as an inevitable response to practical exigencies on Earth and in space.

The arguments for creating research facilities on other planets are also couched in terms that reflect agreed-upon scientific wisdom, external to the psychological motivations of scientists themselves. It is said, for instance, that discovery of life on Mars would strengthen our grasp of the biological principles governing life on Earth and would serve to isolate those genetic ingredients which are uniquely human. This information in turn might help prevent and treat crippling diseases, help avoid genetic defects, and even help reduce the biological and psychological stress associated with the colonization of outer space. Who would dare challenge such praiseworthy, altruistic aims? The reasons outlined by the scientific and engineering community to justify space programs, then, are external to them as individuals. The rest of us are led to see in their plans no connection whatever to their personal motivations as scientists. If such undertakings are to be supported by the general public, they must be seen as the answer to society's accepted priorities: There must be a set of well-defined external circumstances that necessitate the expenditure of funds; and this political reality may explain why public relations has become such a vital component of large-scale space programs.

Many nonscientists, however, think that space programs are not at all driven by societal demands but are being pushed only to outfit expensive playgrounds for testing the esoteric ideas of astronomers and engineers. When matched against the immediate social needs of humanity, research proposals are seen as sorely wanting; they are just another devious means to satisfy the peculiar quirks of the scientific mind. So people who do not share an abiding concern with outer space also commit the Fundamental Attribution Error by assuming that dispositional, inner causes are behind such venturesome proposals. For this reason the scientific community must present counterarguments through rather elaborate marketing efforts.

In answering the concerns of the layperson, either scientists bend over backward to woo critics by referring more vigorously to the impending benefits of space research, or else they attempt to turn the outsider's use of dispositional attributions to their own advantage. In following the latter course, they carry on with all the phraseology the community wants to hear. Common slogans used to defend the expenditure of huge sums of public funds often include the phrases "national pride," "thrill of discovery," and "human destiny." A strong play on the emotions of public officials is most effective when their personal beliefs correspond to those behind the scientific program. Otherwise, of course, the entire effort to sway public policy can backfire badly. The politician who does not believe that the ultimate destiny of the human race is to conquer and populate the Earth, Solar System, and Galaxy is understandably reluctant to vote in favor of excursions into outer space, unless social benefits can be guaranteed.

Perhaps it is not so shocking to learn that equally rational individuals have opposing views of exactly the same "facts." Even when they adhere to the cold logic of science, alternative theories of a phenomenon lead to very different, and sometimes contradictory, interpretations. This friction is also prominent in the ongoing debate between the optimists and the pessimists who have considered the prospects for discovering alien civilizations by eavesdropping on their radio transmissions. Before considering this debate in the context of attribution theory, however, I think it will be helpful to review a parallel case from the annals of social psychology.

A classic study was published thirty-three years ago by Albert Hastorf and Hadley Cantril. As professors at Ivy League colleges (Dartmouth and Princeton), they were aware of the two schools' traditional athletic rivalry, and on one Saturday afternoon a rare opportunity presented itself for investigating the effect of school loyalty on perception. Princeton and Dartmouth played a football game which, from all accounts in the local news media, was particularly rough and emotional. Princeton won the contest, but there were postgame repercussions. Amid the uproar Hastorf and Cantril showed a movie of the game to students from both schools and asked them to record all the infractions they detected by each side. Although they all saw the same movie, the students' perceptions were clearly at odds. The Dartmouth partisans saw an equal number of infractions committed by both teams, whereas the Princetonians saw about twice as many perpetrated by Dartmouth players as by Princeton players. In the postgame fuss the student newspapers exchanged accusations, making the point that "facts" were being seen accurately by only one side—their own, of course—and that the opposition must have seriously misperceived the truth, probably because its view of the game was distorted by blind loyalty to the home team.

It is this sort of discrepancy between perceptions of the same scientific facts that accompanies the use of the radio telescope in the search for extraterrestrial intelligence. Both optimists and pessimists claim that they are forming opinions based on the true situation: To the optimists, the scientific data are sufficiently stable to merit a full-scale search; the pessimists see the same data as too scant and uncertain to justify embarking on any such wild-eyed venture. Each side attributes the other's position to faulty preconceptions—an irrational feeling about the possible success or failure of the project—rather than to an objective appraisal of the relevant facts. Each side accuses the other of viewing the same game through distorting lenses, and thereby each commits the Fundamental Attribution Error.

The novel aspect of the SETI example is that the attribution process is actually turned inside out. Normally a person acts and then others try to ascertain what lies behind the observed behavior, suggesting causes of a dispositional and/or environmental nature. In the case of aliens, however, behavior has never been observed: We have no firm evidence for the existence of intelligent beings residing on other worlds. Despite recent attempts to capture radio signals sent by extraterrestrials, so far nothing at all has turned up. Therefore, the present enterprise rests on making determinations of the physical circumstances in outer space and of how these are perceived by hypothetical organisms. That is, do aliens attach the same importance we do to the electromagnetic spectrum, life on planets, and contact with other life-forms? If we correctly guess the physical and psychological conditions (alien motivations) in outer space, we expect to observe certain behaviors as a consequence. The standard order of events has been inverted.

Optimists and pessimists differ in how far they are willing to go in listing details about relevant conditions in outer space, but the key issue is whether Earth's conditions are typical and frequently repeated throughout the universe or rather are anomalous and seldom encountered in any other place or time. Are mankind's physical, biological, and psychological theories constrained by the idiosyncratic ways we sense and conceptualize our immediate surroundings, or do these scientific models transcend local barriers and apply throughout a larger envelope of time and space? Optimists act on the premise of universality, pessimists on the premise of particularity; skeptics don't bother. So let's bypass the skeptics for the moment and concentrate on the two extreme positions.

First, assume that conditions on Earth are distributed throughout the universe. Therefore it is necessary to specify them only once. Then, as optimists see it, the chances of finding another technical civilization within reach of our radio telescopes justify a conscious effort to make contact. Moreover, optimists suggest, the region along the electromagnetic spectrum in which to look is within the so-called watering hole—in the vicinity of the twenty-one-centimeter radio wave emitted by hydrogen, the most abundant element in the universe and the essential component of water-based life. The romantic reason for choosing this part of the electromagnetic spectrum is that water-based life elsewhere can be expected to congregate at a spot so necessary for its own survival. The practical and scientific reason is that background noise is less there than in other regions of the spectrum, and the relevant microwaves are thus able to penetrate the Earth's atmosphere and be resolved by our radio telescopes.

Several NASA-sponsored publications have even conjectured about the exact form of such signals. They argue that in order to conserve energy and alert another civilization to its presence, a sender should concentrate a beam of energy within a small band of wavelengths or should transmit intermittent pulses of high energy at a fixed wavelength. Implicitly adhering to the principle of psychological symmetry—they are like us—the optimists show that they expect aliens to employ the same strategy, if their level of technical expertise is close to ours. The attribution of causality demonstrated here concerns the physical, external conditions faced by aliens.

In addition, the optimist must believe that aliens "want" to find another species, not necessarily us, but some organisms with a style of thought that leads them to reciprocate. Perhaps their sending program will be a natural extension of ongoing research in physics and astronomy; perhaps they are in desperate straits and seek outside assistance to rescue a sinking civilization; or they might be engaged in the business of sending messages only for the fun of it. Whatever the exact circumstances in outer space, we must develop an opinion about alien motivational states if we are to justify our own effort to gain entry into the galactic club of communicating societies. This argument represents the personal (dispositional) side of the attribution process.

Because physical scientists are conducting the search, they usually assume that the content of any messages will pertain to scientific matters. Optimists attribute human personality styles and occupational interests to extraterrestrials, so the messages anticipated by astronomers and engineers would read pretty much like a shopping list of unsolved scientific problems. It is assumed, at least implicitly, that the hierarchy of science perceived by the physics community on this planet will be reflected in the principles of science discovered by aliens. That is, mathematics and physics will have first priority, somewhat later the conversation may turn to chemistry and biology, and much later talk may extend into the looser arenas of social science. Indeed, the optimists contend, it is in the softer areas of social science that we probably share the least with extraterrestrials, and it may take millions of years even to get around to alien psychology, sociology, and politics.

This brand of attribution strikes a sympathetic chord among those with the requisite knowledge to join in on a scientific dialogue, but a cooler reception seems likely from nonscientists possessing a value system that does not include an interest in outer space. One could certainly argue just as persuasively that physics will be relegated to the lowest priority by a civilization accustomed to communicating over the vast expanses of time and distance separating the stars and planets. To be able to accomplish this feat implies superior mastery over material obstacles, which thereafter can be safely ignored. What probably amuses this civilization now are more esoteric topics—for example, how to preserve a thriving culture, its arts, its social and political values.

I have a physicist friend in California whom I occasionally call from New Hampshire. Luckily, the engineering skills of the telephone company make our contact possible at any time of day or night, but this fact doesn't make it any more likely that our conversation will take up the physical means by which speech is transmitted across a continent. I can't recall us ever spending a single minute discussing telephones! Most information transmitted over phone lines is unrelated to science or engineering, computer lines notwithstanding. I suspect that the time devoted to social topics such as friendship, love, weather, sports, and gossip far surpasses the time alloted to scientific matters. Even the conversation between two scientists collaborating on a research problem is likely to touch on social amenities before moving on to substantive issues. On the interstellar time scale it may take centuries to get beyond the pleasantries that typically characterize social gatherings, an arrangement that would totally invert the scientists' expected order of discussion topics.

Still, it is pointless to quibble over what aliens will and won't want to discuss. The point I am moving toward is this: If the optimists are correct that aliens are influenced by the same physical conditions we are, and possess a similar desire to communicate, then perhaps they are in no danger of committing the Fundamental Attribution Error after all. While I have no evidence to support this view, it seems to me that an observer is least likely to suggest dispositional, inner causes to explain the behavior of someone else when that other is in all critical respects identical to the observer. Returning to the UFO example, if someone like me says that he or she saw a flying saucer in the sky, and if I myself have witnessed UFOs in the past, it is probable that I will believe the report is of an actual physical event. I am unlikely to think the witness is crazy, because this judgment would imply that I am crazy as well. Therefore, the SETI approach might well succeed eventually if psychological symmetry holds true for aliens. If "they" really are like us, then we need only to proceed on the assumptions held by engineers and astronomers when considering the possibility of extending human culture into outer space.

Those who express pessimism over SETI have quite a different perspective on the homogeneity of the physical universe and on the probable desire of aliens to seek contact. When thinking of the small pockets of the universe capable of intelligent thought and consciousness, pessimists anticipate great diversity and uniqueness. Each factor in the Drake formula discussed in chapter 5 is assigned a low probability, so there are assumed to be fewer opportunities for intelligent life to arise. But the chief problem is that these isolated pockets have very little in common. On the basis of what amounts to an evolutionary position, the astrophysicist John A. Ball concludes that there is an incredible range of intellectual levels in the universe, or even within the Galaxy, and consequently that it is unlikely we would ever run across an alien civilization whose technical and psychological state was even remotely similar to ours. Different geophysical environments can be expected to drive biological evolution in characteristic ways. Even on Earth the various life-forms barely notice each other, except on those occasions when one creature interferes with another's access to food, shelter, or personal safety. In particular, we have had only minor success in communicating with our closest intellectual relatives, chimpanzees and dolphins. According to Ball, contact with extraterrestrials would be something like a conversation between a person and a clam—where the stupider one is us. It is doubtful that clams have a very accurate picture of human nature, and the same inadequacy would be expected of our evaluation of an intellectually advanced being from quite another sphere of existence.

Finally, I should mention that the hard-core skeptic of SETI has great difficulty imagining what it is like to be an alien. The argument in this regard is not hard to follow. Because we have no reason to suppose that extraterrestrials are trying to reach us or any other species, the pessimist thinks it downright silly to fabricate attributions about alien perceptions and desires: No behavior, therefore no attribution. On the other hand, most fair-minded skeptics would be instant supporters of the search if a single bit of hard data came to light. If a crippled spacecraft landed on Earth and its navigator stayed around long enough to make our acquaintance, we can be sure that most, though not all, of the world's population would grant the enormous significance of the event and would thereafter enthusiastically support the SETI program. A signal embedded in radio waves would be somewhat less persuasive, but still a very powerful inducement to enlist public support. Whatever the eventual conditions leading to communication with extraterrestrials, we can anticipate at least one reaction: Once contacted, the human race will consider itself a "chosen" people; the relevance of physical conditions in outer space will be minimized in favor of assumptions about the personal dispositions of aliens.

REFERENCES AND FURTHER READINGS

Aronson, E. *The Social Animal*. San Francisco: Freeman, 1976.
Ball, J. A. Extraterrestrial Intelligence: Where Is Everybody? *American Scientist*, 1980, *68*, 656–663.

Bruno, G. On the Infinite Universe and Worlds. In D. Goldsmith (Ed.), *The Quest for Extraterrestrial Life: A book of Readings,* pp. 5–7. Mill Valley, Calif.: University Science Books, 1980.

Hastorf, A. H., & Cantril, H. They Saw a Game: A Case Study. *Journal of Abnormal and Social Psychology,* 1954, *49,* 129–134.

Heider, F. *The Psychology of Interpersonal Relations.* New York: Wiley, 1958.

Lord, S.; Dixon, R.; & Healy, T. (Eds.) *Project Oasis: The Design of a Signal Detector for the Search for Extraterrestrial Intelligence.* Santa Clara, Calif.: University of Santa Clara, technical report, 1981.

Mahoney, M. J. Psychology of the Scientist: An Evaluative Review. *Social Studies of Science,* 1979, *9,* 349–375.

Milgram, S. Behavioral Study of Obedience. *Journal of Abnormal and Social Psychology,* 1963, *67,* 371–378.

Milgram, S. Some Conditions of Obedience and Disobedience to Authority. *Human Relations,* 1965, *18,* 57–76.

Nisbett, R., & Ross, L. *Human Inference: Strategies and Shortcomings of Social Judgment.* Englewood Cliffs, N.J.: Prentice-Hall, 1980.

Oliver, B. M. (Ed.) *Project Cyclops: A Design Study of a System for Detecting Extraterrestrial Life.* CR 114445 NASA/Ames Reseach Center, 1971, Code LT, Moffett Field, Calif. 94035.

Rood, R. T., & Trefil, J. S. *Are We Alone? The Possibility of Extraterrestrial Civilizations.* New York: Scribner, 1981.

Sagan, C. *Cosmos.* New York: Random House, 1980.

Schneider, D. J.; Hastorf, A. H.; & Ellsworth, P. C. *Person Perception.* Reading, Mass.: Addison-Wesley, 1979.

Singer, B., & Benassi, V. A. Occult Beliefs. *American Scientist,* 1981, *69,* 49–55.

Story, R. *The Space-Gods Revealed.* New York: Barnes & Noble, 1980.

Tversky, A., & Kahneman, D. Judgment Under Uncertainty: Heuristics and Biases. *Science,* 1974, *185,* 1124–1131.

Von Däniken, E. *Signs of the Gods.* New York: Berkley, 1980.

CHAPTER 9

PATTERNS IN THE EYE
OF THE BEHOLDER

The conscious experience of objects on the ground below or in the sky above depends not only on the proper functioning of sense organs but also on the perception of relations among objects and on the familiarity engendered by seeing the same patterns over and over again. A luminous disc lying on the kitchen floor may be seen as a one-inch coin of some monetary value, whereas this same visual stimulus hovering above the distant horizon may be appreciated as the harvest Moon of high romance. Hence the apprehension of the external world of objects and events is molded by what these objects are as physical stimuli and by the observer's inner state at the moment of perceiving. The contents of this cognitive state depend mightily on past experience. The relevance of both physical and cultural contexts in determining the perception of "reality" is as valid for the unusual as it is for the ordinary, as valid for the careful scientist as it is for the casual observer. The layperson's report of a UFO in an otherwise ordinary setting results from the principles of visual perception that guide the astronomer's report of a signal culled from the radio noise of outer space.

Because of this underlying similarity in human psychology, the laws of perception apply to all facets of our dealings with outer space, whether the discussion centers on UFOs, satellite probes, ancient astronauts, space colonies, or radio telescopes. Although two people may be exposed to exactly the same physical evidence, their special view of the world, as conditioned by past experience, will ultimately affect how they perceive and interpret that evidence. More particularly, a person's intelligence profile and value orientation ("intellivalue") colors perception of the most basic stimuli: ordinary lights, sounds, smells, and so forth. In the same way, individual intellivalues influence the perception of complex physical events, such as unusual lights in the sky, ancient pyramids in the desert, or patterns of energy in radio emissions. In this chapter I spell out some applications of the principles of perception, with special attention devoted to the search for alien intelligence through application of radio astronomy. From now on this topic will command most of our attention.

A better starting place, however, is the UFO phenomenon, because at first blush it appears to contradict flatly the laws of perception. In the course of daily life objects occupy typical positions in the environment in respect to each other and the visual horizon. Treetops and the roofs of tall buildings are generally seen above the horizon, while household items such as chairs, tables, and rugs are seen near at hand, well below the horizon. Once the perceptual learning of childhood is completed, most of the daily scenes we encounter contain familiar objects perceived in appropriate, expected surroundings. After repeated exposure to any arrangement of things, we adapt to a point of indifference regarding constituent elements; the details of the physical scene barely manage to reach conscious awareness. But if a strange event were to occur—say, a kitchen table floated to the ceiling—it would attract immediate attention. Novel events violate expectations and, for that reason, never fail to stimulate interest and curiosity.

By definition, a UFO is a strange object in a familiar setting. A person anticipates seeing certain things in the sky—the Moon and stars, planes and birds—but is then suddenly confronted with something quite different. It is here that the paradoxical eclipses the commonplace. Nonetheless, the same celestial event may well be perceived as a UFO by one observer and as a natural occurrence by another, depending on their respective knowledge base and past experiences. The seasoned air traffic controller who is accustomed to seeing planes approach from various angles under an assortment of weather and lighting conditions is less likely to label an aerial event as "unidentified" than a person who has never visited a major airport. In the darkness, a plane's body and wing lights can dance about or remain perfectly still for lengths of time that stretch credulity. A person unfamiliar with the nighttime scene at an airport may well think that a plane seen in other surroundings, perhaps above a moonlit wheat field, is a genuine UFO with either threatening or benevolent intentions. This conclusion is certainly valid when considered within the framework of the viewer's learned expectations about events that do and do not happen in the night sky.

If only a fleeting glimpse of an object is possible, this fragment still may be used unconsciously to construct a more detailed version of the event which fits sensibly into the existing context. The perceptual system fills in the blanks to create a meaningful whole. An immediate example is printed text. The reader should have no trouble understanding the words THE I3AT. But look carefully at the letters! The letter A in THE is physically the same as the A in BAT, and yet it is read read as an H in the first word and as an A in the second. The context furnished by the flanking letters directs the proper inference about the word's meaning despite the incomplete evidence in the raw physical stimulus.

Notice, also, that the letter B in BAT is incompletely depicted as I3. Such perceptual effects are not confined to well-rehearsed letters and words; that is, the symbol I3 doesn't always appear as a B. To verify this claim, take a look at these easy additions: $2 + 5 = 7$, $1 + 4 = 5$, $8 + 7 = 15$, $6 + 7 = 13$. Here the numerical context easily identifies the symbol as 13. Ambiguous cases can be easily contrived as well: Does $A + E = I3$ refer to an algebraic sum designated by the quantity 13 or by the variable B?

Analogously, a person may see only part of an object in the sky, but automatically construct in the mind's eye the outline of a full-fledged spaceship, outfitted with windows, side fins, and rockets. The inferred object often will resemble something that is already quite familiar. Many UFOs have been described by witnesses as if the object in question came off the assembly line of a high-tech company specializing in flying machines, be they balloon airships of 1890 vintage, sleek rockets of the 1970s, or spherical landers of the 1980s. It would be amusing to learn that the first sighting of a flying saucer occurred on the heels of a game of backyard Frisbee, or toward the end of a family quarrel enlivened by the tossing of dinnerware. Whatever the precipitating details, ovals and circles are classic visual shapes and in perceptual theory are "good," readily perceived figures. More complex shapes are seldom noted. No one has ever seen a UFO that resembles a Swiss chalet, a Volkswagen bus, or a baby carriage, for the plain reason that in our daily experience these objects appear to rest on the floor or ground and are never encountered next to airborne birds and treetops.

It would be wrong, however, to think that incorrect inferences about the source of UFOs signify a perceptual system gone awry. Most such percepts are undoubtedly truthful renditions of reality, no more a misperception of events than is the natural inference of the letter A in the word BAT. Physical scientists, feeling obliged to "correct" the misapprehensions of laypeople, who report the lion's share of UFO sightings, ask them to put aside their familiar impressions of the night sky in favor of the scientific scene depicted by aeronautics and astronomy, an expanse densely populated with satellites, planets, and stars that can undergo dramatic changes in location, color, and illumination over the course of a single evening. But the familiar context of the astronomer is not synonymous with the familiar context of the general public. Many people choose to retain the popular opinion about the nature and origin of UFOs; that is, they are not of this world. The public support given to such opinions, together with a lack of knowledge about astronomy, makes this conclusion eminently logical.

The past experiences of the observer influence how an object is perceived, whether the percept arises from complete or partial cues from the environment. Our experiences also condition the way we imagine what structures might have existed in an earlier epoch and how we try to explain their reason for being there, who built them, and the like. Here the remnants consist of physical bits and pieces that have somehow weathered the storms of geophysical forces and human negligence. In this instance, the values of today's society affect the way an observer forms a coherent view of the past. This is certainly the case when individuals of diverse cultural backgrounds consider the monuments of ancient civilizations and reflect on whether their architects were human or, instead, extraterrestrial visitors on a mission of unknown purpose. In this sense, the human reconstruction of the event provides as much insight into the values of the modern observer as it does into the historical "facts" of the past.

The persuasive influence of culture on perception has been amply confirmed by experimental psychologists and field anthropologists. We are well aware that the city dweller has a different impression of the environment than the rural farmer; the person from the open plains sees the world differently than someone living in the mountains.

One of my favorite stories of how culture molds perception was related over twenty years ago by the anthropologist Colin M. Turnbull, who spent a year with the BaMbuti Pygmies of the Ituri Forest, located in central Africa. Toward the end of his stay Turnbull left the forest for the great African savannah in the company of his Pygmy guide, Kenge, who had always lived in dense surroundings that afforded views only of objects closer than one hundred feet. With the vast, rolling plains before him Kenge had difficulty making sense out of the scene and, in particular, was unable to recognize some of the animals he saw. Upon spying a small herd of grazing buffalo some two miles off, he turned to Turnbull and asked, "What insects are those?" For his entire life the forest canopy had restricted his perception to nearby objects, so this was his first occasion to see buffalo at such great distances. Their miniature visual images depicted foreign animals on quite a smaller scale.

Turnbull elaborates on this misperception and tells of the man's reaction to other objects in the scene:

Out here in the plains, however, Kenge was looking for the first time over apparently unending miles of unfamiliar grasslands, with not a tree worth the name to give him any basis for comparison. The same thing happened later on when I pointed out a boat in the middle of the lake. It was a large fishing boat with a number of people in it but Kenge at first refused to believe this. He thought it was a floating piece of wood. [*The Forest People*, p. 252]

Strictly speaking, these visual anomalies are not a consequence of the Pygmy culture but rather arise from the special environment in which that culture exists. But Kenge's reaction illustrates very nicely how long-term experience in one setting profoundly affects perception in another. In an analogous way, cultural heritage and professional training bias a person's re-creation of events from the past. Now consider this influence with respect to modern views of the structures discussed in chapter 2: the Egyptian pyramids, the statues of Easter Island, and the figure drawings in the Nazca desert of Peru. In part because of the sketchiness of the facts regarding how and why these structures came about, it is possible to imagine several scenarios that fit the evidence tolerably well, even though the predominant view is that they were constructed by people without any alien assistance.

The Egyptologist views the Great Pyramid in a personal context of historical scholarship, including the study of language and political and social systems—all of which can be contrasted with today's counterparts. The engineer faces the same pyramid and is struck by its physical size and architectural symmetry, which suggest typical engineering questions: Where did the stones come from? How were they hauled to the site and lifted into place? The political and religious inscriptions on the stones are of less interest to the engineer, except insofar as they reveal something unique about early construction methods. The personal image of the Egypt of four thousand years ago simply is not the same for the Egyptologist and the engineer, because their interpretations of the past bear the inescapable imprint of their respective professions. Their personal world views support different perceptions of the same physical evidence.

Whereas scientists and scholars are willing to grant and encourage pluralism among themselves, they are less willing to extend this courtesy to the nonprofessional. So when the indomitable Erich von Däniken lobbied for a reassessment of history, with allusions to visiting aliens, genetic mixing of human and alien stock, and airfields in the desert, he was ridiculed and censored for the naiveté of his perceptions. As far as I can tell, however, the modest facts from that period allow at least some leeway in developing plausible interpretations of what actually took place.

In or out of science it is always a matter of opinion how much the known facts should constrain flights of imagination. Each theory carries the indelible mark of the subculture within which the theorist lives and works. A society's view of the past is not a given constant because people in that society are obviously different from one another, just as perception of the present or prediction of the future does not conjure up the same images for us all. The practical relevance of truth and falsehood evaporates when the facts are not firm enough to settle the issue to everyone's satisfaction.

Now picture for a moment the Egyptologist, the engineer, and von Däniken strolling together among the ruins of ancient Egypt and contemplating the profile of the Great Pyramid. They each "see" something different, and when they envision what the culture that created it must have been like, their images are biased by the idiosyncracies of their own training. For the Egyptologist, the pyramid is the crown jewel of a dead civilization, one where autocratic power committed armies of slaves to the singular vision of their masters, where the chasm separating the elite and the oppressed was wide, and where concern with the hereafter occupied the minds of the ruling class. For the engineer, it was quite another era in history: a period when civilization first applied sophisticated building techniques on a grand scale, a period when block and tackle, levers and pulleys, transport sleds and human energy worked in concert to produce engineering marvels. For the writer von Däniken it was more a time of profound change in the whole human condition, a turning point for the race, as the coffers of science were enriched by alien benefactors. The sudden improvement of technical competence lifted humans onto a level of achievement that von Däniken believed was the forerunner of today's excursions into outer space.

Who can say which of these "learned" perceptions of the past is correct—and does it really matter? Regardless of what one thinks about von Däniken's theories, the realization of his vision of the future seems to be fast approaching. When scientists discuss what a satellite probe would look like and do if sent to poke around for signs of life in distant parts of the Galaxy, they are confronted with a situation that has much in common with that met by the historian trying to weave together the conflicting threads from the past that underlie the fabric of present-day society. In both instances, the final outcome rests on incomplete information in the present. To talk sense in the context of space probes or space colonies is synonomous with having in hand a program that works on a practical level: The probe must arrive intact at its destination and transmit data back to Earth; the colony must support a community for an extended, maybe indefinite, stay under the harsh conditions of outer space.

Because the images of life in outer space are necessarily a function of knowledge derived from experience on Earth, utopian colonies will in fact closely match what we are accustomed to seeing in communities here. The formidable surroundings will determine the form and detail of the structures but will have little impact, at least initially, on the personalities and behavior of the colonists. All the joys and travails associated with participation in a social group on Earth will be transported to space.

In the foregoing I have alluded to imagination as well as perception. The capacity for visual imagery is an important human faculty. Perception and imagination are tightly coupled. The experimental psychologist's most accessible subjects, college students, are adept at conjuring up pictures of objects in familiar settings, even though in everyday life the object and the setting may not have coexisted. Still, the imagined scenes very often reflect the person's experience with actual scenes.

The results of laboratory studies of this ability are clear-cut. For example, Stephen Michael Kosslyn has asked people to estimate how far away an animal—say, an elephant—is when it totally fills the visual field. Undergraduates perform this task reliably, even though most have never seen an elephant at the imagined distance and probably would not care to experience the thrill of doing so. By asking the same question for a variety of animals (e.g., goat, mouse, alligator, giraffe), Kosslyn computes the dimensions of the visual field used in framing all objects in the mind's eye of imagination. This computation is possible because we tend to locate animals at an appropriate distance depending on actual size; that is, an elephant would have to be farther away than a goat if both occupied the same proportion of the visual field.

The significance of this finding is that imagination obeys the same rules as the perception of real objects. Both processes adhere to the geometric link between an object's physical size, distance, and projected visual size. This outcome suggests an experiment. Although it would be fruitless to ask someone to imagine an alien that filled the visual field and expect to get a straight answer, it still would be interesting to know what people assumed was the size and shape of the creature. If a person were asked to dream up a fictional alien, I would guess its salient properties would be recognizably human. A single head probably would sit atop a larger body, complete with extremities resembling arms, legs, or maybe prehensile flippers. Imagination of the unknown generally coincides with perception of the known. Even that master of the imagination, Jules Verne, conjured up aliens which were very humanlike, apart from their size. In *A Journey to the Center of the Earth* he describes an encounter:

Not more than a quarter mile off, leaning against the trunk of an enormous tree, was a human being—a Proteus of these subterranean regions. . . . It was no longer a fossil whose corpse we had raised from the ground in the great cemetery, but a giant capable of guiding and driving these prodigious monsters. His height was above twelve feet. His head, as big as the head of a buffalo, was lost in a mane of matted hair. [p. 206]

By the same token the familiar principles of science and technology are the cultural heritage that will determine the specifics of satellite probes and space colonies. Gerard K. O'Neill has been explicit on this point. The colonies he envisages can be designed, built, and sent into space by applying current knowledge about the chemistry of lunar resources, propulsion methods for moving matter about in the vacuum of space, and construction techniques for building the colonies. No esoteric, unrealized scientific or engineering skill is required. From a social science standpoint it seems virtually certain that the space pioneers who occupy colonies like O'Neill's will exhibit all the personality traits found in a typical cross-section of the population: rich, poor, beggar, thief—both male and female. This is admittedly an untested opinion which could be disproved. Just as the engineer is constrained in thinking about life elsewhere by the agreed-upon laws of physical science, the social scientist (in this case, I myself) is influenced in speculating about the psychological consequences of life in space by what is found on Earth. Both may be correct in their predictions, but it may take several centuries of life in space before we know for sure whether conditions on Earth are typical of conditions throughout the rest of the Galaxy.

The psychology of human perception also has a pivotal role in the Earth-bound quest to find meaningful signals in radio waves from outer space. This venture really is a sequence of steps, each requiring a creative mix of scientific theory, engineering hardware, and astute observation. The radio telescope must be pointed at just the right star at just the right time; the instrument must be sensitive enough to register the signal; and finally, a recognition device must distinguish the signal from uninformative noise, from naturally occurring astronomical phenomena, and from radio interference generated here on Earth. Only then can we begin to decipher the meaning of the message—that is, begin the job of signal identification. Until that point, we continue to devise and operate some sophisticated equipment to identify strange events in the by-now-familiar radio context of the Galaxy. As far as perceptual theory is concerned, this situation places the astronomer in exactly the same position as a person who stands watch every night in hopes of sighting a UFO amid the familiar context of the Moon and stars.

The UFOlogist's problem in drawing valid inferences from incomplete visual data is the one faced by the astronomer who must interpret the radio space portrayed on a computer console. Therefore, human variables affecting the sighting of unidentified flying objects are the very ones affecting sightings of unidentified flying radio waves.

Astronomers tell us that the patterns we are looking for will be represented as differences in energy picked up by radio telescopes, acting in concert with computers that can monitor the energy present in millions of wavelengths simultaneously. The energy pattern across wavelengths can then be transformed into any type of stimulus one wants: most likely light or sound, but possibly vibration and even chemical odors and tastes (astronomers, with good reason, perhaps have not considered the latter viable alternatives). Specifically, we could arrange matters so that the greater the physical energy at a given wavelength, the brighter the light at a particular location on a TV screen. Consider what such a visual pattern would look like. A given instant (say a second) in time would be depicted as a long row of a million points of brightness, each level representing the energy present at a single wavelength. The entire pattern stretched out over time would consist of a string of such rows extending from the top to the bottom of the screen.

Suppose, then, that we believe certain wavelengths convey messages from alien civilizations. If a beam of intense energy were received at a single wavelength over an extended period, it would create a line of bright light down the screen. The immediate problem is to detect and recognize such patterns of light when they are of weak intensity and lie hidden in background noise. What are the appropriate methods for proceeding, and how do our methods rely on familiar context and preconceptions of signal type? In the broadest sense, the answer is this: The methodological resources at our disposal are animals and machines, and effective use of either strongly depends on expectations created by past experiences. More specifically, before examining these options we should have a better idea about what is meant by "detection" and "recognition." It is often thought that a pattern can be detected but not recognized and that a recognized pattern need have no particular meaning. I hope to convince the reader to think otherwise.

Assume that a machine is built for the sole purpose of detecting patterns. The details of its physical realization, whether a computer program, a smart robot, or whatever, must incorporate definite notions about the sorts of patterns to be detected. An electronic counter offers a good example. Suppose we want a counter to tally the cosmic rays penetrating the Earth down to an underground laboratory. Quite obviously, such a counter would be powerless to detect automobile traffic or buffalo grazing on the grasslands above. So the major decision that must be incorporated into the counter turns on the particular events to be recorded. The equipment is then built to accomplish that specific task; use in alternative detection roles may be totally impractical. There is no such thing as a piece of hardware that performs all-purpose signal detection.

Similarly, the recognition of a pattern, once detected, implies preknowledge of that pattern's features. By "recognition" we imply an apprehension of something already experienced. If a pattern must be known beforehand, its eventual labeling doesn't reveal anything new, except its presence in a different setting. More important, a familiar pattern perceived anew must already have meaning, since it was seen before and remembered in a meaningful context; in this sense, background noise is a meaningful context, and extraterrestrial signals must stand out from this context. Applying this logic to the search for extraterrestrial intelligence I reach the pessimistic conclusion that a search cannot begin in earnest until we know what it is we are looking for. But the very nature of alien signals is still at issue, and this makes the detection problem distinct from all others addressed by scientists grappling with the riddles of perception occurring under ordinary circumstances. In SETI we seek a needle in a haystack when nobody knows what the needle looks like, and everyone hopes (and some pray) that the haystack is the radio activity of the Galaxy and not some other familiar context, such as the visible light spectrum.

The situation is like asking someone to fetch an object without giving the person the benefit of knowing whether the object is alive or dead, big or small, red or blue, friendly or dangerous. Moreover, we refuse to answer any queries regarding its distinguishing properties. The chances are slight that the mystery object will be retrieved under these conditions. The comparable problem in SETI requires that educated guesses be made about the appropriate devices to detect and recognize patterns that may or may not exist.

One thing we can do to improve the validity of these guesses is rely on our perceptual resources: animals, humans, and their physical artifacts. The sensory receptors of animals are quite varied and through evolutionary pressures have come to serve the diverse survival needs of their host organisms. Although the sensory capabilities of humans are reasonably adequate compared with those of other animals, specific advantages in the operating range and sensitivity of some animals are well documented. To reel off a few examples, the hawk has four times the visual acuity of the human, both dolphin and bat can hear and produce sound frequencies well above the upper limit of the human ear, dogs have an exceptional sense of smell, and so forth.

Animals have evolved sensory receptors for detecting special patterns. These receptors work together as tiny physiological templates, much in the way one stencils pictures on a piece of cloth by using a cardboard template which allows paint to get on the material in certain places and not in others. A classic biological example is the groups of cells in the frog's eye which respond vigorously whenever a small spot of light or dark falls on them, spots of a size that would be seen in the natural world as a bug located within reach of an agile tongue. The visual systems of primates, on the other hand, are especially sensitive to sharp boundaries of light and dark. Straight lines and angles projected onto the light-sensitive part of the eye (retina) are encoded by matching templates composed of hundreds of receptor units. Other mammals have exceptional hearing. The bottle-nosed dolphin can detect and produce streams of auditory clicks of ultra high frequency, and cells in the auditory brain of the cat respond selectively to a continuous rise or fall in pitch. These physiological antennae determine the types of patterns an organism will notice in the natural environment. If an impinging stimulus does not effectively excite one of the available templates, the animal simply will not react to its presence.

The ultimate role of these selective receptors is to alert creatures to events of survival value. Either the arousal of sensory templates leads to an automatic behavioral response, or else learning intervenes before the information extracted from the environment can direct the behavior necessary to meet the animal's needs. An instance of an automatic response to a visual pattern is the frightened chicken who flees the shadow cast by a hawk without having to be taught that hawks are not the chicken's best friend. Another example is the frog's reflexive tongue flick to snare a passing fly. The classic experiments by the Nobel laureate Roger Sperry showed that if the frog's eyeball is inverted surgically, but the original neural connections between the eye and brain/motor areas are kept intact, the frog always aims downward to catch a fly that now is actually overhead, and vice versa. Unfortunately for a hungry frog, and thankfully for the fly, no amount of practice seems to undo this inborn but surgically redirected reflex. The frog will starve to death before adjusting to the bizarre nature of its perceptual world. In the essential activity of securing food, the perceptual-behavioral connection is relatively fixed. In sum, all animals are restricted in the types of patterns they can detect and recognize by the specialized receptor units they possess.

In the same way, the search for signals in radio waves is framed by the astronomer's imagination in being able to anticipate the most likely patterns; and these will bear a close resemblance to that which is already familiar. Under these circumstances, it would be beneficial to enlarge the repertory of pattern detectors to include examples from the wider pool of cells present throughout the animal kingdom. Assuming the radio energy recovered from space could be transformed to make it suitable for any brand of sense organ, the automatic, unlearned behavior of animals might then signal the presence of patterns that are interesting from the standpoint of the animals who react to them. Despite most animals' inability to exercise much control over the affairs of other species, earthly communication with extraterrestrial life will affect all creatures' well-being and ways of life. This global, biological perspective on SETI is often overshadowed by thoughts about the long-awaited human rewards of a search.

Since the range of sensory-behavior reflexes in even the highest primates has not been fully cataloged, it would be best to employ the perceptual systems of as many species as possible. In order to conclude that a pattern had been detected by an animal we would still have to see a consistent behavioral act associated with an identifiable pattern, but the preknowledge necessary to define a pattern would not have to be acquired beforehand, since it would flow naturally from the organism's innate receptive abilities. Because of the uncertainties involved in transforming the energy of radio waves into suitable forms for various animals, and because we have only a rudimentary understanding of their natural reflexes, this approach would have to be buttressed by a fresh influx of basic and applied research. The option should not be discarded for this reason, though in the current political climate, it probably will be. I mention this rather far-out strategy to highlight a few of the alternatives that are overlooked by astronomers whose training does not predispose them to consider options outside their areas of expertise. Like everyone else, they tend to be confined by their familiar perceptual world to well-worn tracks that simply fail to reach all the possibilities.

It is also conceivable that we could teach some of the smarter animals, such as dogs, cats, monkeys, and dolphins, to be selectively vigilant for patterns in auditory or visual displays. Perceptual learning is easier to orchestrate with these creatures than it is with humans, because by today's standards of morality, the freedom of animals is regulated by human needs and priorities. Whatever one's personal feelings on this matter, it is true that animals can be induced literally to dedicate their lives to a boring task. Animal lovers are reminded of their inadvertent power to teach their pets the association between food and environmental prompts. The sound of the can opener, the rattle of the food dish, and the opening of the refrigerator all come to have timely import for a hungry pet. One of the overweight cats sharing my home spins expectantly on hind legs whenever a person nears his food dish, and the sound of the can opener is a potent signal to encourage his instant return to the house from any spot in the neighborhood.

Having decided on the patterns we expect to discover in radio waves, it would be possible to train animals to react appropriately, that is, to sound the alarm whenever that pattern was encountered. Laboratory experiments also have shown that once such reactions are learned, they will persist in the absence of food incentives. But the target patterns would still be chosen at our discretion and thus would mirror all the biases inherent in the scientific logic behind the search for messages from outer space.

In the end, patterns are likeliest to be found by human beings, who by dint of superior adaptability can achieve levels of perceptual mastery beyond the reach of other animals. The chief reason to enlist humans is that minimum training is required, and the search process itself motivates long-term dedication. Our tolerance for boredom is low, but we are able to let machines do the horribly repetitive tasks; if this were not true, astronomers would not entertain the idea of searching in the first place. An added plus is the human ability to generalize and recognize the same pattern in alternative contexts. The letter A can be written in lower (a) or upper (A) case, upside down (∀) or lying on its side (⋗), and yet the reader always sees the marking on the page as a valid A. Such flexibility tremendously extends the range of stimuli that we can perceive and recognize.

Equal flexibility is not found in machines programmed to identify patterns, and this explains why SETI is not just a trivial exercise in computer science. Machines have a terrible time adapting to shifts in physical context. The automatic reading of bank checks is an excellent case in point. The digits on bank checks are of a standard size, form, and location to permit reading by a machine that has stored in its memory an appropriate set of templates, one for each digit. The match between the digit and the template must be exact, since no provision is made for reading a different format, such as handwriting. Computer scientists feel that it will be quite a while before the handwriting on a check will be accurately read by machine tellers.

On the other hand, it will be difficult to maintain animal or human alertness over extended periods of time. People will become bored; animals will require retraining to stay on the job. The high-speed computer is a detector that is never bored and always vigilant. One way to circumvent its "context problem" is to pre-program a substantial number of templates, one for each possible context it might encounter. With a machine that reads digits on bank checks, for instance, the templates could be increased to include a variety of digit sizes, orientations, locations on the check, and so forth. As long as the digits were written in one of these set formats, they could be accurately processed. Of course, this machine could not learn anything to help it deal with other sorts of patterns, such as letters of the alphabet or pictures of familiar objects. To handle new categories, more templates would be needed and the machine would have to be correspondingly larger and more powerful. This is pretty much an expensive method that relies on brute force to accomplish its goals.

If a match-template approach is tried, the physical features to be represented would have to be decided upon in advance. With enough money and resources a computer template could be programmed to mimic every feature detector known to exist in the sensory realm of animals, but this approach is wildly hypothetical and divorced from economic reality. A more practical method is to isolate the distinguishing attributes of likely signals, as pinpointed by scientific argument, and then construct templates to realize this smaller pool of options. Employing the computer in this way does not improve the chances of detecting unusual patterns, because human bias is only transferred to the machine. On the other hand, the computer's speed, durability, and even temper give it some important advantages over people employed in an "on-line" capacity.

This definitely would be the way to go if we knew what the patterns were beforehand, but unfortunately, this is precisely the information we lack. The dominant attitude to date in SETI has been to sidestep the issue by proceeding as if the signals will be simple in form and easily detected. For example, one frequent assumption is that computers can be programmed to find radio beacons composed of bands of wavelengths within narrow regions of the electromagnetic spectrum. This strategy is justifiable on economic grounds, but in my opinion the scientific argument for following it is harder to come by.

How well a computer can meet the broader aims of a search program will depend heavily on a factor beyond its control—the impact of background noise. Any pristine radio signal emanating from an extraterrestrial source will be jostled about and distorted in transit, arriving here in the company of random noise. Through an ability to recognize the same pattern in many contexts, human observers are not easily fooled by background interference. It is for this reason that computers cannot carry the entire burden of signal detection. Contrary to what many physical scientists think, pattern detection by machine is far below the standards attained by human beings. Therefore, an optimum detection system should foster a synergistic, complementary relation between human and machine, the speed and power of the computer being supplemented by the superior ability of humans to notice patterns in different contexts.

What else might be said about the human side of this search team? In the view of most scientists SETI is not a high research priority. Speaking as a psychologist, I expect that individuals associated with this project must be prepared to tolerate friendly teasing from some quarters and not so friendly psychological pressure from more conservative colleagues. For this reason alone, I suspect that the present ranks of SETI are filled with people who are sincere and deeply motivated. An even greater commitment can be expected from future scientists who will have grown up with the facts of satellite probes, space colonies, and radio search programs.

Such commitment is a mixed blessing. Maintaining interest over periods of drought, consisting of a long string of failed projects, is a prerequisite for the eventual success of the enterprise, but this devotion may impede the very program some astronomers are trying to advance. Because the target signals have never been encountered before, the repeated failure to discover them could seriously weaken the urge to continue. Even the most ardent fisherman loses interest in a lake that has never yielded a single fish to anyone, ever. This negative experience will make it difficult to recognize a strike if and when it occurs: "This tug on the line can't be a fish. It must be a weed or a tire, since nobody has ever caught a fish in these waters, and I'm here only to enjoy the solitude and refreshment of the great outdoors."

At the same time the thought of a major payoff accruing from detection of signals more than counteracts the negative impact of early setbacks. For suppose it was clear that one's entire life would be changed by catching a single fish, no matter how small, from this particular lake, and that as a consequence future generations would prosper; and disease, famine, and pestilence would disappear, along with political and religious conflicts. Well, one might be prepared to spend the necessary hours on shore, casting out in hopes of enticing at least one fish onto the line. The potentially great rewards of contact with aliens, including knowledge for its own sake, will act as a strong motivator, infusing a steady supply of enthusiasm into SETI.

After the detector system is in place and running smoothly, a troublesome problem will still remain. People, animals, and computers have their own inherent properties that lead to false reports of signals that are not really there. If we examine millions of radio frequencies for hours at a time, there is a high probability by chance alone that bogus signals will be generated by the background noise and thereby will be mistaken for genuine signals. If the alarm is sounded, it always will be necessary to investigate more carefully to determine its actual cause. We really know nothing about how alien civilizations might wish to contact others. The messages might be hidden in radio waves, in the currents of the oceans, in the light from a nearby cluster of stars, or in the meowing of a house cat. It is a depressing but defensible thought that under such uncertainty all detection devices are equally good, and each will trigger plenty of false alarms to keep their operators busy.

There is one sure way to reduce the false-alarm rate, and that is to insist on a narrow definition of signal types. If we were convinced that aliens were identical in thought and deed to us then we could assume they would send the types of signals we would expect. But how narrow should we get in our definition of potential signals? Let's suppose that tonight I dream that extraterrestrial messages will arrive aboard a beam of green light shining through my bedroom window at seven o'clock tomorrow morning. This is a very specific statement. If I awake to check on the prediction, it is doubtful whether I will confuse any other aspect of the environment with the green beam. Either the light will appear or it won't. But although a false alarm is unlikely, most people would agree that the probability of success based on such a narrow definition of a message is also infinitesimal.

Now let's explore the opposite extreme. I am told in the dream to pay close attention to the woods behind my house because a message will be found in the uncharacteristic movement of a single leaf. Unfortunately, my cat wakes me before I learn which tree or leaf is critical. Behind my New Hampshire home there are thousands of candidate trees, each with numerous leaves, and they are continually rustled about by the wind. Whenever it suits me I can observe potential messages, but even if the dream speaks the truth, I will spend the majority of my day examining leaf movement that indicates nothing of relevance. The message may be there someplace, but how to find it is the devilish part.

Although the purpose of SETI is to find signals that have meaning for the human species, most of the positive reports in a noisy environment will be false alarms. Because we lack a firm idea about the nature of the signals, we must throw a wide net to make certain no candidates slip by. As the net widens it captures more true signals but simultaneously tosses more bogus events into the same bin. The dilemma, then, is this. If we carefully define the probable signal types and build specialized devices to note the presence of this small list of possibilities, the risk goes up for missing true signals. They might not fit the pattern templates we happen to select. This appears, nonetheless, to be the current strategy of SETI enthusiasts. Speaking in their defense, if the detection devices are made too general and respond to all manner of activity, we will waste a thousand lifetimes weeding out false alarms. Background noise is an anathema to the search process because it can occupy all the detection resources while true signals remain sunk within a morass of noise.

That nonscientists hold such a wide-net attitude is probably responsible for the numerous reports of UFOs, and the subsequent scientific checking of their validity is very time-consuming. The demands of time may explain why few scientists are willing to devote effort to this kind of detective work. There may have been occasions in the past when spacecraft from other planets visited Earth, but their presence would have been lost amid the false alarms. The same fate could befall a wide-net strategy for SETI.

Without the luxury of theorizing about potential signal types no search can be initiated. This much is evident. Fashioning a scientific argument to justify a limited search strategy should not disguise what is going on here. The current SETI program is geared to look for a small class of expected signal types, admittedly chosen on the basis of scientific knowledge (e.g., the efficiency of transmission at different wavelengths, the filtering effects of the atmosphere, and background radiation). Our chance for success stands or falls on the adequacy of the choices. This reality should not deter the search, but it does suggest that modesty is in order when making claims about the probable success rate of the venture. Not only must we assume the existence of extraterrestrial civilizations with a desire to advertise their existence through radio messages, but in addition we must assume that these messages match the educated guesses of a handful of human engineers and radio astronomers. I for one would rather see some fraction of these guesses emerge from the joint advice of parties with quite different backgrounds: social scientists, writers, artists, and devotees of animal husbandry, to name a few. At present, the compartmentalization of disciplines, along with the fierce competition for limited research funds, makes collaboration of this sort extremely unlikely.

REFERENCES AND FURTHER READINGS

Baird, J. C.; Blake, T.; Healy, T.; & Schimandle, J. Human Pattern Detection and Recognition in the Search for Extraterrestrial Intelligence. *Bulletin of the Psychonomic Society,* 1982, *20,* No. 2, 74–76.
Baugher, J. F. *On Civilized Stars: The Search for Intelligent Life in Outer Space.* Englewood Cliffs, N.J.: Prentice-Hall, 1985.
Coren, S.; Porac, C.; & Ward, L. M. *Sensation and Perception.* 2nd ed. New York: Academic, 1984.
Kosslyn, S. M. *Image and Mind.* Cambridge, Mass.: Harvard University Press, 1980.
Lettvin, J. Y.; Maturana, H. R.; McCulloch, W. S.; & Pitts, W. H. What the Frog's Eye Tells the Frog's Brain. *Proceedings of the Institute of Radio Engineers,* 1959, *47,* 1940–1951.
Lord, S.; Dixon, R.; & Healy, T. (Eds.) *Project Oasis: The Design of a Signal Detector for the Search for Extraterrestrial Intelligence.* Santa Clara, Calif.: University of Santa Clara, technical report, 1981.
Oliver, B. M. (Ed.) *Project Cyclops: A Design Study of a System for Detecting*

Extraterrestrial Life. CR 114445 NASA/Ames Research Center, 1971, Code LT, Moffett Field, Calif. 94035.

O'Neill, G. K. *The High Frontier: Human Colonies in Space.* New York: Morrow, 1977; Bantam, 1978.

Sperry, R. W. Mechanisms of Neural Maturation. In S. S. Stevens (Ed.), *Handbook of Experimental Psychology,* pp. 236–280. New York: Wiley, 1951.

Turnbull, C. M. *The Forest People.* New York: Simon & Schuster, 1961.

Verne, J. *A Journey to the Center of the Earth.* New York: Airmont, 1965.

Von Däniken, E. *Chariots of the Gods?* New York: Putnam, 1969.

CHAPTER 10

THE SOFT AND HARD OF
CULTURAL MEMORY

Perception of the environment is a continuous process unfolding in time as well as space. If the recognition of events at one point in space-time is to be compared with events at another, some psychological means must be provided to encode and preserve representations of the world for more than the moment. Indeed, the apprehension of the present is inevitably shaped and directed by memorial remnants of the past. The spatial and temporal scales of such memories are marked in units appropriate to the daily activities of humans, from centimeters to kilometers, from seconds to years. Other units, such as nanoseconds (billionths of a second) or light-years (the distance light travels in a year), have no psychological correlate in human experience, and yet either of these units could be important in trying to communicate with aliens; indeed, a light-year seems to be the most appropriate unit.

The scale bounded by a person's lifetime may be pitifully small when considering dialogue between extraterrestrial cultures, where we may face a realm of time and distance that far exceeds the sum experience of the human race throughout its existence on this planet. This enlarged reference scale creates unique problems, requiring as it does the use of long-term memory devices that are presently unavailable and probably will remain so into the foreseeable future. The difficulty is not simply one of allocating sufficient room to store facts collected over long time spans; in addition, it involves the intelligent arrangement of these facts to ensure rapid access and easy use. On the human scale such storage and retrieval processes are exercised on a regular basis, and the psychological principles apparent there may apply as well to the larger space-time vistas dealt with in a SETI program. This chapter examines the possibility.

I do not discuss here the very latest physical memory devices available to the SETI researcher. Although recent advances have led to increases in computer storage space and speed of retrieving information from memory, the storage is still small with respect to the potential amount received by a radio telescope over the course of a single evening of observation, and in any event, these advances do nothing to enhance our understanding about which particular information should be targeted for long-term storage and efficient retrieval. It is not simply a matter of "more is better."

The retrieval problem can best be appreciated by example. One adult I remember very well from childhood was a family friend who never seemed to throw anything away. He acquired and squirreled away all manner of odds and ends, everything from thumbtacks to discarded outboard motors, from faded photographs to pieces of string and old newspapers. Although my friend made a weekly pilgrimage to the town dump, he often returned with more than he left behind, being especially pleased to discover electrical and mechanical gadgets—old toasters, washing machine parts, small motors, and the like. His sentiment was that one could never tell when some rusty scrap of technology might come in handy, and when that occasion arose, he would be well equipped to meet the challenge. At least that was the plan in theory. Unfortunately, there were physical constraints that rendered the ideal thoroughly unworkable. In the first place, he lived with his family in a modest house on a quarter-acre lot, and although both the cellar and the garage were chock full, there was after all a finite amount of space. At some point he had to curb his acquisitive urge and stem the growth of a sprawling mass of goods that threatened to take over the entire neighborhood.

The second constraint he ran into was practical access. The items were not organized to aid retrieval, being pretty much stored in the order in which they arrived on the premises. This season's "finds" were piled on top of last season's. With both house and garage overflowing with things gathered at random over many years, it was impossible to recover anything on demand. And whenever he launched a time-consuming search for something and couldn't track it down, he was never sure whether it ever existed on the premises, whether it was moved by himself or some other member of the family, or whether it had been—God forbid—taken to the dump.

There is a parallel here to human memory in that we have both a storage and a retrieval problem when we attempt to encode information over time in a form that allows us to recall it on demand. My friend's plight also parallels that facing the human species as it tries to connect with faraway civilizations. If we send a space probe to another star system, the satellite will be sending messages back to Earth throughout a long voyage and for some additional period thereafter, assuming an encountered target warrants attention. If we were visited in the past by aliens or find ourselves hosting future engagements, the significance of such occasions, though great, will probably ebb and flow over the centuries; and if we ever do make radio contact, the ensuing dialogue may proceed at different rates over the course of millions of years. My focus in what follows is on this last eventuality and, in particular, the implications for SETI of human memory limits. A related story line could be spun for other ways of seeking out alien contacts: space colonization, UFOs, or satellite probes. With minor adjustments, the gist of my argument holds for these forms as well.

There is no telling what the magnitude of the time scale will be for the reception and interpretation of messages from outer space. It will most likely be lengthy in comparison with the time over which we have had the technology to receive messages, which many scientists mark from the birth of radio astronomy about forty years ago. Even to achieve the modest goal of signal detection may require constant vigilance, stretching over many generations of astronomers, psychologists, and politicians. Moreover, the information in a message string may be temporally extended and hence not understood unless we keep complete, durable records. Such records raise unusual memory problems for the search program because humans generally are not adept at storing large sums of data in an accurate form for a long time.

The formal discipline of history must always contend with problems of memory. Those on the forefront of this comparatively young social science are still groping to establish methods to describe the sequence and interconnection of events from the past. The disagreements among historians attempting to identify the factors behind major world incidents occurring one hundred, fifty, or as few as twenty-five years ago suggest that the loss of cultural knowledge in the short run is notable and over the span of modern civilization is substantial. Nonetheless, society's increased awareness of the value of historical reasoning, mostly brought about, I suppose, by the advent of superior memory devices, such as film, television, records, and computer tapes, may help us cope with the memory demands that are sure to accompany a full-scale SETI effort. So let's push on to ask exactly how memory devices might help and/or hinder this effort.

There are several options for storing and transmitting knowledge for very long times—say, greater than fifty years and less than two thousand years. The oldest, but least understood, is the "soft" option afforded by the human brain, which has the potential for saving enormous amounts of knowledge through the efficient use of roughly 100 billion biological cells. If the Earth's population were recruited to collect messages from outer space, the available brain cells would be the number of volunteers multiplied by 100 billion—a staggering number of opportunities for saving critical facts. However, it would be hard to find even a single brain willing to devote all its resources to the cause of storing the collective wisdom of aliens, and in any case, the contents of memory would have to be transmitted to another brain every sixty or seventy years, on each occasion laying open the possibility for encoding errors and the loss of information. The original information might be badly distorted after only a few generations.

Unfortunately, brain tissue does not preserve well, biological cells die, and so far as we know the mental contents dissipate along with the physical matter. Despite the many hurdles blocking its use, human memory will certainly play a focal role in SETI and thus will set constraints on the type of information recalled and on the degree to which it can be accessed, updated, and maintained. Therefore, it is reasonable to look into what is known about human memory.

Psychologists find it convenient to classify memory into three categories: sensory, short-term, and long-term. Sensory memory is extremely brief, able to hold new information on the order of a second or so. It appears to serve as a temporary storage medium allowing the brain more time to process the deeper meaning behind what a person perceives. That is, when we look at a scene and then turn away, there remains an image of that scene in the visual system, but this image persists in a usable form for only about a quarter of a second, and after a second, it has disappeared altogether. While this snapshot memory has not been extensively studied in other sense modalities, such as the ear, nose, or tongue, sensory images no doubt occur there as well, and the rate of memory decay might well depend on the modality. In all instances, however, the effective retention of incoming information is probably brief.

One of the positive features of sensory memory is its exceedingly large capacity. Judging from experiments by the psychologist George Sperling, the visual system retains faithful images of complex visual scenes, but these images fade very rapidly. So from what we understand about sensory memory it seems likely that SETI researchers will use it only for driving to work safely and for walking around their radio telescopes without tripping over wires and bumping into computer terminals. This snapshot memory has the capacity to hold a tremendous amount of information, but for such a brief time as to make it unusable as a device to store messages from the stars.

It is true that an occasional individual seems to possess a so-called photographic memory, but such people are rare and have not been the subject of much study. The Russian psychologist Aleksandr Luria discussed one such person, a professional mnemonist blessed with the talent for recalling complex material for months and even years after being exposed to it for only a few minutes. He could easily reproduce tables of fifty one-digit numbers or a comparable string of letters. Apparently, the mnemonist converted the material into an elaborate memory image assembled from the contributions of all the sense modalities: sound, smell, touch, taste, and vision. Luria examined his performance over the course of thirty years and was continually amazed by his feats of memory. The man's synesthetic reactions, involving all the senses, are described by Luria in this excerpt from his book: "What this meant was that S. [the mnemonist] was one of a remarkable group of people, among them the composer Scriabin, who have retained in an especially vivid form a 'complex' synesthetic type of sensitivity. In S.'s case every sound he heard immediately produced an experience of light and color and, as we shall see later in this account, a sense of taste and touch as well" (*The Mind of a Mnemonist,* p. 24).

Many instances of this vivid imagery are thoroughly discussed in Luria's report. As we can see from the quotation above, S's "photographic memory" was in fact dependent on sensory associations. This fellow also had peculiar associations with numbers, as he once explained to Luria:

> For me 2, 4, 6, 5 are not just numbers. They have forms. 1 is a pointed number—which has nothing to do with the way it's written. It's because it's somehow firm and complete. 2 is flatter, rectangular, whitish in color, sometimes almost a gray. 3 is a pointed segment which rotates. 4 is also square and dull; it looks like a 2 but has more substance to it, it's thicker. 5 is absolutely complete and takes the form of a cone or a tower—something substantial. 6, the first number after 5, has a whitish hue; 8 somehow has a naive quality, it's milky blue like lime . . . [P. 26]

One might think that life would be a cinch for someone who could remember everything that ever passed his way, but this was far from the case for S. One of his major shortcomings was that he could not selectively forget, and hence his mind became filled with a jumble of superimposed images. He also had trouble noticing basic logical connections among the items he had memorized. He reacted to a table of digits arranged in increasing order of magnitude (1, 2, 3, 4, . . .) in the same manner as a random list of digits. In both cases, the pattern of numbers was recorded in memory as a series of sensory experiences, devoid of any special meaning among the elements—a meaning that most of us would see instantly. For this reason, it is doubtful if Luria's gifted subject would have been especially useful as a detector of patterns received by a radio telescope and displayed on a video screen for his perusal. He would have lacked the integrative skill to grasp the pattern inherent in a sequence of separate scenes. A photographic memory is not a prerequisite, or a particular advantage, for either pattern detection or recognition.

The second soft storage system, short-term memory, has a more impressive operating range than sensory memory, on the order of twenty to thirty seconds. Facts kept in this medium must be rehearsed if they are to be held intact. A familiar use of short-term memory occurs whenever you look up a telephone number and keep it in mind between the moment your eyes leave the page and your fingers finish dialing. I myself have trouble remembering new phone numbers for more than a few seconds, and people who don't suffer such memory lapses tell me they rehearse during the time between seeing and dialing the number. Any outside interference or even an extraneous thought may disrupt concentration and erase the number from memory.

If humans ever serve as perceptual devices in SETI, they will be scanning video screens, listening to loudspeakers, and poring over tables of astronomical data. One strong cue indicating that a message is present would be a pattern that repeated itself over and over in a regular sequence. If this ever happened, short-term memory would set upper bounds on how long information could be retained so that comparisons could be made from one sample of the pattern to the next. If it took more than a half minute or so for a single event to unfold, an observer would be unlikely to recognize it as familiar, and rehearsal would not help because the observer might not realize that the early phase of a message was really part and parcel of a larger picture. That is, there would be no way to decide what should be rehearsed until the entire pattern was revealed, and that is precisely the knowledge we would lack.

Computers can be programmed to compare patterns that emerge over longer periods, but the machine still must be told what to lay aside in its memory banks in order to make such comparisons. There simply is not enough storage space in today's computers to save all the data collected at the millions of frequencies (wavelengths) received by a radio telescope directed to scan the radio emissions from thousands of stars. To keep careful records of all the incoming data would be prohibitively expensive and inefficient.

On the other hand, once a pattern was extracted from the background noise, it could be stored in the third major soft system, long-term human memory, and reclaimed later for use in matching the familiar aspects of new information. Despite the prodigious growth of computer memory in recent years, the human being is still the best pattern-recognizing device on the market. Visual memory for familiar patterns, such as human faces, written text, or city buildings, is quite remarkable.

The psychologist Ray Nickerson was among the first to verify this superiority. He presented adults with two hundred photographs of faces for five seconds each. He later asked them to distinguish between photos they had seen previously and ones they had not. Accuracy was at the 95 percent level a few minutes after seeing the pictures, and dropped only to 63 percent when people were queried after a full year had elapsed. Roger Shepard independently found that people recognized 99 percent of six hundred magazine pictures that they had been shown two days previously, and that almost 60 percent of the pictures still were recalled after four months. Even more extraordinary are the results of L. Standing, who studied a few gifted individuals able to recognize 70 percent of ten thousand different pictures!

The brain is capable of storing complex patterns in long-term memory, so long as these patterns are comprehensible and easily distinguished one from the other. So if we know what to look for in SETI, and can separate targets from background noise, we should be able to recognize the same patterns on future occasions with great fidelity.

In point of fact, however, if the targets are known beforehand, it probably will be better to instruct a computer to seek them out, rather than employ a team of bored humans for the task. The human observer may identify an interesting signal in the first place, but a computer would prove more efficient in subsequent searches to isolate the same signal again, provided the pattern were not observed in a new context. So it seems likely that a synergistic relationship will evolve between human and machine pattern recognizers, each doing what they do best.

Whatever the memory system, the maintenance of stored knowledge is a problem when the separate facts do not fit together as a meaningful whole. Without a meaningful context, rehearsal is absolutely essential. Several cognitive psychologists have demonstrated the need for frequent rehearsal if information is to be maintained over periods of years, that is, if long-term memory is to be used effectively.

In a longitudinal study of her own memory, Marigold Linton learned the Latin names of six hundred plants. After viewing pictures of the plants and learning the proper Latin names for each, she tested her memory after the passage of various time intervals. The idea was to determine how often one must rehearse in order to remember accurately. Since she knew little about botanical terms before the experiment, she mastered the six hundred plant names by rote. Under these conditions she found that memory for a particular item must be refreshed at intervals of anywhere from two weeks to several months if material already learned is to be recollected during a test session. Without adequate rehearsal, what was once known infallibly will fade from long-term memory—unless the material is incorporated into an existing, meaningful context. One may confidently state that one saw an item previously, but then fail to recall its name. It is doubtful if people could properly name six hundred novel faces presented as stand-alone photos, even though they could confidently say in a large percentage of cases whether they had seen them before.

When it comes to remembering new material, there is no substitute for a context of relevant knowledge, safely registered in long-term memory. An intriguing example is furnished by the game of chess. The Dutch psychologist Adrien De Groot and the Americans W. G. Chase and Herbert A. Simon have conducted studies of players and their ability to reconstruct the positions of pieces on a chessboard. De Groot found that master chess players consider fewer moves in a game than do novices and that for them the most appropriate alternatives simply pop to mind as the best choices. They do not waste time considering bad moves! Does this mean that the master chess player's memory is better than the novice's? Apparently not. Chase and Simon tested the aptitude of a master player, a good class A player, and a beginner. Each was shown a board with pieces located in positions that routinely occur in actual matches, and after viewing the board for five seconds, they tried to reproduce it from memory. The master player was best at this task, the class A player second best, and the novice worst. When, however, the pieces were randomly arranged on the board in unlikely game positions, the experts had no special advantage over the beginner. In fact, the master player recalled the positions of the fewest pieces. In other words, the context provided by the rules of chess and by the meaningful grouping of pieces allowed the most advanced player to recall the groupings on the board better than players of lesser caliber, but this superior performance could not be laid at the doorstep of memory. When the meaningful context was eliminated, the experienced master was on a par with the rank novice.

The potential implications for SETI are these. If an astronomer happens to observe a series of patterns that do not cohere into a meaningful whole, these patterns will be promptly forgotten unless they crop up again within the time frame needed to renew their representation in long-term memory. The repetition of these individual patterns, however, may also permit the astronomer to grasp a higher-order sense of things, obtained by seeing many parts of the puzzle within a short time frame. The astronomer will be successful only if the critical information is imprinted in memory, so that it can be quickly retrieved and matched against incoming patterns. This brings us to the question of how well one can recover information already saved in memory.

There is a popular idea in some quarters of clinical psychology that anything learned simply stays in memory indefinitely. According to this view, we don't really forget anything; once material is mastered it is retained by the brain forevermore. The indisputable fact that people do indeed forget things is explained away by blaming retrieval mechanisms. By this line of reasoning, information may be in memory but inactive and inaccessible. The brain's catalog system is likened to my friend's garage: Whatever is put there stays, but one can't unearth it from beneath the mass of irrelevant information. In practical terms, some memories might just as well be lost, because they cannot be brought to conscious awareness.

If the human brain really did work this way, the implications for SETI would be great. Presumably, a person monitoring a stream of radio signals (meaningful or not) could store everything seen or heard in long-term memory. If a genuine ETI signal were noted and stored, it would be necessary only to retrieve it from memory at one's leisure. In fact, however, this task may not be easy.

It has been claimed that methods exist to bypass the drawbacks of memory retrieval. For example, electrical stimulation of the brain elicits apparent recall of events, hypnosis supposedly reveals deep-hidden memories, and psychoanalysis has long been recommended for dredging up memories of painful or repressed experiences from the past. Apparently, judging from the prevalence of news releases on these topics, the validity of these sundry methods is widely accepted by the lay public. We are bombarded with fresh cases every day. Bold headlines frequently tout the claim that hypnosis, in particular, is an effective means to revive permanent memories which for some reason or other have been lost to conscious awareness.

Many poignant examples are described in Eugene Block's book

Hypnosis: A New Tool in Crime Detection. Block tells us of the purported successes of police departments throughout the world in using hypnosis to crack a variety of unsolved, notorious cases. It is not surprising that people will grasp at any hopeful straw when all else fails. From the psychoanalyst's couch to the physician's medicine cabinet, people are eager to try anything, orthodox or not, in search of relief from physical and emotional stress. And whether a cure for a disease or the solution of a crime is actual or imaginary is irrelevant in at least one respect: If the individual feels better and thinks matters have improved, the treatment or advice will be seen as well worth the money.

I have no quarrel with the psychological practitioner. Hypnosis may be a fine way to encourage people to verbalize what is bothering them, and thereby help clear up their personal problems. However, the fact that a personal malady is alleviated does not imply that the patient under hypnosis has actually recalled events from the past with any degree of accuracy.

The Australian Kevin McConkey, an expert in hypnosis, tells me that it is true that individuals in a trancelike state are able to give exquisitely detailed descriptions of events from the past, but that in some instances people under hypnosis also carry on about events which could not possibly have happened. For example, when the eyewitness to a crime is put into a hypnotic trance he or she may describe the unique features of the protagonist's face: "The guy had long hair, a moustache, and a scar on his left cheek." It might be easily shown, however, that such details would have been impossible to make out from the point where the observer claims to have been standing. Perhaps the witness wouldn't have had an unobstructed view, or perhaps the visual system could not resolve details of a face from such a distant point.

More impressive are cases where someone under hypnosis can be coaxed to report on childhood experiences and to fantasize about what will happen in the future. In "age regression" the person may tell stories that are impossible to validate one way or the other. Nonetheless, the reports are delivered with confidence and are often tinged with what appears to be genuine emotion. In "age progression," attempting to gaze into the future, the person may fabricate many "facts" about hypothetical events and people—even though he or she obviously has never had the opportunity to experience the facts which are disclosed with such authority and conviction.

That someone is able to give a careful and full account of a previous event does not mean that the person is reporting on a true experience. The tendency to lie under hypnosis may be quite innocent and unconscious. Still, regardless of the good intentions of those wishing to cure some of humanity's ills through hypnosis, I think we can safely say that this technique should have no prominent role in the search for alien intelligence.

Stricter criteria for success must be applied when seeking a reliable memory device in SETI. To be a serious contender, a method such as hypnosis must leave no shred of doubt concerning its effectiveness. It must be reliable and well understood on scientific grounds. In this regard, laboratory experiments into the nature of human memory are not encouraging. The findings indicate that we do not store faithful representations of everything that happens to us, and therefore, breakdowns in the brain's retrieval mechanisms cannot be the only reason we fail to recall past events. Furthermore, much of what is supposedly recovered through hypnosis bears little resemblance to the original event, a conclusion reached as well from experiments on the function of human memory.

The most telling evidence on these matters has been gathered by Elizabeth and Geoffrey Loftus of the University of Washington. Their view is that reported memories are mainly reconstructions of the original occurrence as inferred from fragmentary information, probably kept in active memory through periodic rehearsal. While recalled scenes are vivid and realistic, they still may bear only a passing resemblance to the actual event. As the novelist Lawrence Block suggests, "The memory is a cooperative animal, eager to please; what it cannot supply it occasionally invents, sketching carefully to fill in the blanks" (*A Stab in the Dark,* p. 30).

The Loftuses note that one common way to produce a distorted picture of the past is through the clever or inadvertent use of leading questions. To illustrate: Suppose you go on a bird-watching expedition in the country. Upon your return home your neighbor asks, "How many red-winged blackbirds did you see?" Although you may have seen nary a one, the very nature of the question makes you think carefully to see if you can dredge up even the slightest evidence to support the idea, now firmly planted in your mind, that you indeed saw a blackbird. Your neighbor's very words, "how many," presuppose that you spotted at least one and probably more than one. So upon further reflection you might remember a small patch of red in a willow tree or a flutter of orange and black in the bushes by the picnic basket. By sheer inference, and quite unconsciously, you decide that these fragments revealed the presence of a red-winged blackbird. In fact, you may recover from memory some birdlike features that you noticed at entirely different points along your walk, but from which you now, when these features are considered together, construct in your mind's eye a realistic image of a red-winged blackbird. You then answer your neighbor with a clear conscience by saying, "Oh, I saw one for sure, and caught fleeting glances of a few others."

If the remembrance of things past depends on making valid inferences from partial information, we would expect many of these inferences to be distorted and inaccurate. This suspicion has been verified experimentally without resorting to hypnosis. Misleading clues introduced well after the fact influence the fidelity of recall. Apart from the importance of such results for evaluating the veracity of eyewitness reports in criminal court cases, experiments on memory highlight the inherent weakness of the brain as a repository for detailed information. Even if it is true that events can be permanently stored in long-term memory, subsequent experiences interfere and change the recall of those events, in some instances leading to marked distortions of the truth.

By the same logic the human brain should not be trusted to give an impeccable rendition of signals obtained in a search for ETI, whether that rendition is based on patterns in radio waves, satellite data, or perceptions of UFOs. Scientific blunders will surely ensue if we forget that human memory is after all an impermanent medium, subject to distortion, influenced by a myriad of environmental factors, and certainly not on a par with physical devices like video, audio, and computer tapes. The brain is not a high-tech videotape recorder.

If, however, scientists are funded by governments or private foundations to look for ETI, the scholarly and economic stakes will encourage leading questions. After a decade of support, I expect a funding agency to inquire: "How many ETI sightings has your research team made during the grant period?" Such a query is sure to send researchers rummaging through discarded data files in hopes of turning up data that can be massaged and molded into a minor success story. If failure to detect means termination of grant support, loss of jobs, and deflation of egos, scientists will resist admitting the whole truth as much as anyone else would. A thorough memory search is likely to uncover at least one jewel to justify continuation of the agency's trust and financial backing. Inferences made from partial information about the presence of signals will not be outright lies, but only the natural result of placing undue weight on an imperfect memory device—the human brain.

Looking on the brighter side, we do know that people are adept at keeping alive traditions of broad cultural significance, without the aid of physical storage devices. For millennia the spirit behind civilized behavior was sustained by communities of people who felt obliged to transfer cultural values to their children. Until comparatively recently, word of mouth was the favored way to relay social rules and customs from one generation to the next. The original facts germane to society's traditions and legends may have undergone change with each telling, but the major thrusts of the messages were preserved and periodically renewed. Most cultural sagas of any age are metaphorical and quite impossible to link with their precipitating causes. The general message may be crystal clear, but the details are foggy.

The literal veracity of the tales found in great religious works has always been questioned. Did events really happen in the way they are described in the Great Book? These works depict a coherent picture of secular or spiritual relevance that is considered by many to embody "the truth." It might even be argued that the moral and unique integrity of a nation depends primarily on its success in convincing youth to adopt time-honored cultural values, apart from the inculcation of social rules that bind communities together over the course of a single generation.

Most assuredly, human memory will remain an effective method for storing and conveying principles relevant to the continued prosperity of civilization, and it is in this social capacity that we can anticipate its general utilization in SETI. The optimistic spirit and potential significance of contact with aliens will be kept alive through verbal communication among people with diverse perspectives: parents and children, scientists and poets, farmers and office workers. Although none of the technical details will be kept in a soft biological medium, human memory will be integral to any search program. The conclusion, then, is that we can gain much by the study of human memory and by staying apprised of its limitations. Only in this way will we be able to take advantage of its full potential in a responsible way.

The "harder" mediums for long-term storage of societal values pose their own special problems. One might consider, for instance, the use of monuments constructed out of material built to last. Classic examples are the Egyptian Pyramids, the Great Wall of China, the Mayan temples of Central and South America, and predating all of these, the megalithic stones of northern Europe. In some of these cases the structure reveals its purpose, as a gathering place to celebrate birth, encourage worship, or respect death. In others, monuments are inscribed with the symbols of written language and other meaningful patterns. Paintings, drawings, pictograms, and the like often tell a story of historical significance. But despite the awe they inspire, there are obvious disadvantages to storing information in such a durable medium. For one thing, stone monuments are expensive to build and maintain, and they are almost impossible to keep current. New information is not easily combined with the old. Ofttimes it is easier to tear down a venerable structure and start over, or wait until the forces of nature take their toll, before attempting to update the record of community achievements and concerns.

Stonehenge is one of the most notable structures of this sort in the world. Located in southwest England, it consists of a large ring of vertical stone slabs originally connected by horizontal capstones. According to the British archaeologist Glyn Daniel, Stonehenge was built in phases covering some seventeen hundred years, from 2800 B.C. to around 1100 B.C., and was most likely a meeting place for both sacred and secular occasions. It is doubtful if the purpose of these meetings remained the same over this enormous time scale, but who can tell? The true reason for building Stonehenge may lie buried with its architects and hence may remain a mystery forever. Since the goal of science is to illuminate, not mystify, an alternative means for long-term storage is desirable.

Other monuments of the same vintage have engravings that indicate the use of written language, but many of these symbol systems have never been decoded—at least not in recent history. Were it not for the lucky break of discovering the Rosetta Stone, we might still be puzzling over the Egyptian hieroglyphics. The great expense incurred in updating symbolic expressions restricts their value for the large time scales we are considering for SETI, and while these stones are physically majestic, the cultural legends they relate are ambiguous and their particular relevance for today's society cloudy.

This ambiguity is apparent in the ongoing debate about the possible role of aliens in the planning and construction of ancient monuments. Even disregarding the arguments noted in chapter 2, the heat of the controversy makes it plain that people of different value orientations arrive at divergent conclusions about the meaning of structures that presumably were built to pass on straightforward messages to future generations. In sum, it seems unlikely that memorial stones would be the medium of choice for preserving any data, general or technical, pertaining to SETI.

Books are a more compact and efficient way to maintain historical records. Unfortunately, they must be duplicated every century or so, and each transcription can introduce distortions of meaning. Languages undergo gradual transformations over the centuries, evolving to the point where earlier forms become obsolete and unintelligible to the modern reader. The stylized versions of religious books, written thousands of years ago, testify to the problems created in trying to understand historical events based on manuscripts handed down and transcribed by successive generations of scholars. Can anyone honestly answer factual questions based on the writings in the Judeo-Christian Bible, the Muslim Koran, or the Hindu Upanishads? Even some religious leaders have abandoned attempts to decipher the original intent of these documents, being satisfied instead to summarize their allegorical relevance for people living today.

A documented contact with extraterrestrial life may someday be set down in books and related storage media—microfiche, film, tapes, videodiscs—but it must be done with the utmost attention to detail if portions of the text are not to be lost or rendered unintelligible. The lifetime of these materials is measured in decades, not centuries. It is curious to think that modern technology relies on relatively flimsy storage media, as compared to the solid edifices that served this purpose in pretechnological society. What we have gained in size, speed, and efficiency seems to have been lost in long-term durability.

Another hard storage medium is the high-speed computer. Because computers and their associated memory devices are flexible and can be dedicated exclusively to communication, they offer a viable alternative to human biology, stone monuments, and books. Again, one must add the caveat that computers are by no means ideal storage devices. Programs written on one machine often "crash" badly on others, understanding and rewriting programs can be unnerving if the original author is not involved, and the lifetime of magnetic tape is not impressive when it is subjected to large fluctuations in temperature. My local computer center recommends that data on magnetic tape be restored every three to five years. Many such transcriptions will be required if SETI facts are kept in this medium over an extended period—say, on the order of a million years—and as is true with the human brain, each updating introduces the chance that error will creep in and alter the original meaning.

Another technical barrier, and one that only computers could possibly address, is posed by very large and complex data files. The current NASA plans to scan the sky for radio messages require the simultaneous storage of the energy in millions of radio frequencies monitored at one-second intervals. At present writing, the largest feasible time period for collecting such an array is about 30 minutes (1,800 seconds). So every 30 minutes we have accumulated enough data to fill a storage bin 8 million elements on one side and 1,800 on the other. Multiplying these two numbers yields a capacity of 14.4 billion cells! If nothing of scientific interest appears within this giant observation window of time and frequency, the memory banks will be erased to make room for succeeding snapshots of radio activity. One can only hope that if a signal is ever detected and understood, we will then see the need to design more efficient methods for saving and analyzing these gigantic files of data. In any case, all the information received by a radio telescope cannot be kept in permanent storage. Even if it were possible, developing a reference system to permit fast access to selected aspects of the information would remain a prodigious, unsolved problem for some time to come.

Further, the organization of data in memory will be just as important as the ability to store it in a usable form. This also is a significant barrier to SETI's ultimate success. We will have a tricky time deciding on a functional catalog system to keep track of data whose eventual use is presently unknown. Until a signal of definite extraterrestrial origin is received, we have no firm ideas about what particular aspect of the radio activity is worth retaining in permanent storage. If we were capable of holding onto all incoming information so that future astronomers could study the files in search of patterns, we still wouldn't know how this information should be arranged today to ensure rapid and accurate access tomorrow. We then would be faced with the same difficulty my friend ran into: a garage full of items but no way to locate anything on demand.

While in no way disparaging the good-faith proposals of engineers and astronomers, I can't help feeling that we have been negligent in not considering the human factors that I think will determine the fate of SETI now and in the near future. It is entertaining to indulge in romantic fantasy about the societal benefits that might accrue if we ever could interact with aliens, but it is quite another matter to develop a viable research plan to convert this fantasy into reality. Any such plan will have to reckon with the finiteness of available human and machine resources. The discovery of meaningful patterns in the present may depend on how well we keep meaningful records of the past, and this, as we have seen, is not a trivial undertaking.

REFERENCES AND FURTHER READINGS

Block, E. B. *Hypnosis: A New Tool in Crime Detection.* New York: McKay, 1976.
Block, L. *A Stab in the Dark.* New York: Arbor, 1981.
Chase, W. G., & Simon, H. A. Perception in Chess. *Cognitive Psychology,* 1973, *4,* 55–81.

Daniel, G. Megalithic Monuments. *Scientific American,* 1980, *243,* 78–90.

De Groot, A. D. *Thought and Choice in Chess.* The Hague: Mouton, 1965.

Glass, A. L.; Holyoak, K. J.; & Santa, J. C. *Cognition.* Reading, Mass.: Addison-Wesley, 1979.

Linton, M. I Remember It Well. *Psychology Today,* 1979, *13,* 80–86.

Loftus, E. F. *Eyewitness Testimony.* Cambridge, Mass.: Harvard University Press, 1979.

Loftus, E. F., & Loftus, G. R. On the Permanence of Stored Information in the Human Brain. *American Psychologist,* 1980, *35,* 409–420.

Lord, S.; Dixon, R.; & Healy, T. (Eds.) *Project Oasis: The Design of a Signal Detector for the Search for Extraterrestrial Intelligence.* Santa Clara, Calif.: University of Santa Clara, technical report, 1981.

Luria, A. R. *The Mind of a Mnemonist.* Chicago: Basic, 1968.

Nickerson, R. S. Short-Term Memory for Complex Meaningful Visual Configurations: A Demonstration of Capacity. *Canadian Journal of Psychology,* 1965, *19,* 155–160.

Sheehan, P. W., & McConkey, K. M. *Hypnosis and Experience: The Exploration of Phenomena and Process.* Hillsdale, N.J.: Erlbaum, 1982.

Shepard, R. N. Recognition Memory for Words, Sentences, and Pictures. *Journal of Verbal Learning and Verbal Behavior,* 1967, *6,* 156–163.

Sperling, G. The Information Available in Brief Visual Presentations. *Psychological Monographs,* 1960, *74* whole No. 498.

Standing, L. Learning 10,000 Pictures. *Quarterly Journal of Experimental Psychology,* 1973, *25,* 207–222.

Wingfield, A., & Byrnes, D. L. *The Psychology of Human Memory.* New York: Academic, 1981.

CHAPTER 11

DECODING THE STRUCTURE
OF LANGUAGE AND THOUGHT

Once a coherent signal is isolated against the radio background of outer space the really hard work will begin—deciphering the intent of the message. It is likely that its substance will denote something other than itself. That is, it is doubtful if a technologically advanced civilization would be exporting information for the sole purpose of advertising its expertise with the radio telescope, or would send intricate patterns for the sake of gaining high marks for aesthetics. Nobody knows for certain, but just as human language conveys facts about events in the world that can be shared by both speaker and listener, the radio speech employed by our alien neighbors probably will point to events that can be observed by sentient beings throughout the Galaxy. The critical question from our side of the fence, then, will be whether we are smart enough to comprehend the information being sent. Will humans be able to relate to the content of an alien message?

The potential barriers to such understanding are easy to anticipate, but difficult to overcome. The most serious barrier is that the information base from which aliens draw messages is likely to be richer and deeper than the base at our command. Further, the sum wisdom of the alien mind, and hence the contextual meaning of the messages chosen for export, might be far more complicated than anything we could ever hope to fathom. Finally, the language and thought processes of humans may be so foreign to those of the sender, or might represent such a minute fraction of their communication resources, as to leave the messages shrouded in mystery, no matter how long or religiously we strive to understand them.

The discrepancy in the size of the information base between the two parties raises the greatest hurdle to fruitful communication. Although the extent of this discrepancy is impossible to guess beforehand, if we are dealing with an advanced civilization, which has evolved under physical conditions quite different from those on Earth, the knowledge gap could be substantial, and even relatively minor differences in accumulated knowledge could defeat efforts to decipher the meaning of alien messages.

This situation reminds me of an enjoyable afternoon spent several years ago with a friend who invited me to observe sunspots from the roof of the local physics building. He rigged up an optical apparatus to project the image of the Sun onto a piece of cardboard so that points of intense energy looked darker on the screen. The sunspots were visible as dark patches superimposed on a large, brighter area. I estimated the size of several spots to be 1 percent of the area projected by the Sun. The full significance of this estimate did not strike home until my friend remarked that the absolute size of the distant mass responsible for each tiny spot was a swirling torrent of energy about the size of the Earth!

This is how our information base might appear when superimposed onto that of some older and wiser civilization. Although scientists are justifiably proud of how much they have learned about the physical universe, their achievements may be a mere speck of truth or mere fabrication when seen beside those of an advanced civilization. Therefore, in order to establish communication, one of two things must happen: Either the more advanced sender will be aware of the inherent limitations of developing cultures and so will compose messages on many intellectual planes, or alternatively, we will be fortunate enough to have the type of knowledge assumed by the sender for purposes of interstellar communication.

Even if the messages denote events that fall within the purview of our experience, this will not automatically reveal the intended meaning. The conception of facts in any discipline depends upon the larger context in which they are considered. The introductory student of physics can master all the ins and outs of Newtonian mechanics and solve problems on a par with the professional, but the latter's familiarity with Einstein's theory of relativity, or with the subtleties of quantum mechanics, brings fresh meaning to the Newtonian "facts." The experienced scholar's view of the simplest issue is colored by the wider intellectual context in which the whole field of physics is inevitably cast.

Cross-cultural evidence of how one's scope of knowledge affects perception was provided fifty years ago by Benjamin Whorf, a principal founder of modern linguistics. To illustrate his theories Whorf drew heavily on the study of Native American Indian languages. A famous Whorfian example of how a person's world view and language affect perception concerns the perennial topic of weather. Because Eskimos experience different types of snow, and each has a distinct implication for behavior, the language follows suit and contains separate words for each type. For the Aztec, however, matters were quite different. Their warm, southwestern climate afforded little opportunity for talk about snow. And so in Aztec there was only a single word denoting the broader category of "cold."

In Whorf's view, this distinction between languages causes Eskimos to conceptualize the environment differently than did their Aztec counterparts to the south. If an Eskimo and a (non-extinct) Aztec were to converse about the weather, the meaning of all the spoken words, even those open to direct translation (e.g., "cold"), would not be the same for both sides, because of the differing perspectives of people raised under different climatic conditions. So it is not just that more words are used in the Eskimo language to denote snow, but rather that the unique coupling of language and environment determines perception of all aspects of one's physical surroundings.

Another linguistic example of the importance of context is the preeminence of sentences over words. As Whorf states: "Sentences, not words, are the essence of speech, just as equations and functions, and not bare numbers, are the real meat of mathematics" (*Language, Thought, and Reality*, p. 258). On another occasion he makes the point more generally: "As we have seen, reference is the lesser part of meaning, patternment the greater" (p. 261). The meaning of individual words depends on the sentence in which they are embedded; that is, semantic meaning depends on surrounding context. In the sentence "The giant alien sat on the coffeepot," we imagine an oversized coffeepot to accommodate the giant, but the same pot is pictured as normal in the sentence, "The baby alien sat on the coffeepot." The alien now is imagined as a creature that could be held in the palm of the hand and therefore could be easily supported by an ordinary coffee-pot. The pot is not intrinsically large or small; its size is arrived at by evaluating the other words in the sentence.

In a similar vein a colossal mismatch could exist between the views of the Galaxy conditioned by alien and human cultures, even though the events under discussion might be "understood" by both parties within their respective scientific domains. Any such difficulty would be exacerbated by the fact that the languages are likely to differ in profound ways. The problem will not be on a par with translation between Eskimo and Aztec, which after all are languages spoken by the same species.

There is no way to anticipate the special mode of communication preferred by an alien species, but we can be aware of the common features of human languages that might affect the probability of successful interaction. It is instructive to trace these common features back to the inborn capabilities of the child.

A wide range of animal behavior is guided more by biological maturation than by learning. A kitten hunts mice and other prey as soon as it can navigate in the environment. The inaugural flights of birds are usually successful, and human infants cry at birth with minimum prompting. Such behaviors are innate. They require biological maturation, but little in the way of opportunities to learn the appropriate behavior to cope with special physical circumstances. A long-standing issue in psychology is the extent to which human and animal behaviors are learned skills or innate dispositions. When considering faculties more closely identified with humans, such as language and thought, it is tempting to assign a greater share of the burden to learning. Recently, however, linguists and psychologists have found that even rather sophisticated human thought has a strong innate component.

The evidence for a "prewired" substrate of language comes mostly from studies of small children. In the late 1960s the biological psychologist Eric Lenneberg noted that while there are hundreds of languages spoken around the globe, children in all cultures climb the same maturational ladder to reach adult levels of competence. Language milestones include the initiation of cooing at around twelve weeks, babbling at six months, the expression of single words and phrases at between twelve and twenty-four months, and the eventual production of grammatical sentences by the age of four or five years. Regardless of the social and economic conditions of a child's upbringing, or the number of speaking adults in the home, youngsters from all cultures attain these milestones at approximately the same age. This common road to language competence suggests the gradual unfolding of a maturational process in the developing child. Apparently, the necessary neural hookups in the brain must be in place before succeeding steps are taken in the progression of language milestones. No one denies the importance of learning in the acquisition and use of specific words and sentences, but the deeper grammar from which thought arises is most likely an inborn, uniquely human, cognitive ability.

Further evidence to indicate that language evolves maturationally comes from the comparative effects of brain injuries on the linguistic ability of young children and adults. The prognosis for recovery from severe brain traumas, owing to accidental falls, blows to the head, brain tumors, and strokes, depends critically on the person's age at the time of misfortune. Recovery is on the side of youth. The younger one is, the better the prognosis is for a speedy and full recovery of normal function. Even with severe brain damage to areas responsible for language, it appears that other parts of the brain can assume new duties and the young child can return quickly to a normal course of linguistic development. If, however, a serious head injury occurs later in life—say, after the age of twelve or fourteen—and it impairs the expression or comprehension of language, the chances for recovery are slimmer. It seems that the brain has compartmentalized its functions by then and has already laid down the neural connections for language. The disruption of this network cannot be compensated for by other parts of the brain because by then they each have their own duties to perform.

A final piece of evidence pertaining to the biological underpinnings of language is the vocal accent so readily detected when people speak foreign languages. Children living in multilingual communities handle several languages with equal ease and without detectable accents. A native speaker could not tell the speech of a bilingual child from that of someone who speaks only one language. On the other hand, adults who master a foreign language down to the finer points of grammar and semantics still retain an accent that indicates their mother tongue. To the native German, American and French accents are readily identified, even if the speakers have been in Germany for years.

When I visit another country, the American children I meet never cease to amaze me. It is not unusual to run across three- and four-year-olds speaking the foreign language like natives, while my own bumbling efforts leave no doubt of my national origin. No amount of practice seems to prevent the revelation of an adult's linguistic heritage, even when the sentences are "technically" correct, whereas the fluidity of the youthful nervous system permits children to converse naturally in several languages. Even professional spies who master accentless versions of a foreign language can be unmasked by the demand to say certain difficult words or phrases.

This behavioral evidence, together with the fact that the size and number of neuronal connections in the brain are undergoing remarkable expansion during the first twelve years of life, indicates a biological substructure for human language. The common progression of language suggests the operation of a universal form possessed by all humans. Since a good deal of logical thought is expressed by language, it too must have a shared core among people: not the exact meanings of single words, but the rules used to combine words into coherent strings that can be understood by others in the same language community. Indeed, according to many linguists, all human languages, despite differences in their surface grammar, share underlying grammatical principles. A single example will suffice to indicate the importance of a shared linguistic grammar. The words "table," "chimpanzee," and "lift" denote an object, an animal, and an action but do little to help us understand any relationship among them. But the sentence "The chimpanzee lifted the table" refers to a sequence of events that gives fresh meaning to the separate words. When people converse and believe that a meaningful exchange of ideas is occurring, it must be that common rules of interpretation are in operation.

The computer scientist Marvin Minsky has emphasized the universality of nouns, verbs, and objects in all languages, and consequently their relevance for establishing communication with like-minded aliens. The more fundamental rules of mathematics, and in particular arithmetic and simple counting, are also seen as sensible choices from which to build a language for communicating with aliens (e.g., the artificial language LINCOS created back in 1960 by the Dutch mathematician Hans Freudenthal). Both Minsky and Freudenthal are quick to say, however, that such systems are intended for communication with beings of humanlike intelligence, though the physiological and anatomical makeup of such beings may be decidedly nonhuman. In the practical world of astronomy this could be a very significant limitation, because aliens might well be markedly different from us.

Roughly speaking, what seems to go on in human communication is this. Someone arranges a string of words into a sentence to embody a thought to be communicated. This sentence is spoken and then heard by another person, who encodes it in a form to be compared with concepts stored in his or her own memory banks. Presently, a concept springs to mind with the meaning of the encoded sentence, and the discussion proceeds from there. As the linguist Noam Chomsky implies, human communication is a resonance between ideas already present in two people. Verbal communication is a very complicated business, but its elements represent implicit knowledge, a shared grammar permitting one person to understand what another is thinking. At present, there is no way to know how close two organisms must be in their brand of intelligence before meaningful communication of this sort can proceed.

The notion of an innate grammar has been popular in philosophy from Plato to Kant, and psychologists have often noted the importance of a universal cognitive structure for the development of perception and learning. At the heart of this notion is a tautology: Humans are absolutely prohibited by the organization of their nervous system from learning concepts whose understanding requires capabilities beyond that nervous system. Only on a superficial plane do we gain new insights from conversing with another individual. In a deeper sense, conversing with extraterrestrials can occur only if we share a grammar that shapes both sets of thoughts and actions. The human nervous system, with its unique language capacity, ultimately limits the interpretation of environmental messages, whether they originate on Earth or elsewhere. Although this observation may appear patently obvious, SETI optimists have given it scant attention. Because these problems need be faced only at some future time, current opinion downplays or ignores the serious difficulties that will almost certainly plague efforts to decipher alien messages. Finding meaning in the message, once detected, may be the most formidable problem we will meet in trying to learn anything interesting about alien civilizations.

So what are the salient features of human language that must be contained in messages—indeed, that must be found in the expressed thought of aliens if we are to gain any understanding whatsoever? Human language is a curious decoration unless seen in the service of thought, and I suspect the ideas exchanged by radio telescope will be no exception. The linguistic factors here include the time scale over which messages are sent, their length, their arrangement in time and space, and finally, their content.

The most singular issue is time. We are accustomed to a restricted time scale for purposes of communication, a scale that follows naturally from the geophysics and biology of this planet. All animals are influenced in this regard by the cyclical changes of the massive bodies of the Solar System, and the influence is evident in major patterns of rhythmic behavior. The length of a thought, a linguistic expression, the patterning of words, and indeed the entire structure of language may depend on temporal rhythms defined by geophysical events peculiar to Earth and the Solar System.

An unusual example is provided by the fiddler crab. Along the New England coast it is easy to catch fiddler crabs at low tide as they emerge from their burrows and scurry around in search of mates, food, and whatever else strikes their fancy. At high tide, they crawl under rocks and wait for the next recession of water from their territory. Crabs can presumably tell when they are covered or uncovered by deep water, and therefore it is not surprising that they all become active and hit the beach simultaneously. What is surprising, however, is that if these creatures are kept in laboratory containers for up to several weeks, miles from the shore, they become hyperactive whenever the tide is low on their home beach! The behavioral biologist James Palmer tells us that nobody is really sure how the crabs achieve such punctual behavior without directly experiencing tidal changes, but quite possibly the cause is geophysical. That is, the relative positions of the Moon and Earth changing in cyclical fashion over time determine the tides, which correlate closely with the activity of the fiddler crab. It is conceivable that this geophysical event is represented in the crab by a biological clock that evolved as a result of the regularity of the tides.

Other examples of geophysical influences on behavior are plentiful. Hibernating animals, such as the ground squirrel and the black bear, exhibit annual rhythms; while others, including humans, go about their business on twenty-four-hour cycles. Circadian rhythms are driven largely by light-dark cycles—daytime activity, nighttime slumber. When the adventuresome among us have secluded themselves in underground caves for several months, their circadian rhythms persist, even without the aid of an alarm clock or the sight of the rising sun. It has been shown that after an initial disruption of habitual behavior, the cave dweller returns to a familiar twenty-four-hour cycle of sleep and wakefulness.

Repetitive geophysical changes must critically affect our time perspective, which may be psychologically bounded at the upper end by the birth-and-death cycle of humans. The rising and setting of the Sun and Moon are readily apparent to sentient creatures in all regions of the phylogenetic scheme of life, and such regularities could profoundly influence our perception of the passage of time. Consider for example a human lifetime of 80 years. There are $80 \times 365 = 29,200$ days, or $29,200 \times 24 = 700,800$ hours in a lifetime. On this scale an hour is $1/700,800$ of the total and certainly represents a healthy chunk of time. An hour is trivial, however, when compared to the million-year lifespan of a species, or the billion-year scales appropriate for the existence of the Earth, Sun, and stars. These latter values could be the relevant time scales when humans seek to discover intended or unintended signs of alien intelligence in outer space. On the other hand, within the perspective of a scientist's lifetime it seems perfectly reasonable to aim a telescope at a target star for only an hour or two. Humans can transmit substantial information in an hour, and a few minutes is sufficient to explain even complex ideas. At this rate, a survey of nearby stars might take a few months, and a five- or ten-year project would be adequate to survey a fairly large volume of space.

Governments engaged in pure research rarely fund projects beyond five years at a clip, and often the scope is more like two, but suppose an alien civilization exists whose members live ten times longer than us, that is, 800 years. Might their time scale for sending messages be greatly expanded? They could see an hour of human time as totally inadequate for saying anything the least bit interesting, and thus the time we would require to detect a pattern in their radio signals would increase proportionally. Instead of a few hours of observation per star, we would be forced to look for hundreds of hours, and instead of five-year grants, we would need a few centuries of guaranteed financial support. Being alert to this possibility implies that a whole range of time scales, both shorter and longer than those we are used to, should be considered by a thoroughgoing SETI effort. The geophysical and biological cycles guiding behavior and cognition on other planets are not likely to be the ones operating here. It would be convenient if conditions here were duplicated there, but it is not something we can bank on.

Within the general time frame needed to transmit messages, meaningful subunits also must be isolated within shorter time frames. Here, too, success could depend on the degree of match between human and alien experience. The essential ideas expressed by human language emerge at the level of the sentence. The single word conveys not enough information, the paragraph too much, to be treated as a primary unit for the expression of thoughts. Quite obviously, a fixed sentence length for conveying thoughts does not exist, but the accepted variability of length does have limits: page-long sentences are rare, and adults, at least, don't communicate in a telegraphic string of one-worders. Most writers have a preferred sentence length, with a characteristic variability above and below some average.

This has been documented by Carrington B. Williams, who counted the number of words in the sentences of such notable authors as George Bernard Shaw and H. G. Wells. The calculation for Shaw was twenty-seven words per sentence, and for Wells, twenty, but both sprinkled their prose with much longer sentences. In this regard, the general form of every writer's prose is the same, though each has a preferred sentence length. If sentences tell complete thoughts, then whatever the language of extraterrestrials, humans will expect a message length that falls within the familiar range of ten to thirty discrete patterns (words). In fact, I suspect that the cryptic nature of scientific writing will lead astronomers and engineers to expect somewhat shorter bursts of discourse.

At the extremes, on the basis of current technology it is impossible for the radio telescope to resolve patterned messages defined over a time span on the order of trillionths of a second, or to record message strings that require decades to unfold. The sum of human knowledge is stored in documents and books that disclose concepts over time scales appropriate for the attention span of people, who almost never survive for more than a century. In this context the time for a message to be presented is measured in seconds, minutes, and hours, but not in years. If messages from outer space do not conform to familiar scales of time and space, it may be impossible to spot their presence.

Equally important are the implications of encountering an alien species whose form of language does in fact resemble ours. If we were able to count the number of distinct symbols in this species' communication and separate groups of symbols into meaningful units corresponding to our sentences, we would be encouraged to assume that we shared the aliens' conception of the universe. Perhaps our only hope is to seek out or anticipate eavesdropping on civilizations who employ the same styles of linguistic expression.

A related consideration is the size of the alien vocabulary. Statistical regularities in the use of words are apparent in human writing and speech, and these regularities depend on the size of the working vocabulary from which the words are taken. In any representative sample of language we would expect the word "the" to occur more often than the word "alien," but the relative frequency of the two words would differ in the language of the child and the adult because of the size of their respective vocabularies. When searching the heavens for meaningful signals we might do well to seek out repetitions of symbols and ask whether the rates of repetition approximate those found in human languages. English is comprised of a working vocabulary of roughly one hundred thousand words. One can imagine the problems arising in communicating with a species that has a vocabulary 1 million times as large. A story as long as the Bible might not contain the same word twice! On the other hand, discovery of message sequences with symbols that repeat at a rate close to that found in human language could imply that we had met a civilization whose cognitive abilities over-lapped ours in one crucial respect. Human expectations of language regularities will affect the probability of noticing any messages exported by alien civilizations, and the discovery of similarities in the structure of the language employed by aliens and humans would be a giant step forward in the quest to understand the meaning of extra-terrestrial messages.

Whatever the local norm followed in expressing ideas, including the cryptic styles of science and mathematics, if that norm corresponds to human language, the messages will probably occur in a familiar spatial and temporal framework. Although the details cannot be predicted, we can anticipate some type of hierarchical structure. Thoughts will be presented at multiple levels, built upon the principle that directs the combination of linguistic components: story, paragraph, sentence, and word. Such a superordinate arrangement is a cardinal feature of human language, as Benjamin Whorf remarked in an exceptionally long but engaging sentence:

> It is as if, looking at a wall covered with fine tracery of lacelike design, we found that this tracery served as a ground for a bolder pattern, yet still delicate, of tiny flowers, and that upon becoming aware of this floral expanse we saw that multitudes of gaps in it made another pattern like scrollwork, and that groups of scrolls made letters, the letters if followed in a proper sequence made words, the words were aligned in columns which listed and classified entities, and so on in continual cross-patterning until we found this wall to be—a great book of wisdom! [*Language, Thought, and Reality*, p. 248]

The abstractions of science do not disprove Whorf's observation. Hierarchies are obvious throughout the fabric of scientific writing. For instance, in mathematics spatial position indicates the successive nesting of magnitudes. Take a number such as 3,215. The left-most digit, 3, represents the highest denomination (thousands); the number in the adjacent position, 2, is an order of magnitude smaller (hundreds); and so forth. The standard pattern of ten digits (0 through 9) is just reapplied within each scale of size. In chemical formulas a molecule is a spatial grouping of symbols that stand for component elements, and the relative position of abstract symbols (variables) is central as well to all mathematical equations. Because people interested in science are accustomed to thinking hierarchically, the degree to which this simple rule is followed by extraterrestrial signals could well affect the probability of their being noticed, recognized, and eventually understood.

This returns us to the main question of whether we will be able to decipher messages from outer space. To get a better handle on the issues involved, we can ask how well one culture understands another whose language is radically different. The modern prototype for "radically different" is Egyptian hieroglyphics, an active language from approximately 7000 B.C. to 100 B.C. During these historical times many cultural, religious, and political events of a lively society were recorded on massive stone slabs and monuments, but over the period of centuries the language slowly evolved to the point where it was impossible to translate between its original and modern forms. For more than thirteen hundred years the linguistic route to this early culture was blocked, so that people were prevented from gaining a clear view of the cultural traditions of a very early civilization.

As is well known, in 1879 a breakthrough occurred when a French artillery officer unearthed a stone slab near the mouth of the Nile River in the city known to the French as Rosetta. The stone contained inscriptions in three languages: fourteen lines of hieroglyphics, thirty-two lines of modern Egyptian, and fifty-four lines of Greek. The longer Greek passage could be made out to be a public decree of sorts, praising Ptolemy V, Epiphanes king of Egypt (205 to 182 B.C.), but the subject of the decree was nowhere near as eye-catching as its duplication in three languages. On the basis of these inscriptions scholars at the time argued as follows: Assuming that the same passage is repeated in each of the three forms, it should be possible to determine the meaning of the hieroglyphic symbols by matching them to known symbols in the Greek. Once the hieroglyphics on the stone are known, the meaning of others might become transparent. This is essentially how matters finally did work out.

When the British captured the city of Alexandria, the Rosetta Stone was confiscated and lodged at the British museum. Shortly thereafter the by-then-famous stone toured the globe, posing an intellectual challenge for scholars intrigued by novel, nontrivial problems. The accepted solution to the puzzle was not long in coming. In Britain the physicist Thomas Young correctly identified the proper names of several familiar gods, as well as six letters of the ancient alphabet. Somewhat later the French linguist Chompollion undertook a successful translation among the three languages by an approach that was deceptively simple and eminently sensible. By noting the position of a word in both the Greek and the hieroglyphic text, he isolated a proper name, such as "Ptolemy" or "Cleopatra." Then, through substitution of the individual symbols comprising the name, he isolated letters of the alphabet. Largely, by a bootstrap procedure, involving independent checks on the validity of his substitutions between languages, a tolerable understanding of the alphabet was achieved.

After centuries of absolute ignorance, people once again could read firsthand accounts of early Egyptian life and history. Despite the concerted efforts of linguists since Chompollion, we still do not grasp the significance of all the Egyptian hieroglyphics, but their major features have been fully recorded for posterity—or for as long as our present-day records are interpretable!

The parallel situation today is this. The immense distances between civilizations with the potential to communicate by radio telescope imply that any signals received may have begun their journey thousands of years ago. The alien astronomers who erected telescopes and composed messages may have long since died, a fate which may have befallen their civilization as well. In this sense, then, we are now at a point in history that predates discovery of a Rosetta Stone from the stars. Rather than inscriptions on stone monuments, we expect signatures from outer space to arrive as radio transmissions, but their interpretation will require the same cognitive skills needed to translate dead languages or to unravel secret codes. The job will be more like translating ancient hieroglyphics than like translating between languages where direct social interaction is possible among native speakers. If we guess at the meaning for a symbol in the alien message, it will not be easy to verify that guess, because the sending party won't be around to offer encouragement and reward correct inferences. Therefore, the very best we can hope for is a problem on a par with the Egyptian hieroglyphics, but probably without a Rosetta Stone. Most definitely, the skill level required to crack this new riddle will be greater than that required to translate English into Russian or Eskimo into Aztec.

Would we be overly optimistic to anticipate a keystone from space to accompany alien messages and assist in their interpretation? Or might there be some way that the principle of the Rosetta Stone could be applied here to provide access to some deeper cosmic code? An alien who followed the principle behind the Rosetta Stone would prepare and send messages in more than one format. Perhaps the bulk of the message would be coded in a single format, but selected parts would appear in alternate versions. For instance, a message might be encoded in TV signals highlighting an outstanding item in the universe (say, a unique star configuration). The meaning of the pictures would also be described in an accompanying language. If we could decipher at least one of these modes of communication, then, like Chompollion, we would gain access to the other forms by linking individual symbols between the unknown and the known. This favorable scenario presupposes that at least one of the cosmic codes would make sense, but even if only part of the communication were understood, we might be able to recover the broad theme intended. Such is the case today regarding a number of languages which are not spoken by anyone now alive. Messages inscribed on wooden tablets on Easter Island remain a total mystery; several languages which flourished centuries ago in the Middle East are only partially understood by scholars. (Consult *Extinct Languages* by the German archaeologist and linguist Johannes Friedrich.)

Another outside possibility is that the key to unlock the mysteries of alien messages is already here on Earth. Erich von Däniken notwithstanding, it is unlikely that ancient astronauts left an obvious physical artifact to help us understand future messages from alien civilizations, but resources available on this planet still might be harnessed to apply the principle behind the Rosetta Stone. In particular, the combined skills of animals and humans might work in concert to decipher the cosmic lingo employed by aliens. Dolphins, chimpanzees, birds, and many other creatures possess rudimentary skills for communication. With minimum expense and considerable coaching, these creatures might be recruited to the SETI cause in a manner discussed earlier (chapter 9). This scenario implies that different species on Earth can exchange complex information by some means or other, and of course most people would admit that we have had minimal success in this undertaking.

To recap, just as the child automatically resonates to the spoken language of its native culture, humans may resonate to the format of messages from outer space. It will be possible only if there is sufficient overlap between the thought and deep grammar of the two parties. Hence, in a fundamental way we cannot make progress unless the sender shares our style of thinking and preferred mode of expression (radio waves). The opportunities for success would brighten if a chain of organisms on Earth could be orchestrated into some kind of "biological Rosetta Stone," where knowledge acquired by each member of the chain was transformed for the benefit of the others. Quite obviously the odds are stacked against this rather fanciful eventuality.

It is also possible that signals from aliens will prove only partially decipherable and that we will inch our way from under a cloud of ignorance over the course of centuries. Whatever the outcome, if the material received is based on knowledge beyond our ken, messages from the stars will forever remain an intriguing but impenetrable mystery. Physicists occasionally imply that some regions of the universe need not obey the physical laws of human science. We may always perceive these regions as random and hopelessly out-of-bounds. If alien messages fall into this category, they may be dutifully recorded on miles of computer tape, but then pass the eons gathering dust on the shelves of some government observatory.

On a point nearer to home one wonders whether the same conclusions hold for interspecies communication on Earth. We are still far from making meaningful contact with mammals we know are intelligent by dint of the ability to adapt and solve novel problems: animals such as dolphins, whales, and chimpanzees. If we can't talk with these creatures who evolved under the same geophysical and biological conditions as humans, how can we expect to converse with a species that almost certainly will be extraordinarily different? The study of animal communication may help us anticipate the best strategies to apply to

SETI, but the resultant payoff may lie far in the future—issues to be addressed seriously by our children's children's children. In the meantime we should retain a humble evaluation of our present capabilities. It would appear that the formula for success must include a search for signal features that are common to human language in the broadest sense, perhaps basic arithmetic or simple mathematical formulas; otherwise, we will be continually frustrated in efforts to understand a single alien thought. Without the establishment of a shared communication format, one civilization's book of universal wisdom will be another's book of universal confusion.

REFERENCES AND FURTHER READINGS

Budge, E. A. W. *Egyptian Language: Easy Lessons in Egyptian Hieroglyphics.* New York: Dover, 1976.

Chomsky, N. *Language and Mind.* New York: Harcourt Brace Jovanovich, 1968.

Freudenthal, H. *LINCOS: Design of a Language for Cosmic Intercourse.* Part I. Amsterdam: North-Holland, 1960.

Friedrich, J. *Extinct Languages.* New York: Philosophical Library, 1957.

Greppo, J. G. H. *Essay on the Hieroglyphic System.* Boston: Perkins & Marvin, 1830.

Lenneberg, E. H. *Biological Foundations of Language.* New York: Wiley, 1967.

Minsky, M. Communication with Alien Intelligence. *Byte,* 1985, 127–138.

Paivio, A., & Begg, I. *Psychology of Language.* Englewood Cliffs, N.J.: Prentice-Hall, 1981.

Palmer, J. D. *An Introduction to Biological Rhythms.* New York: Academic, 1976.

Whorf, B. L. *Language, Thought, and Reality: Selected Writings of Benjamin Lee Whorf.* Edited by J. B. Carroll. Cambridge, Mass.: M.I.T. Press, 1956.

Williams, C. B. Writers, Readers and Arithmetic. *New Scientist,* 1967, 35, 88–91.

CHAPTER 12

LEARNING WHAT IS MEANT

If and when meaningful signals are extracted from the radio environment of outer space, they will have embarked on their journey hundreds, thousands, or perhaps even millions of years ago. Traveling over enormous distances at the speed of light, these signals may well represent the last vestiges of the ancient culture who sent them, and in any case, the great span of distance and time separating us precludes any kind of lively interplanetary give-and-take. Because the interaction is definitely a one-way affair, we expect to be on the receiving end for a very long time without feeling the need to return the favor and begin sending information for the benefit of others. What this means in practical terms is that any social or scientific learning resulting from the receipt of cosmic messages will by necessity be achieved without the customary aid of immediate feedback from the teacher. It simply is unrealistic to think that we will have the patience to decipher an extraterrestrial message, send back an answer, and wait for a reply. The briefest sort of exchange could take millennia.

The situation would be something like receiving a message in the heyday of the Roman Empire, returning an acknowledgment that would reach its destination in the Middle Ages, and then awaiting a follow-up reply somewhere around the turn of the twenty-first century. The motivational problem created by this type of drawn-out correspondence is more serious than anything the human race has ever faced before. Most learning on this planet is speeded by the use of immediate positive or negative feedback from a sympathetic "teacher."

All learning does not fall under the same heading, and the type of feedback ranges from the starkly simple to the extremely complex. An example of the elementary sort is a rat quickly learning to press a lever in its cage to acquire a food pellet which satisfies a biological need and simultaneously informs the animal of the correctness of its response. An example of a more subtle character is the learning that occurs when we read a magazine article to keep abreast of current world events or pass an evening watching a television report. Here, the sheer interest aroused in tracking a complex issue is rewarding enough to encourage us to continue. To check on how well we have mastered the material presented, we compare it with what we already knew. If the new facts fit well into the old, we assume we understood what we read or watched. If not, we may question either the credibility of the material or our ability to comprehend it, and in this case, we may actively seek out feedback concerning the adequacy of our understanding from a source other than the teacher. When attempting to verify the truth of an alien message, the major source of feedback will be that which is already familiar—for example, current physical theories of the cosmos or astronomical observations.

It is difficult to imagine what it would be like to learn under conditions in which feedback is sporadic, weak, or absent, but some idea of what this situation would be like occurs whenever we try to communicate with another species. By examining this familiar case, we obtain a glimpse into what it might be like when one-way messages are eventually received from outer space. One common example that comes to mind is the everyday conversations carried on between millions of people and their pets. Although profound discussions are occasionally reported, most of us would agree that two-way pet conversations focus on matters closely allied to food and play. Even with the warmest rapport, the quality of pet conversations is usually not stimulating enough to sustain burning interest on either side for more than a few minutes. The intellectual potential of a species, however, cannot be gauged by its willingness to be a good pet.

Rather, we should look to animals with the necessary intelligence, motivation, and means for communicating with humans, coupled with a desire to consider topics of mutual interest. Two species that more or less fulfill these requirements are the chimpanzee and the dolphin. Neither is a very desirable pet, the chimpanzee because its adult strength and personality make for a dangerous house companion, the dolphin because its body size and water needs can't be met within the resources of the typical household. Nonetheless, study of the language ability of chimps raised in people's homes and the communication power of dolphins kept in water laboratories has intensified in recent decades. The establishment of at least one workable trans-species link involving either of these organisms might foretell the pitfalls and benefits resulting from contacts with aliens living elsewhere. Ignoring probable differences in intellectual level, and putting matters bluntly, if we can't communicate with animals on Earth, how can we expect to communicate with aliens who are thousands of light-years away in both directions, past and future?

To undertake the study of animals it is important first of all to overcome the chauvinistic belief in the uniqueness of the human being in regard to intelligence, communication skill, and knowledge about the universe. Such chauvinism hampers any scientific investigation and may underlie the reluctance of many nonscientists to support SETI. The results of a survey I once conducted among Dartmouth students showed that those who believed in the uniqueness of the human species and in the biblical story of creation were the least likely to believe in the possibility of extraterrestrial life or intelligence. If aliens are equally chauvinistic, no fruitful contacts will ever be possible with them. This would be a pity, because an alien civilization that has withstood the test of time and continued to flourish might have invaluable advice regarding the survival of a youthful civilization like ours.

The most thorough research into animal communication has focused on the chimpanzee, our nearest genetic relative. Several million years ago there were several species of hominids roaming about, and some may have been more akin to *Homo sapiens* than the chimpanzee. Although it would be fascinating to engage one of these fellows in conversation, so far as we know they are all dead. Chimpanzees are the best substitutes. Their intellect is keen and their attention span sufficient for us to communicate beyond the stage of mutual acknowledgment.

Some of the earliest work on chimp intelligence was done by the great German psychologist Wolfgang Köhler, who as a young man went to the island of Tenerife, off the North African coast, and directed a research station established by the German Academy of Sciences. At the time, Great Britain controlled the island, and when World War I broke out Köhler was forced to remain there, while still being allowed to pursue his research. For three years he investigated the problem-solving and social behavior of captive chimps. He soon discovered how ingenious these apes could be at surmounting obstacles blocking their access to food. The more clever animals stacked boxes in order to grasp bunches of bananas suspended from the roof of the cage, and his star pupil, Sultan, would insert bamboo sticks into each other to make a wand for retrieving food from the ceiling or from the ground outside the cage. The chimps also revealed their intelligence in playful moments. One of their favorite sports was to tease the chickens who ambled about the yard. Köhler reports that one chimp would hold out an inviting handful of grain to attract a chicken's attention, and if the bird approached to peck, a second would wield a bamboo stick, delivering a blow to the victim's hindquarters. The poor chicken's scrambling and squawking would always send the colony into exuberant celebration.

In addition to describing the chimpanzee's sense of humor, Köhler made it clear that this animal was smarter and more insightful than anyone had previously believed. This work destroyed some of the myths that had formerly surrounded attempts to initiate any deeper discussions with chimps. More recent observations have verified his conclusions about their problem-solving talents and have gone further to determine their language aptitude. As in Köhler's time, the animal's interest in the test is piqued by food inducements, although playful tickling, hugging, and related social rewards also are used effectively; that is, learning depends on some type of feedback from the teacher.

Keith and Cathy Hayes were among the first to study the ability of chimps to understand and speak a human language. They reasoned that one could not expect an animal—or a child, for that matter—to speak if it had been raised in the wild or had never been exposed to a community of human speakers on a continuous basis from birth. The Hayeses provided an infant chimp called Viki the opportunity to develop language in the same way a child might. Viki was raised in their home and was the subject of daily language training conducted by her foster parents. But despite intense efforts to teach the animal to speak, she never really acquired a usable vocabulary, except for the words "mama," "papa," and "cup." Besides their familial designation, "mama" and "papa" also referred to various toys and food—not much of an accomplishment when compared with that of a human child provided with similar linguistic coaching.

Despite this inauspicious start, language research with chimpanzees has progressed. Although the idea of teaching a chimp to vocalize words has been abandoned, a certain degree of success has come from employing alternative modes of expression. In fact, several animals have acquired the rudiments of American Sign Language, while others can communicate by arranging plastic symbols to represent objects and actions.

David Premack and his colleagues taught an artificial language to a young chimpanzee named Sarah. Individual words were coded as abstract plastic shapes of different colors, with metal backing allowing their attachment to the surface of a magnetic board. Either Sarah or her trainers could express ideas by placing the individual shapes on the board in a meaningful sequence. Sarah's preference was to arrange the shapes in a vertical column, and so her trainers quickly learned to abide by her wishes and do the same.

In early experiments, the chimp was taught to use the symbols for "same," "different," "yes," and "no" in appropriate contexts. For instance, two bananas might be placed side by side with an intervening question mark. Sarah could replace the question mark with her special plastic symbol for "same." She also could substitute "different" when the two flanking objects were indeed different and could answer and pose yes-no questions herself, such as (reading down):

MARY	SARAH
GIVE	TAKE
SARAH	HONEY
BREAD	CRACKER

That is, the shapes representing these words would be attached to the magnetic board.

Somewhat later in her training Sarah could successfully identify a few colors and distinguish between quantities such as "none," "one," and "several." In all such tasks, though, she had to receive some type of reward, usually food, for making the correct choices. "Feed-back" was indeed the right term to describe the reason Sarah complied with her trainers' wishes.

After awhile the chimp began to create sentences out of the available set of symbols. This advanced performance was laboriously trained in a sequence of small, digestible steps. She might initially be taught the symbol for "fruit," and next trained to discriminate between "apple" and "banana." For instance, the two symbols might be presented by the trainer, and if Sarah chose the correct alternative she would receive the genuine article, which was promptly consumed. After she mastered this distinction, reward was forthcoming only if she placed the trainer's name before the fruit symbol. For example,

MARY
APPLE

Having accomplished this step, she was rewarded only if a verb was added, followed by the appropriate proper nouns, such as:

MARY   MARY
GIVE   GIVE
APPLE   APPLE
            SARAH

Compound and conditional sentences were taught by the same incremental process of rewarding compliance with minimal language demands, which were progressively increased.

At the conclusion of Premack's study Sarah had learned 130 symbols, but approximately half of this vocabulary was associated with her trainers, the dispensing of food, or social rewards. Although it is indisputable that communication of some kind occurred between human and chimp, the type and level of discourse were limited by the chimp's biological and social needs. Whether more abstract conversations are possible through the application of Premack's technique remains an open question.

Similar constraints on the complexity of messages are apparent when chimps are taught to converse using American Sign Language, an ingenious and practical system composed of approximately two thousand hand positions and gestures, each depicting a unique concept. This special language has allowed deaf people to communicate rapidly and accurately among themselves, as well as with those who can hear. When immersed in a human culture where everyone "signs," a chimp can learn the elements of this visual language. Beatrice and Allen Gardner taught a chimp named Washoe a variety of signs through the use of social and food rewards: tickling, smiling, and feeding. These rewards were administered whenever Washoe correctly mimicked the signs of her trainers. The chimp also combined signs into short sentences, such as "sweet drink," "go out," and "come Roger tickle."

More recently the animal psychologist Herb Terrace raised a chimp called Nim in a New York City environment, albeit a well-protected one, and by the judicious use of rewards was able to teach him a variety of hand signs. Terrace made videotapes of all stages of training, and in later analysis traced out the major steps of language development. His conclusions provoked some controversy because they were at odds with expectations based on the earlier work by Premack and the Gardners.

Although Terrace found that Nim acquired a fairly rich vocabulary, there was no evidence that he combined individual signs into meaningful sentences in the way a child would. Over the first four years of life young children display a steady increase in vocabulary size and in their ability to form lengthy word phrases and sentences. In contrast, the average length of Nim's sentences never exceeded a few words. Moreover, Nim's utterances, unlike children's, lacked novelty. Most of his multiple hand signs added little to the particular sequence expressed a moment earlier by the trainer. It is Terrace's opinion that chimps can learn signs to stand for objects and actions but that sequences of signs are learned by rote and, in any case, are close imitations of the sequence most recently produced by the human trainer.

Therefore, the chimp's ability to generate a sentence composed of familiar signs does not imply that it grasps the full meaning as a human would. In summarizing all the results to date on teaching languages to chimpanzees, Terrace and his colleagues sound a pessimistic note:

Projects devoted to teaching chimpanzees and gorillas to use language have shown that these apes can learn vocabularies of visual symbols. There is no evidence, however, that apes can combine such symbols in order to create new meanings. The function of the symbols in an ape's vocabulary appears to be not so much to identify things or to convey information—as it is to satisfy a demand that it use that symbol in order to obtain some reward. [Terrace et al., "Can an Ape Create a Sentence?" p. 900]

One possible outcome of SETI is that we succeed in detecting a signal and in recognizing a pattern therein, but remain totally incapable of deciphering the correct meaning of the communication. We can easily conceive of a situation where we *think* that the message is understood but in fact it is not. We may be no better off than Nim when it comes to understanding more than the essentials necessary to simply mimic the teacher's signs.

But does the same conclusion apply to all animal learning pertaining to communication? Are dolphins, for example, limited in the same ways? From the experiments done thus far we have reason to believe that dolphins are clever, but can they express their ideas to us? The dolphin is not our nearest neighbor in the biological scheme of evolution, and yet, in a very crucial way, we are close relatives. Its brain is approximately 20 percent larger than ours, but with the animal's adult length of roughly eight feet, the ratio of body to brain size is about the same as ours. It is this ratio which some biologists feel is a telling indicator of intelligence, and the similarity has led to speculation about the possibility and benefits of human-dolphin communication. Each species may possess information of significance to the other; the problem is to figure out how to exchange it. This, of course, also is the preeminent concern of the SETI program, which is why I raise the subject in this context.

Unlike the chimp, the dolphin has a remarkable ability to generate and perceive complex sounds; its hearing is far superior to that of humans. For the sake of comparison, the frequency range (pitch) of the human ear is from 20 to 20,000 cycles per second, whereas the dolphin's upper threshold is at least 150,000 cycles per second and according to Russian scientists may extend much higher than that. These animals are most aware of frequencies in the region of 40,000 to 70,000 cycles per second, well above the limit of the most sensitive human ear.

Therefore, special electronic equipment is needed for humans to monitor whatever communication is taking place within the dolphin community. By these means it has been determined that they rely on a keen acoustic sense in procuring food and avoiding predators. Like bats, they employ a biological sonar system: Emitted sounds are bounced off objects in the water, and by noting the temporal and featural characteristics of the returning echo they can distinguish between objects and locate them with uncanny accuracy.

When alarmed or frightened, dolphins emit a variety of strange sounds, described as "clicks," "squawks," and "blats," and it has been suggested that their high-pitched "whistles" signify a mode of within-species communication. This hypothesis is supported by the observation that each dolphin has a unique whistle that could well serve as a "call sign" for purposes of individual identification.

Despite this marvelous battery of perceptual faculties, there are no firm data to suggest that dolphins have an equally rich natural language for talking among themselves. According to Louis Herman, a leading figure in the field, the scope of dolphin vocalizations is not significantly greater than that possessed by other species, for instance, the chimpanzee.

Nonetheless, Herman and others are trying to teach artificial languages to dolphins, and in a relatively brief period they have collected results at least as promising as those obtained with the chimpanzee. As is true in teaching chimps, however, dolphins do not spontaneously express the will to learn words and phrases of special relevance to people. Both their bodily movements and their linguistic utterances must be followed immediately by fish rewards if one is to see repeat performances. Whatever the ultimate understanding reached through the collaboration of human and dolphin, it appears that explicit rewards must be used to achieve interspecies communication. Unless we are able to unlock some hidden desire motivating these mammals to interact with us for the sheer fun of it, appropriate rewards and feedback will be the indispensable ingredient for maintaining any contact at all.

Without more cooperation, as we define it, from dolphins and chimpanzees, we will soon lose interest in communicating with them. If research efforts go unrewarded for too long, the human motivation to continue the language studies will wane and we will retain our chauvinistic position as the sole representative of a life-form on Earth that communicates by the rules of our language.

Assuming that the communication between intelligent life throughout the universe bears some resemblance, in form if not substance, to interspecies communication on Earth, the lessons learned from studying chimps and dolphins might prove valuable when the occasion arises to converse with an alien species. The failures that have plagued this research so far make it clear that we should not expect too much from alien contact unless the aliens happen to be very close to us in value orientation and intelligence. If we are lucky, the intellectual level and emotional empathy of our first cosmic "teacher" will be just a notch above ours. Unfortunately, the more likely situation is that envisioned by the astronomer John A. Ball, who thinks the occasion will be something akin to how an oyster might feel in trying to rouse the attention of a human.

The reason for this dire prediction is that we have enjoyed the outreach of radio telescopes for only forty-five years or so. Hence, initiation into the circle of advanced civilizations still leaves us at the bottom rung on everyone's ladder of universal intelligence. A special-education expert in School Galactica probably would see us anchoring the "dull" end of the learning continuum. What we don't know is whether this limited intellect qualifies us for special training, relegates us to a pastoral existence in a natural park (the Solar System), or simply means that we will continue to be ignored by any advanced species frequenting our region of the Galaxy.

In any event, we should become accustomed to the role of student, not teacher, and such role reversal never occurs in the psychology laboratory. Whether the organism being taught is a rat, a chimp, or a dolphin, these animals' appraisal of our motivation is considered irrelevant. Taking a cue from the language experiments, astronomers involved in SETI might consider what it is like to be a chimp or a dolphin in the company of a human whose reason for hanging around the other's home territory is not at all apparent. Scientists could be in a similar position in trying to fathom the motivations and pronouncements of aliens.

*

From the learner's standpoint there are three major steps to complete a successful communication. The first is to notice that some "thing" wants attention, the second is to recognize the method by which information is conveyed, and the third is to decipher the meaning of the messages. The chimpanzee probably is able to pass the first two hurdles, but it is doubtful whether true understanding has occurred to date in any of the studies intended to forge human-chimp interaction by use of a language-based communication system.

In John A. Ball's judgment a superior civilization would have no trouble alerting us to its presence, once having chosen to do so. On the other hand, it would be almost impossible for us to notice that civilization if it wished to stay concealed. Although a group of alien civilizations may participate in an active communication network, their use of physical energy is probably extremely efficient; that is, it may be impractical to eavesdrop on their conversations, because no energy is wasted and leaked to the curious outsider. This is a major reason for believing that we will not detect the presence of aliens by noting television broadcasts that they have inadvertently propagated through outer space, a point made recently by a telecommunications expert, Joseph F. Baugher. After all, if humans did not purposefully capture animals to serve as subjects for language instruction, these creatures would have no cognizance that another species was interested in them. And after the training is begun, the "learners" must still be perplexed about why there is such a fuss over the trivial acts of making hand signs in the air, slapping flippers on the water, or vocalizing sounds, acts apparently required to obtain adequate nourishment under the disagreeable regimen of captivity.

It is doubtful if chimps would have voluntarily sought communication with humans, and it is even stranger to think of a chimp's interest being piqued by human attempts to strike up conversations with another species, such as a dolphin. Of course, it can be argued that humans in fact do want to establish contact with a superior intelligence and are definitely curious about whether a higher-order galactic communication network already exists. Then we are more like the eager child than the bewildered chimp. As with children in the classroom, however, we may be ready for instruction in a general sense but perhaps not prepared to learn the specific material the instructor wants to teach. Once having realized the situation, the teacher may decide not to continue until the learner has advanced to a point where high-level discussion is possible. It is a bit astonishing that academics speaking out on SETI have not considered the standard school curriculum as a model for alien communication. The student entering the fields of physics or chemistry must first attend grade school, or otherwise master elementary mathematics and science, then complete high school, and then follow up with four years of intensive work in college or university. Only at this juncture will most physics departments even look at a student's qualifications for graduate training.

Moreover, the student's ability to continue is assessed periodically by examination. If this standard sequence is thought of as a model for learning from advanced aliens, it is possible that signals sent to Earth might be by intention extremely difficult to understand. The argument from the alien side would go something like this: "If another species is to talk with us, it must demonstrate an intelligence that equals our own. We have no real interest in talking with organisms who can never understand what is most dear to us. Therefore, any messages we send into outer space will be made purposely difficult." Such an attitude might snuff out all our hope of success through the search methods presently under consideration. For example, communication via radio waves would be too obvious, so that option would be ruled out; repetitive signals with redundant formats could be understood by a relatively unintelligent species, so that option would be eliminated; and so forth.

In efforts to communicate with other species on Earth, considerable thought goes into identifying and using their preferred mode of expression: visual signs for the chimp, sound waves for the dolphin. No discussion is possible unless both members of the pair observe the same rules. The major thrust of SETI concentrates on the electromagnetic spectrum as the physical means for sending and receiving messages, and a subsidiary preference is to single out radio waves as the most promising region of that spectrum. If an extraterrestrial wants to make contact on common scientific grounds, it had better be aware of our technological preferences and limitations. We in fact have only modest control over radio waves, and even less skill at recognizing patterns within them. Once more, the prognosis is that no meaningful contact with aliens is possible unless "they" are attuned to the communication wishes and technical capabilities of emerging civilizations like ours.

The third critical step in establishing a communication link is the most difficult: understanding the intended meaning of the messages received and being able to formulate interpretable replies. Suppose we realize that an extraterrestrial civilization is beaming messages at Earth, and suppose their channels for doing so are radio waves that can be intercepted and analyzed by our telescopes and computers. To accomplish this much would be great, but still a long way from meaningful discourse. I doubt if we would ever be fully satisfied until we could decipher the intent conveyed by alien messages.

This step might well be insurmountable, forever outside the realm of the human nervous system. In the early experiments designed to teach language to chimps it was believed that they were capable of producing both words and sentences. However, Terrace has raised the nagging question whether these productions make any sense to the chimp who generates them. Do Nim's hand signs and Sarah's arrangements of plastic shapes have the same meaning for them as they do for their human trainers? Terrace's telltale videotapes suggest that the word strings that Nim expressed by a sequence of hand signs were carbon copies of the sequences just demonstrated by his trainer. It has been known for a long time that some creatures imitate others very well—monkey see, monkey do! It now appears that chimps have trouble organizing individual words into novel sentences to convey deeper meaning of the sort that distinguishes human language from other types of animal communication.

Now consider this difficulty in the parallel context of a scientist puzzling over a sequence of signals that ostensibly were beamed to us from outer space. With luck, the signals will consist of a regular pattern that can be recognized as such. An easy example would be a staccato dot-dash sequence that repeated itself at predictable time intervals. Indeed, the pattern could be so regular as to make it a trivial job for a computer to mimic its detailed character, down to the last dot and dash—

computer see, computer do! But while happily progressing this far we still may not have the slightest idea about the meaning behind the sequence. Being able to observe and generate message strings that closely resemble those sent by an alien civilization is not synonomous with deciphering the essential point intended by the sender.

Therefore, we could well end up in Nim's corner, scratching our collective heads to figure out the meaning implied by another organism's language productions. I would bet that Nim didn't realize he was feigning comprehension when copying his trainer's signs. By the same token humans may not be clever enough to realize when they are in the dark about the meaning of messages from outer space. Can we avoid deceiving ourselves under these circumstances? I want to think so, but the evidence from animal studies makes me very skeptical.

Even if these problems are resolved we still might not learn anything new from communication with aliens. Has twenty years of research taught chimps and dolphins anything worthwhile that they did not already know? Perhaps we have told them a little about the sorts of activities humans value, but from the animals' standpoint most topics of conversation turn on ungainly ways to obtain common foodstuffs. So far as we can tell no abstract concepts have been transmitted, no mathematics or fine arts, no fundamentals of physical, biological, or social science. Our nearest genetic relative may never learn anything about these areas of preeminent human concern. I don't suppose anybody believes that we have taught the chimp to enjoy a ripe banana or have educated the dolphin palate to appreciate fish delicacies. The quality of these animals' lives certainly has not improved because of human intervention in their affairs. On the contrary, they have been removed from their natural habitats in even greater numbers since humans have taken a fancy to studying their intellectual abilities and language competence within the confines of the research laboratory. A similar fate could await the human species, once it enters into open communication with an alien species.

The potential rewards pushing humans to seek and maintain contact with aliens are not food and drink, at least not directly. From all indications, the chief scientific reason for searching out life elsewhere is to satisfy our thirst to learn more about the physical universe: more mathematics, physics, and chemistry. Biology is occasionally included in a list of space-age priorities, but scant reference is ever made to the social sciences or to humanistic concerns. Physical science seems convinced that what fascinates an alien communicating via radio waves will capture the imagination of the physical scientists here as well. So being shown the esoteric proof of a mathematical theorem may be equivalent in reward strength to a chimp's receiving a bunch of fresh fruit, and unveiling a new physical law may be equivalent to a dolphin's receiving a surprise shore dinner.

Without tangible rewards of some kind, the search for the alien mind could easily drift into the realm of mystery, magic, and mysticism. Judging by the terrestrial examples of teaching languages to other species, the mathematics and physics acquired from extraterrestrial teachers will not extend very far beyond current knowledge. Teachers of young children, in or out of the classroom, are well aware of the importance to learning of building a bridge between the familiar and the novel. If new concepts are presented too quickly or on too lofty a plane, we won't get a word of it. In all likelihood this situation would trigger a worldwide rise in occult beliefs about aliens that would tend to displace the cooler tone of scientific logic. As noted, we might be technically able to mimic messages and might unconsciously feign comprehension without grasping the underlying meaning. Let's hope, therefore, that School Galactica eases us into the stream of things with a course of study we can master.

Returning to feedback and learning, it is not obvious how we will effectively cope without receiving some indication of the correctness of our interpretations. Humans, like all animals, are used to getting feedback fairly soon after they behave. In the case of signals sent hundreds or thousands of years ago, immediate feedback concerning the success or failure of interpretations is out of the question. It is a hindrance to learning unlike any encountered previously by the species. Even when nineteenth-century linguists were struggling with Egyptian hieroglyphics, there were plenty of physical artifacts around to aid interpretation and, luckily, a Rosetta Stone to solidify the bridge between the old and the new.

There may be ways to avoid or at least attentuate this concern. The teacher-sender could include instructions in the message string to the effect that the recipient should conduct certain well-specified experiments and note the results. Of course, the proposed experiments might be weird, dangerous, or impossible to carry out. If we took the risk, however, then at some later point in the stream of incoming information validating answers might appear. This would be like teaching yourself mathematics by reading the text, doing the exercises, and looking up the answers in the back of the book. It is critical that the time frame be right: It would be frustrating to wait a thousand years before seeing the answers! A civilization might send redundant messages and offer duplicate answer sheets at numerous points following presentation of the laboratory exercise. This practice would accommodate the diverse needs of fast and slow learners, as well as those operating in long and short time frames.

It would be helpful if the alien senders anticipated and counteracted difficulties that are sure to hamper an understanding of the message at the receiving end. It seems likely that awareness of the limitations of others would be reflected in messages beamed intentionally at us. This would be less likely in the case of a civilization's technical by-products that might be discovered amid the background noise received from outer space. At least we can say that we would be considerate of others caught in the same straits. Even with intentional communication, however, validating feedback could be complicated and could require a substantial amount of time to journey here and be understood. If we ever overcame these obstacles and could decipher the messages, however, the social/psychological impact would indeed be dramatic.

REFERENCES AND FURTHER READINGS

Adams, J. A. *Learning and Memory: An Introduction.* Homewood, Ill.: Dorsey, 1976.

Ball, J. A. Extraterrestrial Intelligence: Where Is Everybody? *American Scientist,* 1980, *68,* 656–663.

Baugher, J. F. *On Civilized Stars: The Search for Intelligent Life in Outer Space.* Englewood Cliffs, N.J.: Prentice-Hall, 1985.

Gardner, R. A., & Gardner, B. T. Comparative Psychology and Language Acquisition. *Annals of the New York Academy of Science,* 1978, *309,* 37–76.

Hayes, C. *The Ape in Our House.* New York: Harper, 1951.

Herman, L. M. *Cetacean Behavior: Mechanisms and Functions.* New York: Wiley-Interscience, 1980.

Johanson, D. C., & Edey, M. A. *Lucy: The Beginnings of Humankind*. New York: Warner, 1981.

Köhler, W. *The Mentality of Apes*. New York: Harcourt, Brace, 1927.

Lesser, G. S. *Children and Television*. New York: Random House, Vintage, 1974.

Lilly, J. C. *The Mind of the Dolphin: A Nonhuman Intelligence*. New York: Avon, 1967.

Norris, K. S. *The Porpoise Watcher*. New York: Norton, 1974.

Premack, A. J. *Why Chimps Can Read*. New York: Harper & Row, 1976.

Premack, D. *Intelligence in Ape and Man*. Hillsdale, N.J.: Erlbaum, 1976.

Sebeok, T. (Ed.) *How Animals Communicate*. Bloomington: Indiana University Press, 1977.

Terrace, H. S. *Nim*. New York: Knopf, 1979.

Terrace, H. S.; Petitto, L. A.; Sanders, R. J.; & Bever, T. G. Can an Ape Create a Sentence? *Science*, 1979, *206*, 891–902.

Tighe, T. J. *Modern Learning Theory: Foundations and Fundamental Issues*. New York: Oxford University Press, 1982.

CHAPTER 13

PSYCHO-COSMIC SEARCH

Whatever the method chosen to contact extraterrestrial civilizations, the search itself fulfills a dual purpose. The manifest intent is to enlarge the perspective of humanity beyond the physical boundaries of the Earth and Solar System within which we happen to be situated. That task falls chiefly to the natural sciences of physics and engineering. The more subtle agenda is to use cosmic search as a tool to examine the social and psychological factors behind the widespread interest in and curiosity about alien presence in the universe. The organization of the human nervous system, both innate and learned facets, sets unalterable limits on the sensory reception, cognitive processing, and social meaning of new information, whatever its point of origin or the intention of the sender. These limits appear in sharper relief when seen close up; that is, we are more likely to understand human capabilities when they are considered under circumstances that push humans to the edge of their intellectual potential. The SETI enterprise is just such an extreme and thereby may provide the conditions for a more realistic assessment of the human state than can be attained from the study of people socializing with each other on the plane of everyday life. Seen in the dual light projected by natural and social science, the search takes on a psycho-cosmic flavor and thus represents one of the most exciting and uplifting activities of the human species.

Despite the difficulties we have in assigning exact values to the probabilities in the Drake formula (chapter 5), the immense number of candidate stars in the universe makes it unlikely that we are the only consciousness seeking contact with civilizations located beyond the borders of its home planet. The chances for actually making contact within the time frame of the next century may be slim, but they are not small enough to stop us from trying. If we are willing to be very patient and periodically renew our efforts in the light of societal attitudes and changes in physical methods taking place on this planet, I feel confident that the search will eventually prove successful. A journey of a thousand years, traveled by a beam of light or by a human society, still must begin with the first step at the first moment. In my opinion, then, we should pursue SETI in all its divers guises. Eventual success may come about through the efforts of radio astronomy on Earth, the launching of satellite probes to other star systems, direct human-alien meetings here or in space, or the future development of some entirely novel means for communicating over interstellar distances—for example, a method that exploits some untapped resource of the human brain.

I am less sanguine about the possibility in the near term of making sense out of an alien encounter of any kind. Unless we are awfully lucky, the nature of the alien mind will be vastly different from that of human beings. This state of mental mismatch need not be devastating if at least some faculties are held in common, for then we may be able to reach a marginal degree of emotional and intellectual understanding. This, in itself, would be a remarkable achievement.

In the preceding chapters I have discussed the various stages of information processing that must occur in order to engage in any fruitful communication on Earth or elsewhere. In the first place, the target pattern must be detected and recognized; therefore the message format must be compatible with human perceptual abilities, even if these are extended in power and scope by physical instruments. Next, to be recognized, the pattern must have been observed previously, either in another familiar context or at some earlier time within the message string itself. A repetitive event from outer space will stand a decent chance of being noticed; a singular event of brief duration will not. Further, if the individual elements of a message are to be grasped as a unitary whole, we will probably need the memory capacity to store large amounts of information over fairly long periods—at least for hours, maybe for years. Present computer facilities might be inadequate for storing the data contained in even a single message.

Finally, if these preliminary requirements can be met, the really tricky work begins. We can only hope that the language system, no matter how abstract, employed by aliens to convey messages is comprehensible, and that we are able to absorb the elements of this language in the absence of direct assistance, immediate feedback, or reward from its originators. Once these perceptual/learning hurdles are overcome, we will be in a position to zero in on the substantive meaning of the communication. What on earth or in space is the topic of discussion? Is the content of any relevance to human beings? Will there be undesirable social and political repercussions as a result of new knowledge acquired in this unique way? Are there special dangers—political, social, biological, or physical—arising as a consequence of translating the message into human action? These are important questions without answers at present, and I raise them to highlight the incredibly complex issues to be resolved in the aftermath of a bona fide contact with extraterrestrial consciousness.

This complexity should be cause for involvement, not despair. One of the more intriguing sides of the problem is whether contact will unlock the door to a hidden reservoir of new forms of intelligence and value orientations. Although the psychological boundaries of human thought and expression may seem manifest, these could all be illusory. The actual potential of the human mind may be realized only when external conditions demand more, in which case the full story of humanity will not be told until we cope with the altogether unique conditions of interacting with an alien being of the same or higher intellect.

One prized outcome of contact would be a significant improvement of all aspects of life on this planet and, in particular, the elevation of the present human condition. A clear motive for initiating a search is the widespread belief that among the early scientific returns will be invaluable hints about how humans can fulfill their most cherished dreams for a richer and more rewarding existence. These dreams are traditionally expressed in a religious context, but recent psychological analysis sets forth basic and higher-order human needs within a wider social context.

The personality theorist Abraham Maslow pointed out that not only are human needs different for different people, but they can be arranged in a definite importance hierarchy. As far as a single individual is concerned, the loftier, human needs will be addressed only after the biochemical necessities are met. Only then can a person think about personal safety, shelter, and general well-being. When in turn these needs are satisfied, those of a higher order enter awareness: for instance, feelings of belongingness, love, and friendship. Still further up the hierarchy are the various esteem needs, such as personal achievement, independence, freedom, and self-confidence. Perched on top of this hypothetical pyramid is "self-actualization," human fulfillment of the noblest sort, which includes an appreciation and acceptance of one's self and others and a superior capacity for experiencing beauty and the truly finer sides of life.

By this reasoning a person's view of the future is strongly affected by his or her present station within the hierarchy of human needs. The hungry person yearns for a Utopian world with infinite food supplies; someone with ample food and shelter, but lacking affection, sees the future populated with loving people who care about their fellow beings and are willing to act positively on those feelings. In a similar vein, it is likely that different individuals will expect different rewards to accrue from contact with aliens. People who are preoccupied with securing the basic necessities cannot be expected to support scientific projects whose primary payoff will be to satisfy intellectual curiosity. The larger question, however, is exactly where humanity as a species is currently situated within a need hierarchy viewed on a galactic scale.

It is interesting to speculate that humans are still undergoing change, certainly in cultural and scientific domains, perhaps in the biological realm as well. If the search goes on long enough—say, for thousands of years—the definition of "humanness" may slowly shift to the extent that the organism that initiated the search in the twentieth century may bear little resemblance to the organism that finally tastes success in some future epoch. Such a continuous change in the human state has its advantages. If life on Earth can meet the challenges of outer space with an ever-fresh visage, it will increase the probability of finding a companion with whom to share and communicate on an equal footing, assuming that the spirit of SETI is maintained or at least updated every now and then. We currently may not be equipped, either culturally or technically, to join Ronald Bracewell's galactic club, but subsequent generations may be more favorably constituted to accept the responsibility of membership, whatever it may entail.

When astronomy does reach full-fledged maturity, it may find itself in the hands of an organism bearing little biological likeness to a human being. Some 3 to 6 million years ago in Africa there were three species of organisms that we are now tempted to label "hominids." Only one of these has survived to ask profound questions about its ancestry and future evolutionary path. Since paleontologists tell us that 99 percent of all species that ever lived are now extinct, the question naturally occurs whether the lone survivor of the hominid line will soon join the ranks of the has-beens by finally bowing to the environmental and biological forces that caused the demise of the others, or whether this particular line is in some way special, in some way able to avoid or postpone the inevitable final chapter in the history of all life-forms.

Emotions are something I have not talked much about in this book, but a case could be made that feelings are a key ingredient for communication. In order to have any kind of interaction, both parties must have the desire to do so. This is as true of individuals who report UFOs and believe in ancient astronauts as it is of engineers intent on sending electronic probes to other star systems or of astrophysicists sitting at the controls of their radio telescopes. Once we strip away the particular means of acquiring knowledge and beliefs, we are left with a common psychological motivation: People are curious about the unknown, especially if it is thought to contain the answers to significant human problems: scientific, political, social, or artistic.

We might argue that the only reason we are even remotely interested in pointing our radio telescopes skyward is to realize our full potential as human beings. Still, where we find ourselves at this moment in the need hierarchy will affect how we plan to attain the next stage of development as a species. It is perhaps self-evident that people would disagree rather strenuously about the means to achieve this goal. Ask an astrophysicist at the Harvard observatory and you will get one answer; ask a social worker in New York City and you will surely get another.

In his recent book *Cosmic Dawn* the astrophysicist Eric Chaisson proposed boundary conditions for human beings which he sees as critical barriers to improving the long-range survival prospects of the species. He points to four major obstacles to future development: the population explosion, genetic engineering, nuclear power, and computer evolution. The first two boundaries, population and genetics, clearly pose a threat to Maslow's lowest needs for food acquisition and physiological well-being. The second two, nuclear power and computer technology, affect our personal safety, one in an obvious way (destruction of all life-forms), the other more subtly (subjugation of humanity to machines).

Chaisson's concerns can be shared by all who care to read or think. Yet in a very real sense these issues are extremely time-bound. Not a single one was seen as critical by people living a century ago. Then, population growth was recognized as a potential threat to survival by only a handful of social scientists, the crucial role of genetic transmission in the continuance of the species and the possibility of deterioration of that gene pool was appreciated by still fewer people, the terribly destructive force of nuclear power was totally unknown, and computers were dreams in the minds of mathematicians hampered by their inability to carry out long and painstaking calculations.

If we grant that the human species has been around for 3 million years, then the past century is approximately three ten-thousandths of that total. The higher-order human needs have changed markedly over the course of this minuscule time frame, and hence it is doubtful that an alien civilization would be sending out advice that would meet our unique needs at this precise moment, unless it sent messages appropriate for multiple levels within a hierarchy that bore some resemblance to the one suggested by Maslow. After all, could we honestly expect an alien culture to transmit information relevant to such a specific set of issues as nuclear power, population control, and the human fear of machines? Yet it will be these specific human issues that will motivate some people at least to search for messages in the first place, and given their tendency to look in one place for one type of message, it may be difficult for them to notice another type of message in another place.

Unfortunately, there is not a shred of evidence to indicate that aliens share Maslow's need hierarchy or that they are even aware of such a hierarchy in the life cycle of other species. Consider a civilization on another planet with a very different set of needs. Perhaps its most pressing desire is to be unconscious 99 percent of the time, or to live dangerously for a trillionth of a second, or to become a black hole or an orange. If we are indeed among the lowliest forms of life attempting to gain entry into a coalition of like-minded societies, our list of desires might occupy the lowest rung of some need hierarchy that encompasses all life in the universe. In this event, of course, there may be little or no information coming our way that could be seen as especially relevant to the human species at this juncture in its history.

The tides of history can change rapidly, however. Once astronomers have detected a message devised by an alien civilization for the benefit of distant others, and computer scientists have unwound the patterns inherent in such messages, and all of us have grasped the breadth and depth of their meaning, the human species will enter a phase of adjustment to what will almost certainly be an altogether new conception of the universe. The means and degree of adjustment will not be the same for everyone; some of us will be elated, others depressed, by the stark news that we share existence with other intelligences residing in faraway places. While each of us comes to grips with the implications of contact, it is to be hoped that we will also be learning more about ourselves.

REFERENCES AND FURTHER READINGS

Bateson, G. *Steps to an Ecology of Mind*. New York: Ballantine, 1972.

Bracewell, R. N. *The Galactic Club: Intelligent Life in Outer Space*. San Francisco: San Francisco Book Co., 1976.

Chaisson, E. *Cosmic Dawn: The Origins of Matter and Life*. Boston: Little, Brown, 1981.

Jastrow, R. *The Enchanted Loom: Mind in the Universe*. New York: Simon & Schuster, 1981.

Johanson, D. C., & Edey, M. A. *Lucy: The Beginnings of Humankind*. New York: Warner, 1981.

Leakey, R. E., & Lewin, R. *People of the Lake: Mankind and Its Beginnings*. New York: Avon, 1978.

Maslow, A. H. *The Farther Reaches of Human Nature*. New York: Viking, 1971.

Maslow, A. H. *Toward a Psychology of Being*. Princeton, N. J.: Van Nostrand, 1968.

Rogers, M. *Biohazard*, New York: Avon, 1979.

Singer, B., & Benassi, V. A. Occult Beliefs. *American Scientist,* 1981, *69,* 49–55.

Author Index

Pages in italics indicate the pages on which the full references appear.

Subject Index